MINNESOTA
COMMUNICATION ARTS/ LITERATURE (5-12)

By: Sharon Wynne, M.S.

XAMonline, INC.
Boston

Copyright © 2011 XAMonline, Inc.

All rights reserved. No part of the material protected by this copyright notice may be reproduced or utilized in any form or by any means, electronic or mechanical, including photocopying, recording or by any information storage and retrievable system, without written permission from the copyright holder.

To obtain permission(s) to use the material from this work for any purpose including workshops or seminars, please submit a written request to:

XAMonline, Inc.
25 First Street, Suite 106
Cambridge, MA 02141
Toll Free 1-800-509-4128
Email: info@xamonline.com
Web: www.xamonline.com
Fax: 1-617-583-5552

Library of Congress Cataloging-in-Publication Data

Wynne, Sharon A.
 Minnesota Communication Arts/Literature (5-12) / Sharon A. Wynne 1st ed.
 ISBN 978-1-60787-075-3
  1. Communication Arts/Literature (5-12)
  2. Study Guides
  3. Minnesota
  4. Teachers' Certification & Licensure
  5. Careers

Disclaimer:

The opinions expressed in this publication are the sole works of XAMonline and were created independently from the National Education Association, Educational Testing Service, or any State Department of Education, National Evaluation Systems or other testing affiliates.

Between the time of publication and printing, state specific standards as well as testing formats and Web site information may change and therefore would not be included in part or in whole within this product. Sample test questions are developed by XAMonline and reflect content similar to that on real tests; however, they are not former test questions. XAMonline assembles content that aligns with state standards but makes no claims nor guarantees teacher candidates a passing score. Numerical scores are determined by testing companies such as NES or ETS and then are compared with individual state standards. A passing score varies from state to state.

Printed in the United States of America   œ-1

Minnesota Communication Arts/Literature (5-12)
ISBN: 978-1-60787-075-3

Table of Contents

DOMAIN I
MEDIA LITERACY 1

COMPETENCY 1
UNDERSTAND STRATEGIES FOR ANALYZING AND EVALUATING VISUAL IMAGES IN VARIOUS MEDIA 3

Skill 1.1: Analyzing messages, meanings, and themes conveyed through various visual images *(e.g., political cartoons, photographs)* **in various media** *(e.g., television, movies/film, the Internet)* 3

Skill 1.2: Analyzing how the elements of visual images *(e.g., symbols, shapes, color, composition, perspective, style, content)* **are manipulated to emphasize or reinforce particular messages, meanings, and themes** 6

Skill 1.3: Analyzing how visual images are used to change behavior and influence public opinion by appealing to reason, emotion, authority, and convention..7

Skill 1.4: Analyzing the role that personal experience and prior knowledge play in interpreting certain visual images......................8

COMPETENCY 2
UNDERSTAND STRATEGIES FOR DEVELOPING AND PRODUCING EFFECTIVE MEDIA PRESENTATIONS 10

Skill 2.1: Demonstrating knowledge of the forms and purposes of media presentations *(e.g., interview, reportage, storytelling)* 10

Skill 2.2: Demonstrating knowledge of appropriate topics and projects for media presentations *(e.g., public service announcement, comic strip, skit)*.. 11

Skill 2.3: Applying strategies for selecting effective media and media combinations to use for various audiences and in various presentations *(e.g., Web site, slide presentation, animation, digital video)*... 11

Skill 2.4: Applying strategies for organizing and developing effective media presentations *(e.g., mapping, storyboarding, script writing)*.. 12

Skill 2.5: Applying strategies for producing effective media presentations *(e.g., designing graphics and backgrounds, selecting font styles and sizes for text)* 15

MINNESOTA

DOMAIN II
READING 17

COMPETENCY 3
UNDERSTAND THE FOUNDATIONS OF READING DEVELOPMENT 21

Skill 3.1: Demonstrating knowledge of phonological awareness skills *(e.g., distinguishing word syllables)* 21

Skill 3.2: Demonstrating knowledge of phonemic awareness skills *(e.g., segmenting, blending)* 21

Skill 3.3: Demonstrating knowledge of the concepts of print and the alphabetic principle 22

Skill 3.4: Demonstrating knowledge of the role of phonics in promoting reading comprehension 22

Skill 3.5: Demonstrating knowledge of the role of fluency in reading development, the components of fluency, and the factors that influence fluency 22

Skill 3.6: Demonstrating the ability to differentiate reading instruction to meet the needs of students at various reading proficiency levels and with various linguistic backgrounds 23

Skill 3.7: Demonstrating the ability to scaffold reading tasks for students who experience comprehension difficulties 24

COMPETENCY 4
UNDERSTAND STRATEGIES FOR DEVELOPING VOCABULARY KNOWLEDGE AND READING COMPREHENSION 24

Skill 4.1: Using knowledge of syntactic rules and word structure and contextual analysis skills to help identify word meanings 24

Skill 4.2: Recognizing relationships between words *(e.g., synonyms, antonyms)* **and issues related to word selection** *(e.g., denotative and connotative meanings)* 29

Skill 4.3: Recognizing factors that influence vocabulary development *(e.g., promoting word consciousness, wide reading)* 29

Skill 4.4: Recognizing factors that influence reading comprehension *(e.g., reader's interest, reading rate)* 29

Skill 4.5: Recognizing an appropriate reading strategy *(e.g., scanning, skimming)* **to use for a particular text and purpose** 30

Skill 4.6: Recognizing appropriate research-based reading comprehension strategies to use before, during, and after reading *(e.g., predicting, self-monitoring/self-questioning and using other metacognitive skills, summarizing)* 31

Skill 4.7: Recognizing appropriate oral and written language activities to use to enhance reading comprehension *(e.g., think-alouds, retelling)* 31

Skill 4.8: Demonstrating knowledge of literal and inferential reading comprehension skills *(e.g., identifying sequence of events in a text, making generalizations from information presented in a text)* 31

COMPETENCY 5
UNDERSTAND STRATEGIES FOR READING INFORMATIONAL AND PERSUASIVE TEXTS 33

Skill 5.1: Recognizing the characteristics of various types of informational texts *(e.g., newspapers, textbooks)* **and persuasive texts** *(e.g., editorials, propaganda)* 33

Skill 5.2: Using knowledge of the organizational features and structure of a text to help enhance comprehension of the text 34

Skill 5.3: Identifying the main idea, purpose, and intended audience of a text 35

Skill 5.4: Distinguishing between facts and opinions and between general statements and specific details in a text 36

Skill 5.5: Assessing the relevance, importance, and sufficiency of evidence, examples, and reasons provided to explain a concept or support an argument in a text 38

Skill 5.6: Assessing the credibility, objectivity, and reliability of various sources used in a text 40

Skill 5.7: Analyzing the use of rhetorical devices and techniques in a text *(e.g., repetition, exaggeration)* 41

COMPETENCY 6
UNDERSTAND STRATEGIES FOR READING TECHNICAL AND FUNCTIONAL TEXTS 42

Skill 6.1: Recognizing the characteristics of various types of technical texts *(e.g., warranties, contracts)* **and functional texts** *(e.g., timetables, application forms)* 42

Skill 6.2: Using information presented in technical texts to gain knowledge and develop skills *(e.g., learning and exercising consumers' and citizens' rights)* 42

Skill 6.3: Using information presented in functional texts to confirm facts and perform tasks *(e.g., planning travel, applying for a job)* 42

Skill 6.4: Interpreting graphic features used in technical texts *(e.g., schematics, flowcharts)* **and in functional texts** *(e.g., keys/legends, diagrams)* 43

DOMAIN III
LITERATURE 49

COMPETENCY 7
UNDERSTAND STRATEGIES FOR ANALYZING AND INTERPRETING VARIOUS FORMS OF LITERARY NONFICTION, FICTION, AND DRAMA 53

Skill 7.1: Recognizing the characteristics of various forms of literary nonfiction, fiction, and drama *(e.g., critical biography, historical novel, morality play)* 53

Skill 7.2: Recognizing the structural elements of literary prose *(e.g., prologue, climax, denouement)* 62

Skill 7.3: Analyzing the use of rhetorical, dramatic, and literary devices and techniques in a work of literary prose *(e.g., analogy, foreshadowing)* 67

Skill 7.4: Analyzing the diction or choice of words in a work of literary prose 67

Skill 7.5: Analyzing the plot, setting, and characterization in a work of literary prose 68

Skill 7.6: Interpreting the point of view, tone, and mood in a work of literary prose using critical theories and text-centered and reader-centered approaches 69

Skill 7.7: Interpreting central ideas or themes in a work of literary prose using critical theories and text-centered and reader-centered approaches 70

COMPETENCY 8
UNDERSTAND STRATEGIES FOR ANALYZING AND INTERPRETING VARIOUS FORMS OF POETRY 71

Skill 8.1: Recognizing the characteristics of various forms of poetry 71

Skill 8.2: Recognizing stanzaic and metrical structures and verse forms in a work of poetry *(e.g., quatrain, iambic pentameter, free verse)* 71

Skill 8.3: Analyzing formal rhyme schemes and sound devices in a work of poetry *(e.g., assonance, alliteration)* 75

Skill 8.4: Analyzing the use of figures of speech in a work of poetry *(e.g., simile, metonymy, apostrophe)*..................75

Skill 8.5: Analyzing the use of poetic and literary devices in a work of poetry *(e.g., imagery, allusion)*..................75

Skill 8.6: Interpreting the point of view, tone, and mood in a work of poetry using critical theories and text-centered and reader-centered approaches..................77

Skill 8.7: Interpreting central ideas or themes in a work of poetry using critical theories and text-centered and reader-centered approaches..................79

COMPETENCY 9
UNDERSTAND THE MAJOR CHARACTERISTICS OF LITERATURES FROM AROUND THE WORLD..................79

Skill 9.1: Demonstrating knowledge of major literary genres, styles, and trends associated with literature from around the world..................79

Skill 9.2: Demonstrating knowledge of the formal, stylistic, and thematic characteristics of major works and writers of literatures from around the world..................82

Skill 9.3: Demonstrating knowledge of the formal, stylistic, and thematic characteristics of major movements and periods in literatures from around the world..................87

Skill 9.4: Demonstrating knowledge of the formal, stylistic, and thematic characteristics of major literary genres and works from the oral tradition..................95

COMPETENCY 10
UNDERSTAND THE MAJOR HISTORICAL, SOCIAL, CULTURAL, AND POLITICAL ASPECTS OF LITERATURES FROM AROUND THE WORLD..................97

Skill 10.1: Examining in literary works references to major historical events and to major social, cultural, and political movements and institutions that have influenced the development of literatures from around the world..................97

Skill 10.2: Examining in literary works the expression of diverse values, attitudes, and ideas of people from various regional, ethnic, and cultural groups..................110

Skill 10.3: Examining how writers from diverse cultural backgrounds and various historical periods have commented on major historical events and influenced public opinion about and understanding of major social, cultural, and political issues through their literary works..................111

Skill 10.4: Examining how social, cultural, and political issues, such as issues relating to age, gender, ethnicity, and human rights, are explored in classical and contemporary literary works..................111

DOMAIN IV
LISTENING AND SPEAKING..................113

COMPETENCY 11
UNDERSTAND STRATEGIES FOR EFFECTIVE LISTENING..................115

Skill 11.1: Demonstrating knowledge of the components of the listening process *(e.g., focusing, decoding)*..................115

Skill 11.2: Identifying the characteristics and purposes of various types of listening, including **critical** *(e.g., listening to determine the speaker's point of view)*, **empathetic** *(e.g., listening to show support or improve mutual understanding and trust)*, **and deliberative** *(e.g., listening to learn information)*..................118

Skill 11.3: Demonstrating knowledge of the barriers to listening effectively *(e.g., internal and external noise, delivery, language, perceptions)* 119

Skill 11.4: Applying strategies for listening actively *(e.g., clarifying, restating, validating, building or reflecting on a speaker's message)* 120

COMPETENCY 12
UNDERSTAND STRATEGIES FOR EFFECTIVE SPEAKING 120

Skill 12.1: Demonstrating knowledge of a systematic approach to preparing a speech *(e.g., selecting a topic, adapting to the audience)* 120

Skill 12.2: Demonstrating knowledge of the forms of speech anxiety and apprehension *(e.g., audience-specific, situational)* **and ways of managing them** *(e.g., practicing, focusing on the topic, using relaxation techniques)* 122

Skill 12.3: Distinguishing among types of speech delivery *(e.g., memorized, extemporaneous, impromptu)* **and styles of language** *(e.g., informal, technical, regional)* **appropriate for various topics, purposes, audiences, and occasions** 122

Skill 12.4: Demonstrating knowledge of rhetorical techniques used to increase clarity and interest in speeches *(e.g., narrating, repeating key words and phrases, establishing common ground)* 123

Skill 12.5: Recognizing the different roles that voice *(e.g., volume, rate, tone)* **and body language** *(e.g., hand gestures, facial expressions, eye contact)* **play in speech delivery** 123

COMPETENCY 13
UNDERSTAND STRATEGIES FOR EFFECTIVE INTERPERSONAL COMMUNICATION 125

Skill 13.1: Demonstrating knowledge of the types *(e.g., dyadic, small-group)*, **characteristics** *(i.e., content versus relational messages)*, **and purposes of interpersonal communication** *(e.g., interviewing, problem solving, debating, forensics)* 125

Skill 13.2: Recognizing the importance of social etiquette, norms, and conventions in interpersonal communication and how these are influenced by factors such as power, intimacy, and culture 125

Skill 13.3: Demonstrating knowledge of the principles of group dynamics and factors that influence group effectiveness *(e.g., group size and composition, environment, group members' roles)* 125

Skill 13.4: Applying strategies for identifying, managing, and resolving conflict in groups *(e.g., compromise, negotiation, collaboration, accommodation)* 125

DOMAIN V
COMPONENTS OF WRITING 129

COMPETENCY 14
UNDERSTAND THE CONVENTIONS OF STANDARD AMERICAN ENGLISH AND THE ELEMENTS OF EFFECTIVE COMPOSITION 131

Skill 14.1: Demonstrating knowledge of the conventions of spelling and capitalization to use when developing text 131

Skill 14.2: Demonstrating knowledge of the conventions of punctuation to use when developing text 133

Skill 14.3: Demonstrating knowledge of proper word usage and grammatical sentence structure to use when developing text 137

Skill 14.4: Recognizing methods of developing an introduction to a text that draws a reader's attention, specifies a topic, and provides a thesis 154

Skill 14.5: Recognizing methods of developing a body of a text that presents, emphasizes, links, and contrasts ideas in a clear, concise, and coherent manner 157

Skill 14.6: Recognizing methods of developing a conclusion to a text that provides a summary or resolution, suggests a course of action, or offers a personal commentary 159

COMPETENCY 15
UNDERSTAND THE WRITING PROCESS 159

Skill 15.1: Demonstrating knowledge of the appropriate form of writing to use for a particular purpose and audience 159

Skill 15.2: Recognizing methods of generating and organizing ideas for writing 161

Skill 15.3: Recognizing methods of drafting text to show logical development of a central idea or theme through the use of relevant supporting details 167

Skill 15.4: Recognizing methods of revising a text to eliminate wordiness, redundancy, distracting details, and extraneous information 168

Skill 15.5: Recognizing methods of editing text to generate interest and clarify meaning *(e.g., varying sentence length and structure, maintaining parallelism, using appropriate transitions, simplifying inflated language)* 169

Skill 15.6: Recognizing methods of proofreading and preparing text for publication 170

COMPETENCY 16
UNDERSTAND THE ELEMENTS OF EFFECTIVE AND APPROPRIATE RESEARCH 170

Skill 16.1: Recognizing methods of selecting and refining a topic for research 170

Skill 16.2: Recognizing methods of composing specific, open-ended questions for a research topic 170

Skill 16.3: Recognizing methods of identifying and locating multiple and various sources of information for a research topic 170

Skill 16.4: Recognizing methods of assessing the credibility, objectivity, and reliability of sources of information 173

Skill 16.5: Recognizing methods of gathering and organizing information from sources systematically 174

Skill 16.6: Recognizing methods of paraphrasing, summarizing, and quoting information from sources appropriately and of integrating a paraphrase, summary, or quotation effectively into a text 175

Skill 16.7: Recognizing methods of citing or acknowledging sources of information appropriately in a text 176

DOMAIN VI
MODES OF WRITING 179

COMPETENCY 17
UNDERSTAND STRATEGIES FOR EXPOSITORY WRITING 183

Skill 17.1: Demonstrating knowledge of the forms and purposes of expository writing *(e.g., explaining a factual subject, reporting an event)* 183

Skill 17.2: Recognizing methods of selecting and limiting a subject for expository writing 183

Skill 17.3: Recognizing methods of formulating a specific question to address through expository writing and of developing a thesis statement that provides a focus for writing 184

Skill 17.4: Recognizing methods of selecting an effective organizational approach to use in expository writing *(e.g., cause and effect)* 184

Skill 17.5: Recognizing methods of selecting effective and appropriate supporting details to use in expository writing *(e.g., statistics, examples)* 186

Skill 17.6: Recognizing methods of developing expository writing that is clear, concise, and coherent 188

COMPETENCY 18
UNDERSTAND STRATEGIES FOR PERSUASIVE WRITING 189

Skill 18.1: Demonstrating knowledge of the forms and purposes of persuasive writing *(e.g., stating an opinion, influencing beliefs)* 189

Skill 18.2: Recognizing methods of establishing a clear position or controlling idea in persuasive writing 190

Skill 18.3: Recognizing methods of selecting an effective organizational approach to use in persuasive writing *(e.g., logical order, order of importance)* 191

Skill 18.4: Recognizing methods of selecting effective and appropriate supporting details to use in persuasive writing *(e.g., facts, reasons, appeals)* 192

Skill 18.5: Recognizing methods of anticipating questions, concerns, and counterarguments for points made in persuasive writing and of incorporating effective responses to them into the writing 193

Skill 18.6: Recognizing methods of selecting an appropriate style, tone, voice, and diction to use in persuasive writing 194

COMPETENCY 19
UNDERSTAND STRATEGIES FOR NARRATIVE WRITING 195

Skill 19.1: Demonstrating knowledge of the forms and purposes of narrative writing *(e.g., relating a personal experience, portraying a character, exploring points of view, imagining an event or situation)* 195

Skill 19.2: Recognizing methods of selecting and limiting a subject for narrative writing 196

Skill 19.3: Recognizing methods of selecting an effective organizational approach to use in narrative writing *(e.g., chronological order, in medias res, flashback)* 197

Skill 19.4: Recognizing methods of developing narrative writing that employs literary devices and techniques *(e.g., figurative language, symbolism)* 200

Skill 19.5: Recognizing methods of developing narrative writing that establishes a distinct point of view, tone, and mood *(e.g., creating interesting dialogue, choosing sensory details)* 200

Skill 19.6: Recognizing methods of developing narrative writing that is creative, compelling, and insightful *(e.g., incorporating an inventive plotline and dynamic characters, explicating a significant theme, building actions around a conflict)* 203

COMPETENCY 20
UNDERSTAND STRATEGIES FOR CRITICAL AND ANALYTICAL WRITING 203

Skill 20.1: Demonstrating knowledge of the forms and purposes of critical and analytical writing *(e.g., critiquing or evaluating a literary work, interpreting a literary work)* 203

Skill 20.2: Recognizing methods of formulating a specific question to address through critical or analytical writing and of developing a thesis statement that makes a significant claim or conveys a purpose for writing 203

Skill 20.3: Recognizing methods of selecting an effective organizational approach to use in critical or analytical writing *(e.g., comparison-and-contrast)* 204

Skill 20.4: Recognizing methods of developing a convincing critique or cogent analysis of a literary work *(e.g., incorporating specific words and phrases from a literary work to support a claim)* 204

Skill 20.5: Relating elements of one literary work *(e.g., character, theme, style, point of view)* **to elements of other literary works** 206

SAMPLE TEST

Sample Test 213

Answer Key 233

Rigor Table 234

Sample Test with Rationales 235

MINNESOTA
COMMUNICATION ARTS/ LITERATURE (5-12)

SECTION 1
ABOUT XAMONLINE

XAMonline—A Specialty Teacher Certification Company

Created in 1996, XAMonline was the first company to publish study guides for state-specific teacher certification examinations. Founder Sharon Wynne found it frustrating that materials were not available for teacher certification preparation and decided to create the first single, state-specific guide. XAMonline has grown into a company of over 1,800 contributors and writers and offers over 300 titles for the entire PRAXIS series and every state examination. No matter what state you plan on teaching in, XAMonline has a unique teacher certification study guide just for you.

XAMonline—Value and Innovation

We are committed to providing value and innovation. Our print-on-demand technology allows us to be the first in the market to reflect changes in test standards and user feedback as they occur. Our guides are written by experienced teachers who are experts in their fields. And our content reflects the highest standards of quality. Comprehensive practice tests with varied levels of rigor means that your study experience will closely match the actual in-test experience.

To date, XAMonline has helped nearly 600,000 teachers pass their certification or licensing exams. Our commitment to preparation exceeds simply providing the proper material for study—it extends to helping teachers **gain mastery** of the subject matter, giving them the **tools** to become the most effective classroom leaders possible, and ushering today's students toward a **successful future**.

SECTION 2
ABOUT THIS STUDY GUIDE

Purpose of This Guide

Is there a little voice inside of you saying, "Am I ready?" Our goal is to replace that little voice and remove all doubt with a new voice that says, "I AM READY. **Bring it on!**" by offering the highest quality of teacher certification study guides.

Organization of Content

You will see that while every test may start with overlapping general topics, each is very unique in the skills they wish to test. Only XAMonline presents custom content that analyzes deeper than a title, a subarea, or an objective. Only XAMonline presents content and sample test assessments along with **focus statements**, the deepest-level rationale and interpretation of the skills that are unique to the exam.

Title and field number of test
→Each exam has its own name and number. XAMonline's guides are written to give you the content you need to know for the specific exam you are taking. You can be confident when you buy our guide that it contains the information you need to study for the specific test you are taking.

Subareas
→These are the major content categories found on the exam. XAMonline's guides are written to cover all of the subareas found in the test frameworks developed for the exam.

Objectives
→These are standards that are unique to the exam and represent the main subcategories of the subareas/content categories. XAMonline's guides are written to address every specific objective required to pass the exam.

Focus statements
→These are examples and interpretations of the objectives. You find them in parenthesis directly following the objective. They provide detailed examples of the range, type, and level of content that appear on the test questions. **Only XAMonline's guides drill down to this level.**

How Do We Compare with Our Competitors?
XAMonline—drills down to the focus statement level.
CliffsNotes and REA—organized at the objective level
Kaplan—provides only links to content
MoMedia—content not specific to the state test

Each subarea is divided into manageable sections that cover the specific skill areas. Explanations are easy to understand and thorough. You'll find that every test answer contains a rejoinder so if you need a refresher or further review after taking the test, you'll know exactly to which section you must return.

How to Use This Book

Our informal polls show that most people begin studying up to eight weeks prior to the test date, so start early. Then ask yourself some questions: How much do you really know? Are you coming to the test straight from your teacher-education program or are you having to review subjects you haven't considered in ten years? Either way, take a **diagnostic or assessment test** first. Also, spend time on sample tests so that you become accustomed to the way the actual test will appear.

This guide comes with an online diagnostic test of 30 questions found online at www.XAMonline.com. It is a little boot camp to get you up for the task and reveal things about your compendium of knowledge in general. Although this guide is structured to follow the order of the test, you are not required to study in that order. By finding a time-management and study plan that fits your life you will be more effective. The results of your diagnostic or self-assessment test can be a guide for how to manage your time and point you toward an area that needs more attention.

After taking the diagnostic exam, fill out the **Personalized Study Plan** page at the beginning of each chapter. Review the competencies and skills covered in that chapter and check the boxes that apply to your study needs. If there are sections you already know you can skip, check the "skip it" box. Taking this step will give you a study plan for each chapter.

Week	Activity
8 weeks prior to test	Take a diagnostic test found at www.XAMonline.com
7 weeks prior to test	Build your Personalized Study Plan for each chapter. Check the "skip it" box for sections you feel you are already strong in. ✗ SKIP IT ☐
6-3 weeks prior to test	For each of these four weeks, choose a content area to study. You don't have to go in the order of the book. It may be that you start with the content that needs the most review. Alternately, you may want to ease yourself into plan by starting with the most familiar material.
2 weeks prior to test	Take the sample test, score it, and create a review plan for the final week before the test.
1 week prior to test	Following your plan (which will likely be aligned with the areas that need the most review) go back and study the sections that align with the questions you may have gotten wrong. Then go back and study the sections related to the questions you answered correctly. If need be, create flashcards and drill yourself on any area that you makes you anxious.

SECTION 3
ABOUT THE MINNESOTA COMMUNICATION ARTS/ LITERATURE (5-12) EXAM

What is the Minnesota Communication Arts/Literature (5-12) Exam?

The Minnesota Communication Arts/Literature (5-12) is meant to assess mastery of the content knowledge required to teach high school communication arts and literature in Minnesota public schools.

Often **your own state's requirements** determine whether or not you should take any particular test. The most reliable source of information regarding this is your state's Department of Education. This resource should have a complete list of testing centers and dates. Test dates vary by subject area and not all test dates necessarily include your particular test, so be sure to check carefully.

If you are in a teacher-education program, check with the Education Department or the Certification Officer for specific information for testing and testing timelines. The Certification Office should have most of the information you need.

If you choose an alternative route to certification you can either rely on our website at www.XAMonline.com or on the resources provided by an alternative certification program. Many states now have specific agencies devoted to alternative certification and there are some national organizations as well, for example:
National Association for Alternative Certification
http://www.alt-teachercert.org/index.asp

Interpreting Test Results

Contrary to what you may have heard, the results of the Minnesota Communication Arts/Literature (5-12) test are not based on time. More accurately, your score will be based on the raw number of points you earn in each section, the proportion of that section to the entire subtest, and the scaling of the raw score. Raw scores are converted to a scale of 100 to 300. It is likely to your benefit to complete as many questions in the time allotted, but it will not necessarily work to your advantage if you hurry through the test.

Scores are available by email if you request this when you register. Score reports are available 21 days after the testing window and posted to your account for 45 days as PDFs. Scores will also be sent to your chosen institution(s).

What's on the Test?

The Minnesota Communication Arts/Literature (5-12) is a computer-based test and consists of two subtests, each lasting one hour. You can take one or both subtests at one testing appointment. The breakdown of the questions is as follows:

Category	Approximate Number of Questions	Approximate Percentage of the Test
SUBTEST 1	50	
I: Media Literacy		20%
II: Reading		40%
III: Literature		40%
SUBTEST 2	50	
I: Listening and Speaking		30%
II: Components of Writing		30%
III: Modes of Writing		40%

Question Types

You're probably thinking, enough already, I want to study! Indulge us a little longer while we explain that there is actually more than one type of multiple-choice question. You can thank us later after you realize how well prepared you are for your exam.

1. Complete the Statement. The name says it all. In this question type you'll be asked to choose the correct completion of a given statement. For example:

   > **The Dolch Basic Sight Words consist of a relatively short list of words that children should be able to:**
   >
   > A. Sound out
   >
   > B. Know the meaning of
   >
   > C. Recognize on sight
   >
   > D. Use in a sentence

The correct answer is C. In order to check your answer, test out the statement by adding the choices to the end of it.

2. **Which of the Following.** One way to test your answer choice for this type of question is to replace the phrase "which of the following" with your selection. Use this example:

> **Which of the following words is one of the twelve most frequently used in children's reading texts:**
> A. There
> B. This
> C. The
> D. An

Don't look! Test your answer. _____ is one of the twelve most frequently used in children's reading texts. Did you guess C? Then you guessed correctly.

3. **Roman Numeral Choices.** This question type is used when there is more than one possible correct answer. For example:

> **Which of the following two arguments accurately supports the use of cooperative learning as an effective method of instruction?**
> I. Cooperative learning groups facilitate healthy competition between individuals in the group.
> II. Cooperative learning groups allow academic achievers to carry or cover for academic underachievers.
> III. Cooperative learning groups make each student in the group accountable for the success of the group.
> IV. Cooperative learning groups make it possible for students to reward other group members for achieving.
>
> A. I and II
> B. II and III
> C. I and III
> D. III and IV

Notice that the question states there are **two** possible answers. It's best to read all the possibilities first before looking at the answer choices. In this case, the correct answer is D.

4. **Negative Questions.** This type of question contains words such as "not," "least," and "except." Each correct answer will be the statement that does **not** fit the situation described in the question. Such as:

> **Multicultural education is not**
>
> A. An idea or concept
>
> B. A "tack-on" to the school curriculum
>
> C. An educational reform movement
>
> D. A process

Think to yourself that the statement could be anything but the correct answer. This question form is more open to interpretation than other types, so read carefully and don't forget that you're answering a negative statement.

5. **Questions that Include Graphs, Tables, or Reading Passages.** As always, read the question carefully. It likely asks for a very specific answer and not a broad interpretation of the visual. Here is a simple (though not statistically accurate) example of a graph question:

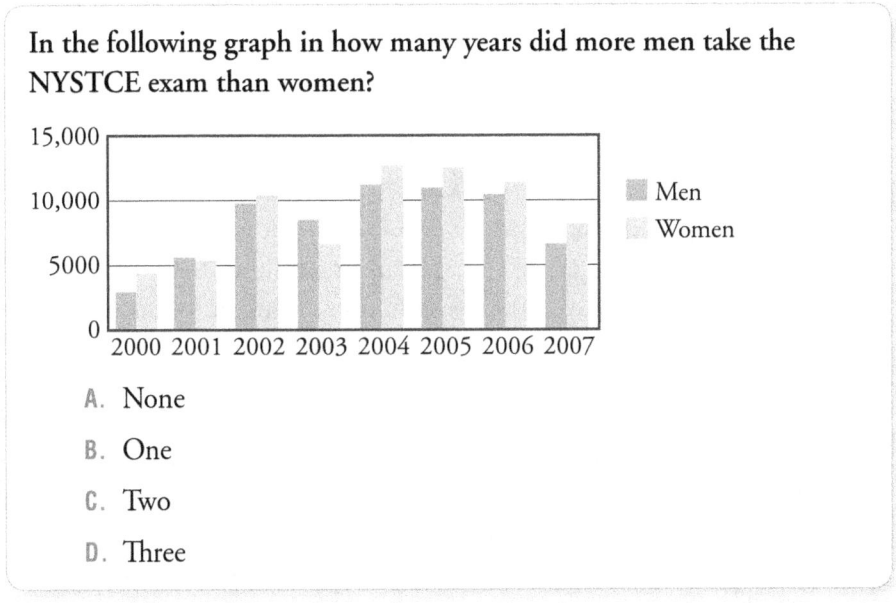

> **In the following graph in how many years did more men take the NYSTCE exam than women?**
>
> A. None
>
> B. One
>
> C. Two
>
> D. Three

It may help you to simply circle the two years that answer the question. Make sure you've read the question thoroughly and once you've made your determination, double check your work. The correct answer is C.

SECTION 4
HELPFUL HINTS

Study Tips

1. **You are what you eat.** Certain foods aid the learning process by releasing natural memory enhancers called CCKs (cholecystokinin) composed of tryptophan, choline, and phenylalanine. All of these chemicals enhance the neurotransmitters associated with memory and certain foods release memory enhancing chemicals. A light meal or snacks of one of the following foods fall into this category:

   - Milk
   - Rice
   - Eggs
   - Fish
   - Nuts and seeds
   - Oats
   - Turkey

   The better the connections, the more you comprehend!

2. **See the forest for the trees.** In other words, get the concept before you look at the details. One way to do this is to take notes as you read, paraphrasing or summarizing in your own words. Putting the concept in terms that are comfortable and familiar may increase retention.

3. **Question authority.** Ask why, why, why? Pull apart written material paragraph by paragraph and don't forget the captions under the illustrations. For example, if a heading reads *Stream Erosion* put it in the form of a question (Why do streams erode? What is stream erosion?) then find the answer within the material. If you train your mind to think in this manner you will learn more and prepare yourself for answering test questions.

4. **Play mind games.** Using your brain for reading or puzzles keeps it flexible. Even with a limited amount of time your brain can take in data (much like a computer) and store it for later use. In ten minutes you can: read two paragraphs (at least), quiz yourself with flash cards, or review notes. Even if you don't fully understand something on the first pass, your mind stores it for recall, which is why frequent reading or review increases chances of retention and comprehension.

5. **Get pointed in the right direction.** Use arrows to point to important passages or pieces of information. It's easier to read than a page full of yellow highlights. Highlighting can be used sparingly, but add an arrow to the margin to call attention to it.

6. **The pen is mightier than the sword.** Learn to take great notes. A by-product of our modern culture is that we have grown accustomed to getting our information in short doses. We've subconsciously trained ourselves to assimilate information into neat little packages. Messy notes fragment the flow of information. Your notes can be much clearer with proper formatting. *The Cornell Method* is one such format. This method was popularized in *How to Study in College*, Ninth Edition, by Walter Pauk. You can benefit from the method without purchasing an additional book by simply looking up the method online. Below is a sample of how *The Cornell Method* can be adapted for use with this guide.

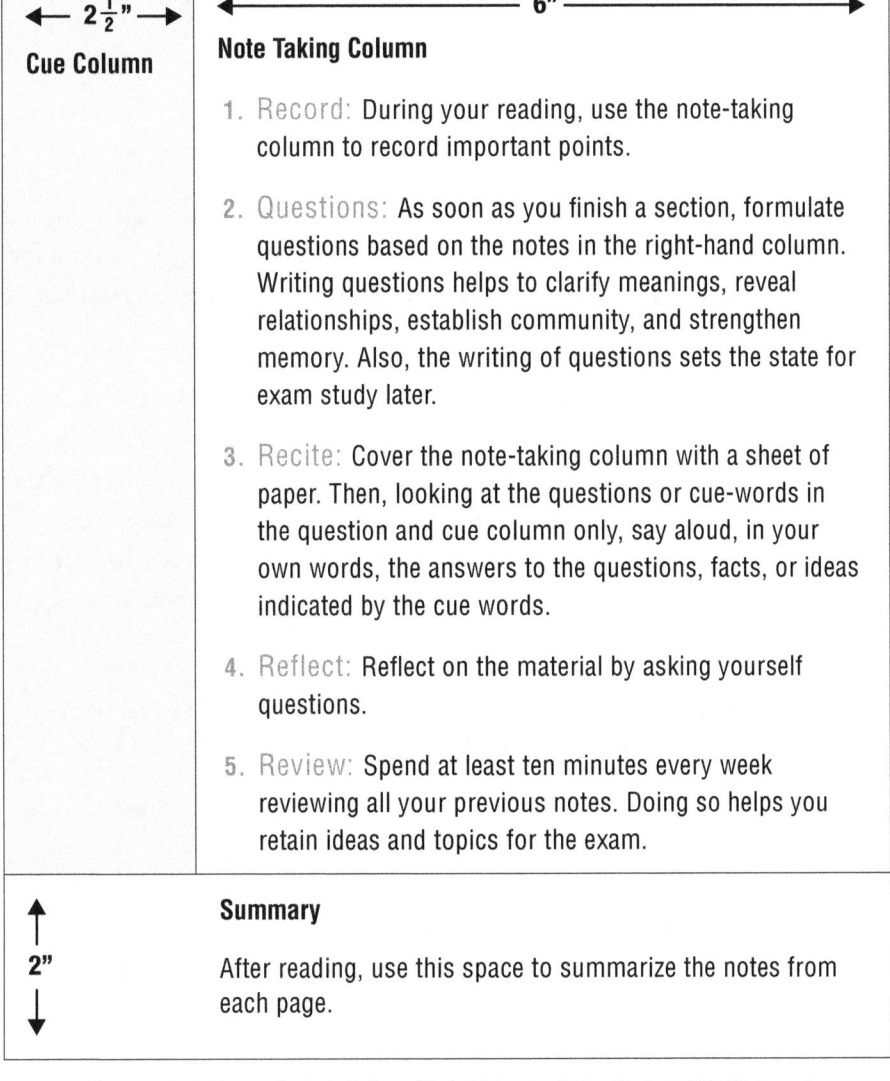

*Adapted from *How to Study in College*, Ninth Edition, by Walter Pauk, ©2008 Wadsworth

> *The proctor will write the start time where it can be seen and then, later, provide the time remaining, typically fifteen minutes before the end of the test.*

7. **Place yourself in exile and set the mood.** Set aside a particular place and time to study that best suits your personal needs and biorhythms. If you're a night person, burn the midnight oil. If you're a morning person set yourself up with some coffee and get to it. Make your study time and place as free from distraction as possible and surround yourself with what you need, be it silence or music. Studies have shown that music can aid in concentration, absorption, and retrieval of information. Not all music, though. Classical music is said to work best.

8. **Check your budget.** You should at least review all the content material before your test, but allocate the most amount of time to the areas that need the most refreshing. It sounds obvious, but it's easy to forget. You can use the study rubric above to balance your study budget.

Testing Tips

1. **Get smart, play dumb.** Sometimes a question is just a question. No one is out to trick you, so don't assume that the test writer is looking for something other than what was asked. Stick to the question as written and don't overanalyze.

2. **Do a double take.** Read test questions and answer choices at least twice because it's easy to miss something, to transpose a word or some letters. If you have no idea what the correct answer is, skip it and come back later if there's time. If you're still clueless, it's okay to guess. Remember, you're scored on the number of questions you answer correctly and you're not penalized for wrong answers. The worst case scenario is that you miss a point from a good guess.

3. **Turn it on its ear.** The syntax of a question can often provide a clue, so make things interesting and turn the question into a statement to see if it changes the meaning or relates better (or worse) to the answer choices.

4. **Get out your magnifying glass.** Look for hidden clues in the questions because it's difficult to write a multiple-choice question without giving away part of the answer in the options presented. In most questions you can readily eliminate one or two potential answers, increasing your chances of answering correctly to 50/50, which will help out if you've skipped a question and gone back to it (see tip #2).

5. **Call it intuition.** Often your first instinct is correct. If you've been studying the content you've likely absorbed something and have subconsciously retained the knowledge. On questions you're not sure about trust your instincts because a first impression is usually correct.

6. Graffiti. Sometimes it's a good idea to mark your answers directly on the test booklet and go back to fill in the optical scan sheet later. You don't get extra points for perfectly blackened ovals. If you choose to manage your test this way, be sure not to mismark your answers when you transcribe to the scan sheet.

7. Become a clock-watcher. You have a set amount of time to answer the questions. Don't get bogged down laboring over a question you're not sure about when there are ten others you could answer more readily. If you choose to follow the advice of tip #6, be sure you leave time near the end to go back and fill in the scan sheet.

Do the Drill

No matter how prepared you feel it's sometimes a good idea to apply Murphy's Law. So the following tips might seem silly, mundane, or obvious, but we're including them anyway.

1. Remember, you are what you eat, so bring a snack. Choose from the list of energizing foods that appear earlier in the introduction.

2. You're not too sexy for your test. Wear comfortable clothes. You'll be distracted if your belt is too tight or if you're too cold or too hot.

3. Lie to yourself. Even if you think you're a prompt person, pretend you're not and leave plenty of time to get to the testing center. Map it out ahead of time and do a dry run if you have to. There's no need to add road rage to your list of anxieties.

4. Bring sharp number 2 pencils. It may seem impossible to forget this need from your school days, but you might. And make sure the erasers are intact, too.

5. No ticket, no test. Bring your admission ticket as well as **two** forms of identification, including one with a picture and signature. You will not be admitted to the test without these things.

6. You can't take it with you. Leave any study aids, dictionaries, notebooks, computers, and the like at home. Certain tests **do** allow a scientific or four-function calculator, so check ahead of time to see if your test does.

7. Prepare for the desert. Any time spent on a bathroom break **cannot** be made up later, so use your judgment on the amount you eat or drink.

8. Quiet, Please! Keeping your own time is a good idea, but not with a timepiece that has a loud ticker. If you use a watch, take it off and place it nearby but not so that it distracts you. And **silence your cell phone**.

To the best of our ability, we have compiled the content you need to know in this book and in the accompanying online resources. The rest is up to you. You can use the study and testing tips or you can follow your own methods. Either way, you can be confident that there aren't any missing pieces of information and there shouldn't be any surprises in the content on the test.

If you have questions about test fees, registration, electronic testing, or other content verification issues please visit *www.mtle.nesinc.com*.

Good luck!

Sharon Wynne
Founder, XAMonline

DOMAIN I
MEDIA LITERACY

MEDIA LITERACY

PERSONALIZED STUDY PLAN

✘ KNOWN MATERIAL/ SKIP IT

PAGE	COMPETENCY AND SKILL		
3	**1:**	**Understand strategies for analyzing and evaluating visual images in various media**	☐
	1.1:	Analyzing messages, meanings, and themes conveyed through various visual images in various media	☐
	1.2:	Analyzing how the elements of visual images are manipulated to emphasize or reinforce particular messages, meanings, and themes	☐
	1.3:	Analyzing how visual images are used to change behavior and influence public opinion by appealing to reason, emotion, authority, and convention	☐
	1.4:	Analyzing the role that personal experience and prior knowledge play in interpreting certain visual images	☐
10	**2:**	**Understand strategies for developing and producing effective media presentations**	☐
	2.1:	Demonstrating knowledge of the forms and purposes of media presentations	☐
	2.2:	Demonstrating knowledge of appropriate topics and projects for media presentations	☐
	2.3:	Applying strategies for selecting effective media and media combinations to use for various audiences and in various presentations	☐
	2.4:	Applying strategies for organizing and developing effective media presentations	☐
	2.5:	Applying strategies for producing effective media presentations	☐

COMPETENCY 1
UNDERSTAND STRATEGIES FOR ANALYZING AND EVALUATING VISUAL IMAGES IN VARIOUS MEDIA

> **SKILL 1.1** Analyzing messages, meanings, and themes conveyed through various visual images *(e.g., political cartoons, photographs)* in various media *(e.g., television, movies/film, the Internet)*

To present their messages effectively, the media employ various approaches to reach their audiences. Some messages are more obvious than others, and students should be taught to analyze all of them to determine the logic and reasoning.

Posters

The power of the political poster in the twenty-first century seems trivial considering the barrage of electronic campaigning, mudslinging, and reporting that seem to take over the video and audio media in election season. Even so, the political poster is a powerful propaganda tool that has been around for a long time. For example, in the first century CE, a poster that calls for the election of a Satrius as quinquennial has survived to this day. Nowhere have political posters been used more powerfully or effectively than in Russia during the 1920s campaign to promote communism. Many of the greatest Russian writers of that era were the poster writers. Those posters would not be understood at all, except in light of what was going on in the country at the time.

Today we see political posters primarily at rallies and protests, where they are usually hand-lettered and hand-drawn. The message is rarely subtle. Understanding the messages of posters requires little thought as a rule. However, they are usually meaningless unless the context is clearly understood. For example, a poster reading "Camp Democracy" can be understood only in the context of the protests against the Iraq War near President Bush's home near Crawford, Texas. "Impeach" posters were understood in 2006 to be directed at President George W. Bush, not a local mayor or representative.

MEDIA LITERACY

Check out the teaching guide for the professional cartoonist index:

www.cagle.com/teacher/

Cartoons

The political cartoon (aka editorial) presents a message or point of view concerning people, events, or situations using caricature and symbolism to convey the cartoonist's ideas, sometimes subtly, sometimes brashly, but always quickly. A good political cartoon has:

- Wit and humor, usually obtained by exaggeration that is slick and not used merely for comic effect
- A foundation in truth; that is, the characters are recognizable to the viewer
- Some basis in fact (even if it has a philosophical bias)
- A moral purpose

Using political cartoons as a teaching tool enlivens lectures, prompts classroom discussion, promotes critical thinking, develops multiple talents and learning styles, and helps prepare students for standardized tests. It also provides humor. However, political cartoons may be the most difficult form of literature to teach. Many teachers who choose to include them in their social studies curricula caution that, although students may enjoy them, it's doubtful whether they are actually getting the cartoonists' messages.

The best strategy for teaching such a unit uses a subskills approach that leads students step-by-step to higher orders of critical thinking. For example, the teacher can introduce caricature and use cartoons to illustrate the principles. Students can identify and interpret symbols if they are given the principles for doing so and get plenty of practice, and cartoons are excellent teaching tools. Using this approach can cut down the time it takes for students to develop these skills, and many of the students who might otherwise lose the struggle to learn to identify symbols may overcome the roadblocks through the analysis of political cartoons. Many political cartoons exist for the teacher to use in the classroom, and they are more readily available than ever before.

A popular example of an editorial cartoon that provides a way to analyze current events in politics is the comic strip "Doonesbury" by Gary Trudeau. For example, prior to the 2004 presidential election, the media-savvy teenager Alex does her best to participate in the political process. In January, she rallies her middle school classmates to the phones for a Deanathon; by August, she is luring Ralph Nader supporters into discussions on Internet chat rooms. Knowledgeable about government, active in the political process, and willing to enlist others, Alex has many traits that educators seek to develop in their students.

Ideally, the purpose of the media (primarily news and documentary programs) in the democratic process would be for the media to convey critical information to the people so that the people could cast more intelligent votes than they would without the input. In this ideal scenario, media objectivity is assumed; the reality is, however, that media objectivity is widely assumed to be missing. Various media broadcasting organizations report information in ways that suggest a bias, a slant, favoring one or another political ideology.

As educators, you should help students critically evaluate information coming from the major news networks and associated channels. Educators can help students recognize bias and can suggest strategies for approaching media input in ways that result in more comprehensive and objective views of issues and situations. For instance, educators can suggest that students gather information on an issue from several media organizations in order to get a better perspective on it.

The media are extremely effective in spreading information quickly. Therefore, the media itself influence the process by the very fact that if candidates for office know of an event with media coverage, they try to make an appearance and an impression. Since time is limited in most media formats, candidates attempt to focus on broadcasting a few points. This phenomenon results in little more than propaganda. Questions posed by newscasters meet with various deflections. Few candidates tip their hands any more than absolutely necessary. One downside of the relationship between the media and candidates is that substance seems to take a back seat to slogans.

Access to the media involves expense, and that creates a problem for the democratic process: Being wealthy becomes a prerequisite for candidacy. Certainly, this emphasis on money creates all kinds of complications for the democratic process. Candidates are in danger of being beholden to sponsors. Instead of following their own consciences, they follow the dictates of the contributors.

Exit polling by the media influences the democratic process by projecting outcomes based on a small percentage of actual votes. Potential voters may alter their choices based on this information, or they may decide not to vote at all. The time differences from the East Coast to the West Coast provide an environment for this distortion. With the advent of mail-in ballots, media speculation based on polling has the potential to exert even more influence on voting patterns.

The media play an extremely important role in the democratic process, and this role is bound to expand as technology evolves. If we are to have a strong democracy, we must become increasingly sophisticated in our evaluation of media input.

MEDIA LITERACY

> **SKILL 1.2** Analyzing how the elements of visual images *(e.g., symbols, shapes, color, composition, perspective, style, content)* **are manipulated to emphasize or reinforce particular messages, meanings, and themes**

Check out the language of media literacy—a glossary of terms:

www.medialit.org /reading_room/article565 .html

A common classroom assignment that applies to this skill is to view the movie version of a book studied by a particular class, to compare and contrast the two media, and to argue which did the better job of conveying the intended message(s).

Conveying the same message across different media is difficult because of the dynamics specific to those media. The degree of difficulty increases as the complexity of the message does. Nonetheless, certain general observations inform the discussion.

A print message has two kinds of unique features. Some seem to be positive. For instance, print messages have longevity; they are also easily portable. Print messages appeal almost exclusively to the mind and allow students to recursively read sections that warrant more thought. Other features of print seem potentially negative. For instance, a print message requires an active reader; without such a reader, print messages are not very effective. Print messages are not accessible to nonreaders.

A graphic message in the hands of a talented artist can produce images that are extremely powerful. More commonly, a graphic message gives a quick overview of some quantifiable situation. Some learners find that graphic information works for them better than print, and many struggling readers find graphic messages more helpful, too. However, compared to print, graphic messages convey a much shorter range of information. If a particular graphic is inspiring, the inspirations conveyed are subject to the descriptions of the various readers who view it. With print, the inspired scripts are already there for the reader, provided the reader is applying active reading skills.

Check out more strategies for developing listening skills:

www.nclrc.org/essentials /listening/stratlisten.htm

An audio message allows for messages delivered with attention to prosody. Students who can't read can access the material. Audio messages invite the listener to form mental images consistent with the topic of the audio. Audio messages also allow the learners to close their eyes for better mental focus. Listening to an audio message is a more passive modality than reading a print message, though. As a rule, people read faster than normal speech patterns, so print conveys more information in a given time span.

An audiovisual message offers the easiest accessibility for learners. It has the advantages of each medium, the graphic and the audio. Learners' eyes and ears are engaged. Nonreaders get significant access to content. Viewing an audiovisual presentation is an even more passive activity than listening to an audio message, however, because information is coming to learners effortlessly through two senses. Activities to foster a critical perspective on an audiovisual presentation serve as valuable safeguards against any overall and unwelcome passivity.

Also see Skill 1.1

SKILL 1.3 Analyzing how visual images are used to change behavior and influence public opinion by appealing to reason, emotion, authority, and convention

The media exert a profound influence on personal and societal values, opinions, and behaviors. One of the main avenues of this influence is advertising. The media depends upon advertising for its economic viability. The advertising industry devotes tremendous resources to the study of how to influence values, opinions, and behaviors.

It should come as no surprise that the techniques used by advertisers to promote their products often have little to do with the pros and cons of the products themselves. Rather, advertisers frequently appeal to sex and status to peddle their wares. In this sense, the media helps foster conspicuous and often mindless consumption.

Educators can help students become more aware of how advertising operates by leading them through analysis of various advertisements to identify the basis of their appeal.

The media directly attempt to influence societal values, opinions, and behaviors through news and documentary programming. The power and scope of the media in disseminating information is not only pivotal, but also is becoming more so as technology continues to make such information instantly available. Alerting students to the need for developing a critical perspective with regard to sources of broadcasting news and information is an important goal of educators.

Behavior models available through dramas, sitcoms, and cartoons comprise another profound influence of the media on personal and societal values, opinions, and behaviors. Young people, in particular, are exposed to a wide spectrum of such models. Increasingly, material that would have been considered too vulgar and risqué is available to them through the media. Since the young are experimenting with various identity models, it is not surprising that some young people adopt these media models and exhibit values, opinions, and behaviors that seem

MEDIA LITERACY

vulgar, rude, and risqué. An educator should be aware of this development in order to avoid being unduly reactive to such student behaviors.

Body image is also profoundly influenced by the media. Trying to meet impossible standards of beauty presented by the media has resulted in suffering and disease for many young people, particularly young women. Countering this trend is another worthy educational goal.

In general, an analysis of the media's influence on personal and societal values leads to the conclusion that educators must be proactive in addressing the negative aspects of this pervasive influence. Helping students develop a critical perspective with regard to all these aspects of media consumption is an essential educational goal.

SKILL 1.4 Analyzing the role that personal experience and prior knowledge play in interpreting certain visual images

More money is spent each year on advertising to children than on educating them. Thus, the media's strategies are considerably well-thought-out and effective. They employ large, clear letters, bold colors, simple line drawings, and popular symbols to announce upcoming events, push ideas, and advertise products. By using attractive photographs, brightly colored cartoon characters, or instructive messages, they increase sales, win votes, or stimulate learning. The graphics are designed to communicate messages clearly, precisely, and efficiently. Some even target subconscious yearnings for sex and status.

Learn more about teaching film, television, and media:

www.tc.umn.edu/~rbeach/linksteachingmedia/chapter8/16.htm

Because so much effort is spent on influencing students through media tactics, just as much effort should be devoted to educating those students about media awareness. A teacher should explain that artists, the aspects they choose to portray, and the ways in which they portray them reflect their attitude and understanding of those aspects. Artistic choices are not entirely based on creative license—they also reflect an imbedded meaning that the artist wants to represent. Colors, shapes, and positions are meant to arouse basic instincts for food, sex, and status, and are often used to sell cars, clothing, or liquor.

To stimulate analysis of media strategies, ask students questions such as:

- Where/when do you think this picture was taken/film was shot/piece was written?
- Would you like to have lived at this time in history, or in this place?
- What objects are present?

UNDERSTAND STRATEGIES FOR ANALYZING AND EVALUATING VISUAL IMAGES

- What do the people presented look like? Are they happy or sad?
- Who is being targeted?
- What can you learn from this piece of media?
- Is it telling you something is good or bad?
- What message is being broadcasted?

Advertising Techniques

Because students are very interested in the types of approaches advertisers use, you can develop high-interest assignments requiring them to analyze commercial messages. What is powerful about Nike's "Just Do It" campaign? What is the appeal of Paris Hilton's eponymous perfume?

TYPICAL ADVERTISING TECHNIQUES	
Beauty Appeal	Beauty attracts us; we are drawn to beautiful people, places, and things.
Celebrity Endorsement	This technique associates product use with a well-known person. We are led to believe that by purchasing this product, we will attain characteristics similar to those of the celebrity.
Compliment the Consumer	Advertisers flatter the consumer who is willing to purchase their product. By purchasing the product, the consumer is recognized by the advertisers as having made a good decision with the selection.
Escape	Getting away from it all is very appealing; you can imagine adventures you cannot have; the idea of escape is pleasurable.
Independence/ Individuality	This technique associates a product with people who can think and act for themselves. Products are linked to individual decision making.
Intelligence	This technique associates a product with smart people who can't be fooled.
Lifestyle	This technique associates a product with a particular style of living/way of doing things.
Nurture	Every time you see an animal or a child, an appeal is made to your paternal or maternal instincts. This technique associates products with taking care of someone.
Peer Approval	This technique associates product use with friendship/acceptance. Advertisers can also use this technique negatively to make you worry that you'll lose friends if you don't use a certain product.
Rebel	This technique associates products with behaviors or lifestyles that oppose society's norms.

Continued on next page

MEDIA LITERACY

Rhetorical Question	This technique poses a question to the consumer that demands a response. A question is asked, and the consumer is supposed to answer in a way that affirms the product's goodness.
Scientific/ Statistical Claim	This technique provides some sort of scientific proof or experiment, very specific numbers, or an impressive-sounding mystery ingredient.
Unfinished Comparison/Claim	This technique uses phrases such as "Works better in poor driving conditions!"

COMPETENCY 2
UNDERSTAND STRATEGIES FOR DEVELOPING AND PRODUCING EFFECTIVE MEDIA PRESENTATIONS

SKILL 2.1 Demonstrating knowledge of the forms and purposes of media presentations (e.g., interview, reportage, storytelling)

Teach your students how to create a graph:
nces.ed.gov/nceskids/createagraph/default.aspx

Still visual media include pictures, drawings, photographs, tables, charts, maps, and diagrams. Techniques employed by still visual media include choosing colors appropriate to the purpose, placing important information in strategic locations within the still, sequencing stills (stages, overlays), sizing stills for optimum effect, placing stills in understandable contexts, and providing sufficient key or legend information.

Moving visual media include movies and videos. Techniques employed by visual media include most of those applicable to still media, plus determining a storyline or presentation rationale. In other words, the moving presentation needs to have an understandable beginning, development, and conclusion. Obviously, choosing effective transitions between scenes and installing a reasonable pace of image movement figure importantly in visual media. If the presentation is in slow motion or going by at warp speed for no discernable reason, the intended impact is diminished.

Oral media include songs, chants, speeches, and readings of stories, poems, and articles. Oral media can be stored on tapes, CDs, and a variety of digital recorders. Techniques employed by oral media include choosing an appropriate volume, applying principles of prosody (pace, pitch, inflection, voice modulation, or accents), employing rhythm and rhyme, and enhancing impact through musical instruments or sound effects.

Also see Skills 1.1 and 1.2

SKILL 2.2 Demonstrating knowledge of appropriate topics and projects for media presentations *(e.g., public service announcement, comic strip, skit)*

See Skill 1.1

SKILL 2.3 Applying strategies for selecting effective media and media combinations to use for various audiences and in various presentations *(e.g., Web site, slide presentation, animation, digital video)*

Visual graphics include a spectrum of artifacts. Pictures, graphs, charts, tables, and drawings are all useful to a greater or lesser degree in a wide variety of educational communications.

Keep in mind several principles regarding these graphic communications. One principle addresses aesthetics: Effective graphics should be pleasing to the eye. This is especially true if the graphic is some type of picture: It should be strategically placed; its colors should be well-chosen; and the size of the graphic should be suited to its intended purpose. Within the graphic itself, design features should enhance the intended communication. At the very least, the graphic needs to be large enough to view easily. Legends associated with a given graphic should be clear and thorough. The graphic, to be most effective, should be presented in a context that allows students to understand its function and importance.

Learn more about presenting effective presentations with visual aids:
www.osha.gov/doc/outreachtraining/htmlfiles/traintec.html

Oral communication as it applies in the classroom includes formal and informal speaking and listening by both teachers and students. Principles of oral communication include attention to such issues as vocabulary levels, appropriate volume, repetition of key points, prosody, and active listening. Students today, in general, have significantly fewer words in their vocabularies than did those of prior generations. Attention must be paid to developing clear definitions for key terms and to expressing ideas in terms accessible to the given student audience.

Speaking clearly and at volumes appropriate for given contexts is, of course, critical to any oral communication effort. When speaking to a whole room, for

MEDIA LITERACY

instance, a speaker has to project his or her voice beyond usual comfort levels in order to be effective. Repetition of key points, including whole class response routines, enhances communication of intended information. Using inflection and modulation enhances communication as well. Finally, there can be no oral communication without a receptive audience. Learning how to listen strategically is an important key.

Audiovisual communications include DVDs and digital recordings, and the principles that apply singly to graphic and oral communications also apply to audiovisual communications. In a classroom context, present audiovisual resources in ways that ensure student engagement. Rather than simply inserting a DVD and playing it for the whole period, pause the DVD at least a few times during the period and leading the class through some type of processing routines. This exercise will build in some accountability and some engagement for the students.

Technologies that incorporate interactive dimensions of audiovisual material are especially effective in communicating information and ensuring adequate student focus, especially in the absence of dynamic, teacher-directed processing.

Also see Skill 2.1

SKILL 2.4 Applying strategies for organizing and developing effective media presentations *(e.g., mapping, storyboarding, script writing)*

Learn more about integrating technology in the classroom:
www.glencoe.com/sec/teachingtoday/tiparchive.phtml/3

Media's impact on today's society is immense and ever-increasing. Children watch programs on television that are amazingly fast-paced and visually rich. Parents' roles as verbal and moral teachers are diminishing as children respond to the much more stimulating guidance of the television set. Adolescence, which used to be the time for going out and exploring the world first-hand, is now consumed by the allure of networking websites, popular music, and video games. Young adults are exposed to uncensored sex and violence.

But at the same time, media's effect on society is also beneficial and progressive. Its effect on education in particular provides special challenges and opportunities for teachers and students.

Thanks to satellite technology, urban classrooms and rural villages can receive instructional radio and television programs. CDs and DVDs enable students to learn information through a virtual reality experience. The Internet allows instant access to unlimited data and connects people across all cultures through shared interests. Educational media, when used in a productive way, enriches instruction and makes it more individualized, accessible, and economical.

UNDERSTAND STRATEGIES FOR DEVELOPING EFFECTIVE MEDIA PRESENTATIONS

Tips for using print media and visual aids:

- Use pictures over words whenever possible
- Present one key point per visual
- Use no more than three to four colors per visual to avoid clutter and confusion
- Use contrasting colors such as dark blue and bright yellow
- Use a maximum of twenty-five to thirty-five numbers per visual aid
- Use bullets instead of paragraphs when possible
- Make sure it is student-centered, not media-centered; delivery is just as important as the media presented
- Keep the content simple and concise (avoid too many lines, words, or pictures)
- Balance substance and visual appeal
- Make sure the text is large enough for the class to read
- Match the information to the format that will fit it best

Tips for using film and television:

- Study programs in advance
- Obtain supplementary materials such as printed transcripts of the narrative or study guides
- Provide your students with background information, explain unfamiliar concepts, and anticipate outcomes
- Assign outside readings based on student viewing
- Ask cuing questions
- Watch along with students
- Observe students' reactions
- Follow up viewing with discussions and related activities

Technology has broadened and enriched the entire communication process. Teachers and students who learn to use technological resources effectively will expand their capabilities inside and outside the classroom.

Multimedia refers to a technology for presenting material in both visual and verbal forms. This format is especially conducive to the classroom, since it reaches both visual and auditory learners.

MEDIA LITERACY

Knowing how to select effective teaching software is the first step in efficient multimedia education. First, decide what the software will be used for (creating spreadsheets, making diagrams, or creating slideshows). Consult magazines such as *PC World, Macworld,* and *Multimedia World* to learn about the newest programs available.

Go to a local computer store and ask a customer service representative to help you find the exact equipment you need. If possible, test the programs you are interested in. Check reviews in magazines such as *Consumer Reports, PC World,* or *Multimedia Schools* to ensure the software's quality.

SOFTWARE PROGRAMS FOR PRODUCING TEACHING MATERIAL	
Adobe	Aldus Freehand
CorelDRAW!	DrawPerfect
Claris Works	PC Paintbrush
Harvard Graphics	Visio
Microsoft Word	Microsoft PowerPoint

MULTIMEDIA TEACHING MODEL	
Step 1	Diagnose Figure out what students need to know Assess what students already know
Step 2	Design Design tests of learning achievement Identify effective instructional strategies Select suitable media Sequence learning activities within program Plan introductory activities Plan follow-up activities
Step 3	Procure Secure materials at hand Obtain new materials

Continued on next page

UNDERSTAND STRATEGIES FOR DEVELOPING EFFECTIVE MEDIA PRESENTATIONS

Step 4	Produce
	Modify existing materials
	Craft new materials
Step 5	Refine
	Conduct small-scale test of program
	Evaluate procedures and achievements
	Revise program accordingly
	Conduct classroom test of program
	Evaluate procedures and achievements
	Revise in anticipation of next school term

SKILL 2.5 Applying strategies for producing effective media presentations
(e.g., designing graphics and backgrounds, selecting font styles and sizes for text)

When designing a media presentation it is important to first keep in mind the purpose of the presentation. Multimedia presentation software is merely a tool to convey information. Do not overwhelm the audience with all of the bells and whistles associated with some of these programs.

Match the Design to the Purpose
Set the purpose. What is the purpose of the presentation? Is it meant to inform, entertain, persuade, or sell? The purpose and the mood of the presentation (formal vs. informal) will set the tone for the pictures, clip-art and font colors and sizes that are used.

Keep It Simple
Too much text, color, changes in font, and animation in one slide will overwhelm the audience and take away from the overall effectiveness of the presentation. The simpler the slides in the presentation, the clearer the message.

Be Consistent
Decide on a stylistic design and stick with it throughout. Changing the visual effects of each slide will only confuse the audience as well as take away from the continuity of the presentation. Again, less is more when designing a presentation.

MEDIA LITERACY

Many media software packages include predesigned slide templates that allow the presentation designer to focus on the content rather than the background color scheme and the visual effects. It is often a good idea to choose a color scheme and background template that matches the message that is being delivered and then stick with the one design that has been chosen.

Also see Skill 2.4

DOMAIN II
READING

READING

PERSONALIZED STUDY PLAN

PAGE	COMPETENCY AND SKILL		KNOWN MATERIAL/ SKIP IT
21	**3:**	**Understand the foundations of reading development**	☐
	3.1:	Demonstrating knowledge of phonological awareness skills	☐
	3.2:	Demonstrating knowledge of phonemic awareness skills	☐
	3.3:	Demonstrating knowledge of the concepts of print and the alphabetic principle	☐
	3.4:	Demonstrating knowledge of the role of phonics in promoting reading comprehension	☐
	3.5:	Demonstrating knowledge of the role of fluency in reading development, the components of fluency, and the factors that influence fluency	☐
	3.6:	Demonstrating the ability to differentiate reading instruction to meet the needs of students at various reading proficiency levels and with various linguistic backgrounds	☐
	3.7:	Demonstrating the ability to scaffold reading tasks for students who experience comprehension difficulties	☐
24	**4:**	**Understand strategies for developing vocabulary knowledge and reading comprehension**	☐
	4.1:	Using knowledge of syntactic rules and word structure and contextual analysis skills to help identify word meanings	☐
	4.2:	Recognizing relationships between words and issues related to word selection	☐
	4.3:	Recognizing factors that influence vocabulary development	☐
	4.4:	Recognizing factors that influence reading comprehension	☐
	4.5:	Recognizing an appropriate reading strategy to use for a particular text and purpose	☐
	4.6:	Recognizing appropriate research-based reading comprehension strategies to use before, during, and after reading	☐
	4.7:	Recognizing appropriate oral and written language activities to use to enhance reading comprehension	☐
	4.8:	Demonstrating knowledge of literal and inferential reading comprehension skills	☐

READING

PERSONALIZED STUDY PLAN

PAGE	COMPETENCY AND SKILL		KNOWN MATERIAL/ SKIP IT
33	**5:**	**Understand strategies for reading informational and persuasive texts**	☐
	5.1:	Recognizing the characteristics of various types of informational texts and persuasive texts	☐
	5.2:	Using knowledge of the organizational features and structure of a text to help enhance comprehension of the text	☐
	5.3:	Identifying the main idea, purpose, and intended audience of a text	☐
	5.4:	Distinguishing between facts and opinions and between general statements and specific details in a text	☐
	5.5:	Assessing the relevance, importance, and sufficiency of evidence, examples, and reasons provided to explain a concept or support an argument in a text	☐
	5.6:	Assessing the credibility, objectivity, and reliability of various sources used in a text	☐
	5.7:	Analyzing the use of rhetorical devices and techniques in a text	☐
42	**6:**	**Understand strategies for reading technical and functional texts**	☐
	6.1:	Recognizing the characteristics of various types of technical texts and functional texts	☐
	6.2:	Using information presented in technical texts to gain knowledge and develop skills	☐
	6.3:	Using information presented in functional texts to confirm facts and perform tasks	☐
	6.4:	Interpreting graphic features used in technical texts and in functional texts	☐

COMPETENCY 3
UNDERSTAND THE FOUNDATIONS OF READING DEVELOPMENT

SKILL 3.1 Demonstrating knowledge of phonological awareness skills *(e.g., distinguishing word syllables)*

Understanding the history and development of their language is one part of students' study of the English language. They should also understand the features and characteristics of their language's structure.

Phonological Awareness

PHONOLOGICAL AWARENESS refers to the ability of the reader to recognize the sound of spoken language. This recognition includes how these sounds can be blended together, segmented (divided up), and manipulated (switched around). This awareness then leads to PHONICS, a method for teaching students to read. Phonics helps students "sound out words."

Instructional methods to teach phonological awareness may include auditory games and drills during which students recognize and manipulate the sounds of words, separate or segment the sounds of words, take out sounds, blend sounds, add in new sounds, or take apart sounds to recombine them in new formations. These drills and games are good ways to foster phonological awareness.

Check out a continuum of complexity of phonological awareness activities:
www.ldonline.org/article/6254

PHONOLOGICAL AWARENESS: the ability of a reader to recognize the sound of spoken language

PHONICS: a method for teaching reading that helps students "sound out words"

SKILL 3.2 Demonstrating knowledge of phonemic awareness skills *(e.g., segmenting, blending)*

Phonemic Awareness is understanding that words are composed of sounds. Phonemic awareness allows a listener to recognize and manipulate specific sounds in spoken words. Phonemic awareness deals with sounds in words that are spoken. The majority of phonemic awareness tasks, activities, and exercises are oral.

READING

Phonological awareness is the ability of the reader to recognize the sounds of spoken language. This recognition includes how these sounds can be blended together, segmented (divided up), and manipulated (switched around).

Phonological awareness skills include:

- Rhyming and syllabification
- Blending sounds into words
- Identifying the beginning or starting sounds of words
- Breaking words down into sounds (also called "segmenting" words)
- Recognizing small words contained in bigger words by removing starting sounds (for example, hear to ear)

SKILL 3.3 Demonstrating knowledge of the concepts of print and the alphabetic principle

See Skill 3.2

SKILL 3.4 Demonstrating knowledge of the role of phonics in promoting reading comprehension

See Skills 3.1 and 3.2

SKILL 3.5 Demonstrating knowledge of the role of fluency in reading development, the components of fluency, and the factors that influence fluency

See Skill 3.2

UNDERSTAND THE FOUNDATIONS OF READING DEVELOPMENT

SKILL 3.6 Demonstrating the ability to differentiate reading instruction to meet the needs of students at various reading proficiency levels and with various linguistic backgrounds

Jumping into a reading assignment may be tempting. Most students just want to get the assignment done and are unwilling to add any steps. Persuading them that they will save time in the end if they take the time to do some preparation for reading a piece will be worth the classroom time.

What can be done ahead of time?

- Looking at the date of publication is useful. Knowing that a story was published in 1930 or in 2005 can reveal a lot about the setting and characters. Knowing what was going on in the world at the time of publication would help a reader, and an encyclopedia can provide a quick overview. Also, knowing something about the author is useful. Most well-known authors have at least a short biography in an appropriate encyclopedia.

- A quick overview of the story before beginning to read might help. Are there chapters with headings? If not, a quick survey of the sections, either chapters or paragraphs, will yield clues that will guide reading and improve comprehension. If the reading assignment is an essay, a quick skimming for paragraph topic sentences and a look at the conclusion will provide useful information before beginning the actual reading. Students should be warned not to make premature judgments based on any of these pre-reading activities, however, and should be advised to let the story or essay speak for itself.

Assuming that the students in your classroom do not have reading disabilities, reading comprehension skills can be taught. This works particularly well if reading comprehension instruction goes hand-in-hand with teaching writing skills. Students need to practice looking for the point of a written discourse just as they need to learn to focus their writing. What was the writer's aim or purpose? Can the writing be said to be persuasive in nature, for instance, or is it simply conveying useful (or not useful) information? Is the piece purely expressive, with the intention of opening up an experience for the reader?

These skills will be taught in the writing classroom and can be reinforced in the reading classroom. If students understand what the possible structures are in a piece of writing, they will be more skilled at comprehending what is being said.

Another tool for comprehension is learning to react to the written information. What does this piece have to do with me? Do I agree or disagree with this writer? Once a reader gets to that point, the ability to comprehend has matured to a useful level.

Check out different reading strategies:

www.greece.k12
.ny.us/instruction
/ela/6-12/OKOKReading
/Reading%20Strategies
/reading%20strategies%20
index.htm

READING

> **SKILL 3.7** Demonstrating the ability to scaffold reading tasks for students who experience comprehension difficulties

See Skill 3.6

COMPETENCY 4
UNDERSTAND STRATEGIES FOR DEVELOPING VOCABULARY KNOWLEDGE AND READING COMPREHENSION

> **SKILL 4.1** Using knowledge of syntactic rules and word structure and contextual analysis skills to help identify word meanings

For students to understand difficult or complex passages, they must use skills to define unfamiliar words and infer meaning from the surrounding text. By understanding how words are formed, students will be better able to analyze challenging vocabulary and phrases.

Learn more about monitoring comprehension:
www.indiana.edu/~l517/monitoring.html

Context Clues

Context clues help readers determine the meaning of words with which they are not familiar. The context of a word consists of the sentence or sentences that surround that word. Read the following sentences and attempt to determine the meanings of the words in bold print.

> The **luminosity** of the room was so incredible that there was no need for lights.

If there was no need for lights, then one must assume that the word luminosity has something to do with giving off light. The definition of "luminosity," therefore, is the emission of light.

> Jamie could not understand Joe's feelings. His mood swings made understanding him an **enigma**.

UNDERSTAND STRATEGIES FOR DEVELOPING VOCABULARY KNOWLEDGE

The fact that he could not be understood made him somewhat of a puzzle. The definition of "enigma" is a mystery or puzzle.

Another way to determine meaning is to identify common morphemes, prefixes, and suffixes. Familiarity with word roots (the basic elements of words) and with prefixes can also help one determine the meanings of unknown words.

Root words

A ROOT WORD is a word from which another word is developed. The second word can be said to have its "root" in the first. This structural component nicely lends itself to the illustration of a tree with roots, so that students can use a concrete image for an abstract concept. Students may also want to construct root words literally by using cardboard trees or actual roots from plants to create word family models. This way, students have the opportunity to own their root words.

An example of a root word is "bene," which means "good" or "well." English words from this Latin root include "benefit," "beneficial," "beneficent," and "beneficiary."

> **ROOT WORD:** a word from which another word is developed

Base words

A BASE WORD is a stand-alone linguistic unit that cannot be deconstructed or broken down into smaller words. For example, in the word "retell," the base word is "tell."

> **BASE WORD:** a stand-alone linguistic unit that cannot be deconstructed or broken down into smaller words

Contractions

CONTRACTIONS are shortened forms of two words in which one or more letters have been deleted. These deleted letters have been replaced by an apostrophe. For example, "hasn't" is the contraction for "has not."

> **CONTRACTIONS:** shortened forms of two words in which one or more letters have been deleted

> *Learn more about word analysis:*
> www.orangeusd.k12.ca.us/yorba/word_analysis.htm

Prefixes

PREFIXES are units of meaning that can be added (or "affixed") to the beginning of a base word or root word. They cannot stand alone. Prefixes are also sometimes known as "bound morphemes," meaning that they cannot stand alone as base words. Some examples of prefixes are "pre," "ex," "trans," and "sub."

> **PREFIXES:** units of meaning that can be added to the beginning of a base word or root word

Suffixes

A SUFFIX is a unit of meaning that can be affixed to the end of a root or base word. Suffixes transform the original meanings of base and root words. Like prefixes, they are also known as bound morphemes, because they cannot stand alone as words. Some examples of suffixes are "ing," "ful," "ness," and "er."

> **SUFFIX:** a unit of meaning that can be affixed to the end of a root or base word

READING

> **INFLECTIONAL ENDINGS:** types of suffixes that impart a new meaning to the base word or root word

> **COMPOUND WORDS:** words that occur when two or more base words are connected to form a new word

Inflectional endings

INFLECTIONAL ENDINGS are types of suffixes that impart a new meaning to the base or root word. These endings in particular change the gender, number, tense, or form of the base or root words. Just like other suffixes, these are also termed "bound morphemes." Some examples are "ette," "es," and "ed."

Compound words

COMPOUND WORDS occur when two or more base words are connected to form a new word. The meaning of the new word is in some way connected with that of the base words. "Bookkeeper," besides being the only English word with three double letters in a row, is an example of a compound word.

Following is a partial list of roots and prefixes. Reviewing these might be useful to you.

Root	Meaning	Example
aqua	water	aqualung
astro	stars	astrology
bio	life	biology
carn	meat	carnivorous
circum	around	circumnavigate
geo	earth	geology
herb	plant	herbivorous
mal	bad	malicious
neo	new	neonatal
tele	distant	telescope

Prefix	Meaning	Example
un-	not	unnamed
re-	again	reenter

Continued on next page

UNDERSTAND STRATEGIES FOR DEVELOPING VOCABULARY KNOWLEDGE

Prefix	Meaning	Example
il-	not	illegible
pre-	before	preset
mis-	incorrectly	misstate
in-	not	informal
anti-	against	antiwar
de-	opposite	derail
post-	after	postwar
ir-	not	irresponsible

Word forms

Sometimes a very familiar word can appear as a different part of speech. You may have heard that *fraud* involves a criminal misrepresentation, so when it appears as the adjective form *fraudulent* ("He was suspected of fraudulent activities"), you can make an educated guess. You probably know that something out of date is *obsolete*; therefore, when you read about "built-in *obsolescence*," you can detect the meaning of the unfamiliar word.

Sentence clues

Often, a writer will actually define a difficult or particularly important word for the reader the first time it appears in a passage. Phrases like *that is, such as, which is,* or *is called* might announce the writer's intention to give the definition. Occasionally, a writer will simply use a synonym or near-synonym joined by the word *or*. Look at the following examples:

> The **credibility**, that is to say, the believability, of the witness was called into question by evidence of previous perjury.
>
> Nothing would **assuage** or lessen the child's grief.

Punctuation

At the sentence level, punctuation is often a clue to the meaning of a word. Commas, parentheses, quotation marks, and dashes tell the reader that a definition is being offered by the writer.

> *A tendency toward **hyperbole**, extravagant exaggeration, is a common flaw among persuasive writers.*
>
> *Political **apathy**—lack of interest—can lead to the death of the state.*

A writer might simply give an explanation in other words that you can understand in the same sentence.

> *The **xenophobic** townspeople were suspicious of every foreigner.*

Writers also explain a word in terms of its opposite at the sentence level.

> *His **incarceration** was ended, and he was elated to be out of jail.*

Adjacent sentence clues

The context for a word goes beyond the sentence in which it appears. At times, the writer uses adjacent sentences to present an explanation or definition.

> *The $200 for the car repair would have to come out of the **contingency** fund. Fortunately, Angela's father had taught her to keep some money set aside for just such emergencies.*

The second sentence offers a clue to the definition of *contingency* as used in this sentence: emergencies. Therefore, a fund for contingencies would be money tucked away for unforeseen and/or urgent events.

Entire passage clues

On occasion, one must look at an entire paragraph or passage to figure out the definition of a word or term. In the following paragraph, notice how the word *nostalgia* undergoes a form of extended definition throughout the selection rather than in just one sentence.

> *The word **nostalgia** links Greek words for away from home and pain. If you're feeling **nostalgic**, then you are probably in some physical distress or discomfort, suffering from a feeling of alienation and separation from loved ones or loved places. **Nostalgia** is that awful feeling you remember from the first time you went away to camp or spent the weekend with a friend's family—homesickness, or some condition even more painful than that. But in common use, **nostalgia** has come to have more sentimental associations. A few years back, for example, a **nostalgia** craze had to do with the 1950s. We resurrected poodle skirts and saddle shoes, built new restaurants to look like old ones, and tried to make chicken a la king just as mother probably never made it. In TV situation comedies, we recreated a pleasant world that probably never existed and relished our **nostalgia**, longing for a homey, comfortable lost time.*

UNDERSTAND STRATEGIES FOR DEVELOPING VOCABULARY KNOWLEDGE

SKILL 4.2 **Recognizing relationships between words** *(e.g., synonyms, antonyms)* **and issues related to word selection** *(e.g., denotative and connotative meanings)*

See Skill 4.1

SKILL 4.3 **Recognizing factors that influence vocabulary development** *(e.g., promoting word consciousness, wide reading)*

See Skill 3.2

SKILL 4.4 **Recognizing factors that influence reading comprehension** *(e.g., reader's interest, reading rate)*

Reading comprehension is a necessary skill that students must acquire to become good readers. There are students who can read fluently, yet do not understand what they read. Teachers should continually ask questions about the text to ensure comprehension.

A lack of background knowledge is often one of the factors that affect comprehension. When students do not understand the topic at hand, they will have difficulty reading about the topic no matter how fluently they read. Other factors that affect the level of comprehension are:

- Lack of word recognition skills
- Inability to determine the meanings of words through context clues
- Insufficient level of vocabulary development

Reading rate can also influence comprehension. A student whose reading rate is slow, or halting and inconsistent, exhibits a lack of reading fluency. Limited fluency may affect performance in the following ways:

- Students read less text than their peers and have less time to remember, review, or comprehend the text
- Students expend more cognitive energy than their peers trying to identify individual words
- Students may be less able to retain text in their memories and less likely to integrate those segments with other parts of the text

READING

SKILL 4.5 Recognizing an appropriate reading strategy (e.g., scanning, skimming) to use for a particular text and purpose

One of the common fallacies students have about reading comes from the ways in which students are taught to read. Sure, as students are being taught to read, they must learn the strategies of careful reading, which includes sounding out words, focusing on fluency, obtaining meaning, etc. However, at points in the learning-to-read process, teachers can help students learn that there are various reasons why people read. Sometimes people read for pleasure, in which case they can decide whether to skim through quickly for the content or read slowly to savor ideas and language. Other times, people simply want to find information quickly, in which case they will skim or scan. In some texts, rereading is necessary to fully comprehend information.

READING STRATEGIES	
Skimming	Skimming is when readers read quickly while paying little attention to specific words. This is often done when readers want a full picture of a text but do not want to focus on the details. Skimming can be done as a preview or a review. When done as a preview, often readers will look to see what it is they can expect from the text. When done as a review, readers will hope to be reminded of the main points through the skim.
Scanning	Scanning is a bit different from skimming. In skimming, readers read connected text quickly. In scanning, readers go straight to specific ideas, words, sections, or examples. They pick and choose what they will read within a text. This is done when the reader does not need to know everything from a text.
In-Depth Reading	In-depth reading is the reading most people think is the only legitimate type of reading. Strangely, though, all types of reading are done by all types of people—all the time! In-depth reading is done when readers want to enjoy a text or learn from it thoroughly. For the most part, in this type of reading, readers will move forward quickly and not stop to focus on a specific word or idea, although sometimes this is necessary. The main idea of this type of reading, though, is that readers do not skip over or read fast to get information. They read everything carefully and thoroughly.
Rereading	Rereading is the final type of reading, which comes in many forms. Sometimes, whole texts must be reread for the concepts. This is usually the case when the text is difficult. Rereading can also be done as someone is doing regular in-depth reading. For example, a word, concept, or a few ideas may need to be reviewed before the reader can go on. Another method of rereading is rereading a whole text months or years after reading it the first time. This is done when readers realize that through their life experiences since the first reading, they will view the text in a different light.

UNDERSTAND STRATEGIES FOR DEVELOPING VOCABULARY KNOWLEDGE

All these methods are acceptable forms of reading, however, all must be done with specific purposes in mind. Generally, it is not a good idea to skim or scan a class novel, but skimming and scanning through a textbook may be acceptable if only a few ideas are crucial.

SKILL 4.6 **Recognizing appropriate research-based reading comprehension strategies to use before, during, and after reading** *(e.g., predicting, self-monitoring/self-questioning and using other metacognitive skills, summarizing)*

See Skill 3.6

SKILL 4.7 **Recognizing appropriate oral and written language activities to use to enhance reading comprehension** *(e.g., think-alouds, retelling)*

See Skills 3.2 and 4.4

SKILL 4.8 **Demonstrating knowledge of literal and inferential reading comprehension skills** *(e.g., identifying sequence of events in a text, making generalizations from information presented in a text)*

Inferences and Conclusions

An **INFERENCE** is sometimes called an *educated guess* because it requires that one goes beyond the strictly obvious to create additional meaning by taking the text one logical step further. Inferences and conclusions are based on the content of the passage—that is, on what the passage says or how the writer says it—and are derived by reasoning. Inference is an essential and automatic component of most reading. Examples include:

- Making educated guesses about the meaning of unknown words
- The author's main idea
- The presence of bias in the author's writing

> **INFERENCE:** sometimes called an *educated guess* because it requires that one goes beyond the strictly obvious to create additional meaning by taking the text one logical step further

Such is the essence of inference—a reader must use his or her own ability to reason in order to figure out what the writer implies. As a reader, then, one must often logically extend meaning that is only implied.

Consider the following example. Assume you are an employer, and you are reading over the letters of reference submitted by a prospective employee for the position of clerk/typist in your real estate office. The position requires the applicant to be neat, careful, trustworthy, and punctual. You come across this letter of reference submitted by an applicant.

> ### To Whom It May Concern:
>
> *Todd Finley has asked me to write a letter of reference for him. I am well qualified to do so because he worked for me for three months last year. His duties included answering the phone, greeting the public, and producing some simple memos and notices on the computer. Although Todd initially had few computer skills and little knowledge of telephone etiquette, he did acquire some during his stay with us. Todd's manner of speaking, both on the telephone and with the clients who came to my establishment, could be described as casual. He was particularly effective when communicating with peers. Please contact me by telephone if you wish to have further information about my experience with Todd.*

Here the writer implies, rather than openly states, the main idea. This letter calls attention to itself because there is a problem with its tone. A truly positive letter would say something such as, "I have the distinct honor of recommending Todd Finley." Here, however, the letter simply verifies that Todd worked in the office. Second, the praise is obviously lukewarm. For example, the writer says that Todd "was particularly effective when communicating with peers." An educated guess translates that statement into a nice way of saying Todd was not serious about his communication with clients.

In order to draw inferences and make conclusions, a reader must use prior knowledge and apply it to the current situation. A conclusion or inference is never stated. You must rely on your common sense.

COMPETENCY 5
UNDERSTAND STRATEGIES FOR READING INFORMATIONAL AND PERSUASIVE TEXTS

> **SKILL 5.1** Recognizing the characteristics of various types of informational texts *(e.g., newspapers, textbooks)* and persuasive texts *(e.g., editorials, propaganda)*

Twenty-first century Americans read many words every day, both in print and in electronic form. Because of this flood of information, readers should be able to discern the various purposes, structures, elements, and meanings of these expository (informational) texts.

We purchase a new cabinet and read the directions for assembling it. If those directions are not easily understandable, we become frustrated and upset. Installing new software on our computers requires that we read a lot of expository text. The writers of this documentation are not trying to persuade us to read it—they are simply providing information that we might need.

Although many have predicted from time to time that the newspaper will become obsolete (replaced by radio, television, or the Internet), it hasn't happened yet. The first printed newspaper was published in 1605, and many people still rely on their daily and weekly newspapers to keep in touch with their communities and the world.

Even so, there is some indication that the proliferation of computer access and the high level of accessibility of news from all over the world is, in fact, affecting the newspaper business. Paid circulation is declining in most countries. Advertising revenue, which makes up the bulk of a newspaper's income, is shifting from print to online, resulting in a general decline in newspaper profits. As a result, the predictions that newspapers may vanish are rife again. Only time will tell whether this traditional feature of daily life will end any time soon.

General-interest newspapers are the most common type and are purveyors of current news such as political events, crimes, business, culture, sports, and opinions (editorials, columns, or political cartoons). The first permanent photograph was produced in 1826, and photography eventually became an important part of news stories. Cartoonists also got into the act in 1843 when *Punch* magazine began to put satirical drawings on its pages. Today, most newspapers include political cartoons.

A newspaper may include the following specific features:

- Weather news and forecasts
- An advice column
- Critical reviews of movies, plays, or restaurants
- Editorial opinions
- A gossip column
- Comic strips and other entertainment, such as crosswords, sudoku, and horoscopes
- A sports column or section

SKILL 5.2 Using knowledge of the organizational features and structure of a text to help enhance comprehension of the text

Language is hierarchal. The lowest level in the hierarchy consists of sounds (spoken) and letters (written), also known as the PHONEMIC STAGE in the hierarchy. The second stage is MORPHEMES, or units of meaning that are not words. The third stage in the hierarchy is WORDS, which are made out of morphemes.

Words are used to make SENTENCES also (which comprise the syntactic level of language). In English, sentences also include *classes* of words (sometimes called parts of speech) that are strictly arranged according to order. English is one of the few languages that depend on word order to convey the intended meaning. For example, Spanish depends on case and inflection in word endings to signal subjects and predicates. Just as the subject of a sentence announces what the topic is, so the verb says something about that subject. The dog (subject) barks (verb).

PARAGRAPHS echo the sentence in that they include a topic sentence that states the subject and include supporting sentences that say something about the topic sentence. The same is true in longer discourses. In an essay, the thesis states the subject of the document. Paragraphs will develop that thesis (say something about the thesis).

As a teacher, keeping in mind that this hierarchical nature of language is innate can be useful; it is embedded in the minds of native speakers, including students. Tapping into this innate characteristic can help students understand the importance of the topic sentence and thesis statement in their own compositions. It's also extremely useful in helping them learn to analyze written text, be it persuasive, expository, descriptive, or narrative. If students understand how

---

PHONEMIC STAGE: the lowest level in the language hierarchy—sounds and letters

MORPHEMES: the second level in the language hierarchy—units of meaning that are not words

WORDS: the third level in the language hierarchy—units of meaning, made out of morphemes

SENTENCES: units of meaning made out of words

language works (including their own) when stating a subject and saying something about it, they can more easily understand how another writer has done that very thing. What is this writer's subject, and what has he or she said about it?

The very notion of a table of contents is based on this hierarchical nature of language. A TABLE OF CONTENTS is a map to the arrangement of a document by topic, sub-topics, and sometimes sub-sub topics. If this hierarchy is understood, then creating a table of contents for a written piece comes naturally. For a writer, the table of contents is a natural extension of an outline. It helps the writer stay on target and develop a cohesive and balanced piece of writing. For a reader, the table of contents provides visual clues by establishing the main ideas and supporting details in a hierarchical format.

To make information easier for readers to comprehend, step-by-step lists help clarify complicated processes or procedures. Just as a cook follows a recipe step by step, a mechanic follows an established procedure. These lists can be bulleted or enumerated, depending on the purpose of the list.

When readers have less time to read, they tend to skim. Just as headlines that do not provide accurate clues to the content of a newspaper article can be frustrating, the same is true of inaccurate chapter headings. This is not usually the time to be creative. Effective chapter headings guide readers through material so that they can more easily locate the information they need.

If the student comes to see written and spoken language in the terms delineated above, then summarizing a piece becomes much easier. The summarizer looks for the "bones" of the piece being summarized and bypasses details that flesh out the main points. Students need much practice in this skill because of the tendency to oversimplify. Practice may not make perfect, but it does lead to deeper understanding of how language works.

> **PARAGRAPHS:** units of meaning made up of a topic sentence and supporting sentences

> **TABLE OF CONTENTS:** a map to the arrangement of a document

SKILL 5.3 Identifying the main idea, purpose, and intended audience of a text

Sometimes a writer will announce the purpose of a document. The responsibility remains with the reader, however, to determine whether the piece of writing fulfills the announced purpose. If the writer does not state the *point* of the written work, the reader must determine it. It's best to read the entire piece of writing from beginning to end and then to ask the questions: What did the writer accomplish? What did the writer *intend* to accomplish? The point of a piece of writing is called a THESIS.

> **THESIS:** the purpose of a piece of writing

READING

Sometimes a piece of writing does not state the thesis anywhere in the text. In these cases, the reader must infer the thesis based on such questions as these:

- Does the writer make a point even though it is not stated?
- What does the paper prove?
- What is the point?

A good thesis statement is very specific. A general thesis statement leads nowhere. Freewriting about a topic often yields several good thesis statements about a particular topic. Once the writer clarifies his or her topic, then the thesis statement needs to be narrowed in scope and intent to fit what the writer wants to accomplish. Composing an effective thesis statement usually requires some whittling and rethinking.

Read more about thesis statements:

www.unc.edu/depts/wcweb/handouts/thesis.html

To develop a thesis statement, a writer provides supporting details. These details can include facts, opinions, statistics, examples, or definitions—anything that clarifies the point of the piece of writing.

In the traditional five-paragraph essay taught in schools, the goal is for students to provide depth and breadth to their thesis statements, and they are encouraged to provide three supporting details. However, this standard can often produce limited or artificial support. Writers may choose to focus on one or two supporting details or to provide a much broader range—whatever is needed to develop the thesis clearly and completely.

> **SKILL 5.4** Distinguishing between facts and opinions and between general statements and specific details in a text

Your students will enjoy sharing their opinions. Some of them may be voicing what they have heard from others, while some are discovering their own voices. All of them, though, are trying to make sense of their worlds. Helping students distinguish between fact and opinion, realize conclusions, and make inferences develops critical reasoning.

FACT: a statement that is verifiable

OPINION: a statement that must be supported in order to be accepted

Facts and Opinions

FACTS are statements that are verifiable. OPINIONS are statements that must be supported in order to be accepted. Facts are used to support opinions. For example, "Jane is a bad girl" is an *opinion*. However, "Jane hit her sister with a baseball bat" is a *fact* upon which the opinion is based. JUDGMENTS are

UNDERSTAND STRATEGIES FOR READING INFORMATIONAL AND PERSUASIVE TEXTS

opinions—decisions or declarations based on observation or reasoning that express approval or disapproval. Facts report what has happened or exists, and they come from observation, measurement, or calculation. Facts can be tested and verified, whereas opinions and judgments cannot. They can only be supported with facts.

Most statements cannot be so clearly distinguished. "I believe that Jane is a bad girl" is a fact. The speaker knows what he or she believes. However, the statement obviously includes a judgment that could be disputed by another person who might believe otherwise. Judgments are not usually so firm. They are, rather, plausible opinions that provoke thought or lead to factual development.

> **JUDGMENT:** a type of opinion; a decision or declaration based on observation or reasoning that expresses approval or disapproval

Use the chart below to identify both facts and opinions in a text and be sure to explain how you know the details you write down are either facts or opinions.

FACT VS. OPINION		
	Text Details and Direct Quotes From the Text	**Explain How You Know Whether the Details Are Facts or Opinions**
Facts		
Opinions		

http://www.greece.k12.ny.us/instruction/ela/6-12/Tools/factvsopinion

Conclusions

CONCLUSIONS are drawn as a result of a line of reasoning. Whether inductive or deductive, a conclusion is an analysis of what the data means. Given all the facts, all the opinions, and all the details, the reader can draw a conclusion.

> **CONCLUSION:** an analysis drawn as a result of a line of reasoning

> *Joe DiMaggio, a Yankees center fielder, was replaced by Mickey Mantle in 1952.*

This is a fact. If necessary, evidence can be produced to support this.

> *First-year players are more ambitious than seasoned players.*

This is an opinion. There is no proof to support that every first-year player feels this way.

READING

> **SKILL 5.5** Assessing the relevance, importance, and sufficiency of evidence, examples, and reasons provided to explain a concept or support an argument in a text

Assessing Relevance

It is important to continually assess whether or not a sentence contributes to the overall task of supporting the main idea. When a sentence is deemed irrelevant, it is best either to omit it from the passage or to make it relevant by one of the following strategies:

STRATEGY	DESCRIPTION
Adding Detail	Sometimes a sentence can seem out of place if it does not contain enough information to link it to the topic. Adding specific information can show how the sentence is related to the main idea.
Adding an Example	This is especially important in passages in which information is being argued, compared, or contrasted. Examples can support the main idea and give the document overall credibility.
Using Diction Effectively	It is important to understand connotation, avoid ambiguity, and avoid too much repetition when selecting words.
Adding Transitions	Transitions are extremely helpful for making sentences relevant because they are specifically designed to connect one idea to another. They can also reduce a paragraph's choppiness.

The following passage has several irrelevant sentences that are highlighted in bold.

> The New City Planning Committee is proposing a new capitol building to represent the multicultural face of New City. **The current mayor is a Democrat.** The new capitol building will be on 10th Street across from the grocery store and next to the Recreational Center. It will be within walking distance to the subway and bus depot, as the designers want to emphasize the importance of public transportation. Aesthetically, the building will have a contemporary design, featuring a brushed-steel exterior and large, floor-to-ceiling windows. **It is important for employees to have a connection with the outside world even when they are in their offices.** Inside the building, the walls will be moveable. This will not only facilitate a multitude of creative floor plans, but it will also create a focus on open communication and flow of information. **It sounds a bit gimmicky to me.** Finally, the capitol will feature a large outdoor courtyard full of lush greenery and serene fountains. **Work will now seem like Club Med to those who work at the New City capitol!**

Evaluating the Logic of Writer's Argument

Fact and fallacy

An **ARGUMENT** is a generalization that is proven or supported with facts. If the facts are not accurate, the generalization remains unproven. Using inaccurate facts to support an argument is called a **FALLACY IN REASONING**. The following are some factors to consider in judging whether the facts used to support an argument are accurate:

1. Are the facts current, or are they out-of-date? For example, if the proposition is, "Birth defects in babies born to drug-using mothers are increasing," then the data included must be the latest available.

2. Another important factor to consider in judging the accuracy of a fact is its source. From where was the data obtained, and is that source reliable?

3. The calculations on which the facts are based may be unreliable. It is a good idea to run one's own calculations before using a piece of derived information.

> **ARGUMENT:** a generalization that is proven or supported with facts
>
> **FALLACY IN REASONING:** using inaccurate facts to support an argument

Even facts that are true and have a sharp impact on the argument may not be relevant to the case at hand, as in the following examples:

1. Health statistics from an entire state may have no relevance, or little relevance, to a particular county or zip code. Statistics from an entire country cannot be used to prove very much about a particular state or county.

2. An analogy can be useful in making a point, but the comparison must match up in all characteristics, or it will not be relevant. Analogies should be used very carefully. They are often just as likely to destroy an argument as they are to strengthen one.

The importance or significance of a fact may not be sufficient to strengthen an argument. For example, of the millions of immigrants in the U.S., using a single family to support a solution to the immigration problem will not make much difference overall, even though such single-example arguments are often used to support one position or another. They may achieve a positive reaction, but they will not prove that one solution is better than another. If enough cases were cited from a variety of geographical locations, the information might be significant.

Number of Facts

How much is enough? Three strong supporting facts are sufficient to establish the thesis of an argument. However, sometimes many more facts are needed, as in the following example:

Conclusion: All green apples are sour.

- When I was a child, I bit into a green apple from my grandfather's orchard, and it was sour.
- I once bought green apples from a roadside vendor, and when I bit into one, it was sour.
- My grocery store had a sale on green Granny Smith apples last week, and I bought several, only to find that they were sour when I bit into one.

The fallacy in the above argument is that the sample was insufficient. A more exhaustive search of literature, etc., will probably turn up some green apples that are not sour.

Sometimes more than three arguments is too many. On the other hand, it is common to hear public speakers, particularly politicians, cite a long litany of facts to support their positions.

Omission of facts

A very good example of the omission of facts in an argument is the résumé of an applicant for a job. The applicant is arguing that he or she should be chosen for a particular job. The application form will ask for information about past employment, and unfavorable dismissals from jobs in the past may be omitted. Employers are usually suspicious of periods when the applicant has not listed an employer.

A writer makes choices about which facts will be used and which will be discarded in developing an argument. Those choices may exclude anything that is not supportive of the point of view the arguer is taking. It is always a good idea for the reader to do some research to spot the omissions and to ask whether they may have an impact on the acceptance of the point of view presented in the argument.

No judgment is either black or white. If the argument seems too neat or too compelling, there are probably facts that might be relevant that have not been included.

SKILL 5.6 Assessing the credibility, objectivity, and reliability of various sources used in a text

See Skill 5.5

UNDERSTAND STRATEGIES FOR READING INFORMATIONAL AND PERSUASIVE TEXTS

SKILL 5.7 Analyzing the use of rhetorical devices and techniques in a text (e.g., repetition, exaggeration)

Tailoring language for a particular audience is an important skill. Writing to be read by a business associate surely sounds different from writing to be read by a younger sibling. Not only are the vocabularies different, but the formality or informality of the discourse needs to be adjusted.

Two characteristics that determine language style are degree of formality and word choice. The most formal language does not use contractions or slang, while the most informal language probably features a casual use of common sayings and anecdotes. Formal language uses longer sentences and does not sound like a conversation. Informal language uses shorter sentences (not necessarily simple sentences, but shorter constructions) and may sound like a conversation.

In both formal and informal writing, there exists a TONE, the writer's attitude toward the material and/or readers. Tone may be playful, formal, intimate, angry, serious, ironic, outraged, baffled, tender, serene, depressed, and so on. The overall tone of a piece of writing is dictated by both the subject matter and the audience. Tone is also related to the actual word choices that make up the document, as we attach affective meanings to words, called their CONNOTATIONS. Gaining this conscious control over language makes it possible to use language appropriately in various situations and to evaluate its uses in literature and other forms of communication. By evoking the proper responses from readers or listeners, we can prompt them to take action.

TONE: the writer's attitude toward the material and/or readers

CONNOTATIONS: affective meanings attached to words

Using the following questions is an excellent way to assess the audience and tone of a given piece of writing:

- Who is your audience (friend, teacher, businessperson, someone else)?
- How much does this person know about you and/or your topic?
- What is your purpose (to prove an argument, to persuade, to amuse, to register a complaint, to ask for a raise, and so on)?
- What emotions do you have about the topic (nervous, happy, confident, angry, sad, no feelings at all)?
- What emotions do you want to register with your audience (anger, nervousness, happiness, boredom, interest)?
- What persona do you need to create in order to achieve your purpose?

- What choice of language is best suited to achieving your purpose with this particular subject (slang, friendly but respectful, formal)?

- What emotional quality do you want to transmit to achieve your purpose (matter-of-fact, informative, authoritative, inquisitive, sympathetic, angry), and to what degree do you want to express this tone?

COMPETENCY 6
UNDERSTAND STRATEGIES FOR READING TECHNICAL AND FUNCTIONAL TEXTS

> **SKILL 6.1** Recognizing the characteristics of various types of technical texts *(e.g., warranties, contracts)* **and functional texts** *(e.g., timetables, application forms)*

See Skill 5.1

> **SKILL 6.2** Using information presented in technical texts to gain knowledge and develop skills *(e.g., learning and exercising consumers' and citizens' rights)*

See Skill 5.1

> **SKILL 6.3** Using information presented in functional texts to confirm facts and perform tasks *(e.g., planning travel, applying for a job)*

See Skills 5.1 and 5.2

UNDERSTAND STRATEGIES FOR READING TECHNICAL AND FUNCTIONAL TEXTS

SKILL 6.4 **Interpreting graphic features used in technical texts** (e.g., schematics, flowcharts) **and in functional texts** (e.g., keys/legends, diagrams)

Graphing Information

Bar graphs and pictographs

Bar graphs and pictographs display data graphically, bar graphs by using horizontal or vertical bars, and pictographs by using symbols, such as smiley faces or apples. To make a bar graph or a pictograph, determine the scale to be used for the graph. Then determine the length of each bar on the graph or determine the number of pictures needed to represent each item of information. Be sure to include an explanation of the scale in the legend.

> Bar graphs and pictographs display data graphically, bar graphs by using horizontal or vertical bars, and pictographs by using symbols, such as smiley faces or apples.

Example: A class had the following grades: 4 As, 9 Bs, 8 Cs, 1 D, 3 Fs. Graph these on a pictograph and a bar graph.

Grade	Number of Students
A	☺☺☺☺
B	☺☺☺☺☺☺☺☺☺
C	☺☺☺☺☺☺☺☺
D	☺
F	☺☺☺

Bar graph

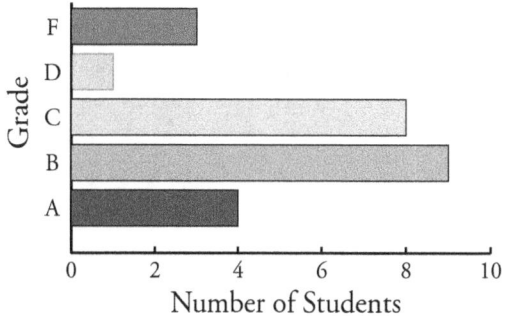

Line graphs

LINE GRAPHS are graphical displays that show change over time. To make a line graph, determine appropriate scales for both the vertical and horizontal axes (based on the information to be graphed). Describe what each axis represents, and mark the scale periodically on each axis. Graph the individual points of the graph, and connect the points on the graph from left to right.

> **LINE GRAPHS:** graphical displays that show change over time

READING

Example: Graph the following information using a line graph.

THE NUMBER OF NATIONAL MERIT FINALISTS PER SCHOOL YEAR						
YEAR	90–91	91–92	92–93	93–94	94–95	95–96
Central	3	5	1	4	6	8
Wilson	4	2	3	2	3	2

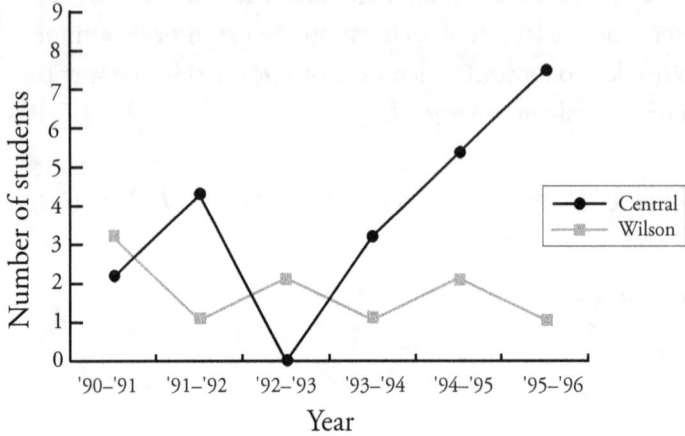

Circle graphs

CIRCLE GRAPH: graphs made up of "pie slices" that show the percent for each category of data

A **CIRCLE GRAPH** is made up of "pie slices" that show the percent for each category of data. Many software programs—spreadsheets, presentation programs, even word processing programs—will create circle graphs automatically. You just need to enter the data.

Here's an example. Let's say that Lydia spends 7 hours a day in school, 3 hours a day doing homework, 5 hours a day playing, and 9 hours a day sleeping. Here is the data that can be used to create a circle graph:

School	7
Homework	3
Playing	5
Sleeping	9

And here is the circle graph displaying the data graphically. Notice that it shows the ***percent*** of her day that she spends in school, doing homework, playing, and sleeping.

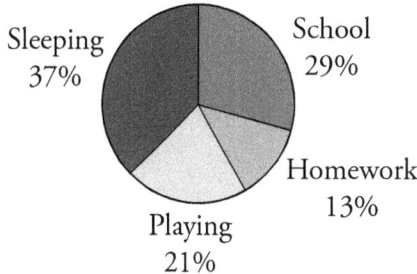

Scatter plots

SCATTER PLOTS compare two characteristics of the same group of things or people and usually consist of a large body of data. They show how much one variable affects another. The relationship between the two variables is their CORRELATION. The closer the data points come to making a straight line when plotted, the closer the correlation.

SCATTER PLOTS: compare two characteristics of the same group of things or people and usually consist of a large body of data

CORRELATION: the relationship between the two variables

Stem-and-leaf Plots

Stem-and-leaf plots are visually similar to line plots. The stems are the digits in the greatest place value of the data values, and the leaves are the digits in the next greatest place values. Stem-and-leaf plots are best suited for small sets of data and are especially useful for comparing two sets of data. The following is an example using test scores:

READING

4	9
5	4 9
6	1 2 3 4 6 7 8 8
7	0 3 4 6 6 6 7 7 7 7 8 8 8 8
8	3 5 5 7 8
9	0 0 3 4 5
10	0 0

Histograms

HISTOGRAMS: used to summarize information from large sets of data that can be naturally grouped into intervals

HISTOGRAMS are used to summarize information from large sets of data that can be naturally grouped into intervals. The vertical axis indicates frequency (the number of times any particular data value occurs), and the horizontal axis indicates data values or ranges of data values. The number of data values in any interval is the frequency of the interval.

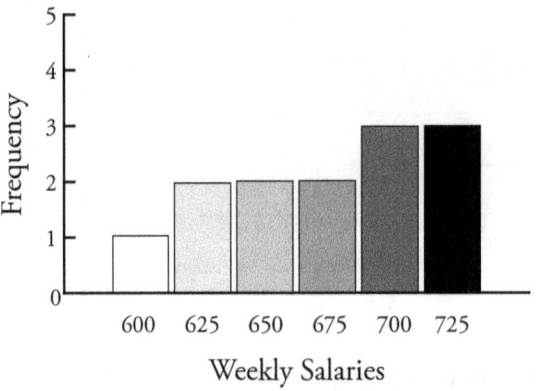

A trend line on a line graph shows the correlation between two sets of data. A trend may show positive correlation (both sets of data get bigger together), negative correlation (one set of data gets bigger while the other gets smaller), or no correlation.

Interpreting Data

INFERENCE: a statement that is derived from reasoning

An INFERENCE is a statement that is derived from reasoning. When reading a graph, inferences help with interpretation of the data that is being presented. From this information, a conclusion and even predictions about what the data actually means are possible.

UNDERSTAND STRATEGIES FOR READING TECHNICAL AND FUNCTIONAL TEXTS

Example: Katherine and Tom were both doing poorly in math class. Their teacher had a conference with each of them in November. The following graph shows their math test scores during the school year.

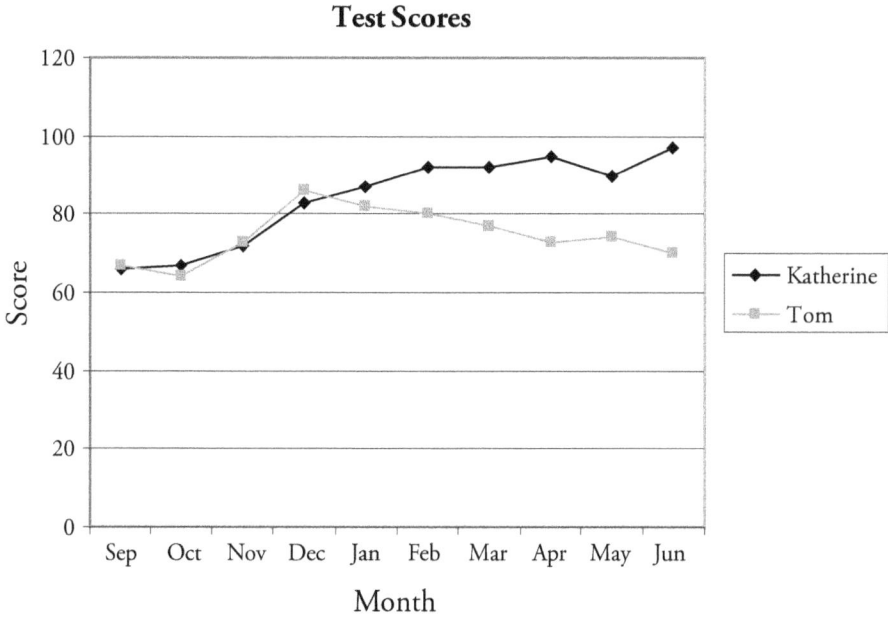

1. What kind of trend does this graph show?

   This graph shows that there is a positive trend in Katherine's test scores and a negative trend in Tom's test scores.

2. What inferences can you make from this graph?

   It can be inferred that Katherine's test scores rose steadily after November. Tom's test scores spiked in December but then began to fall again and became negatively trended.

3. What conclusion can you draw based upon this graph?

   One can conclude that Katherine took her teacher's meeting seriously and began to study in order to do better on the exams. It seems as though Tom tried harder for a bit, but his test scores eventually slipped back down to the level where he began.

READING

DOMAIN III
LITERATURE

LITERATURE

PERSONALIZED STUDY PLAN

✗ **KNOWN MATERIAL/ SKIP IT**

PAGE		COMPETENCY AND SKILL	
53	**7:**	**Understand strategies for analyzing and interpreting various forms of literary nonfiction, fiction, and drama**	☐
	7.1:	Recognizing the characteristics of various forms of literary nonfiction, fiction, and drama	☐
	7.2:	Recognizing the structural elements of literary prose	☐
	7.3:	Analyzing the use of rhetorical, dramatic, and literary devices and techniques in a work of literary prose	☐
	7.4:	Analyzing the diction or choice of words in a work of literary prose	☐
	7.5:	Analyzing the plot, setting, and characterization in a work of literary prose	☐
	7.6:	Interpreting the point of view, tone, and mood in a work of literary prose using critical theories and text-centered and reader-centered approaches	☐
	7.7:	Interpreting central ideas or themes in a work of literary prose using critical theories and text-centered and reader-centered approaches	☐
71	**8:**	**Understand strategies for analyzing and interpreting various forms of poetry**	☐
	8.1:	Recognizing the characteristics of various forms of poetry	☐
	8.2:	Recognizing stanzaic and metrical structures and verse forms in a work of poetry	☐
	8.3:	Analyzing formal rhyme schemes and sound devices in a work of poetry	☐
	8.4:	Analyzing the use of figures of speech in a work of poetry	☐
	8.5:	Analyzing the use of poetic and literary devices in a work of poetry	☐
	8.6:	Interpreting the point of view, tone, and mood in a work of poetry using critical theories and text-centered and reader-centered approaches	☐
	8.7:	Interpreting central ideas or themes in a work of poetry using critical theories and text-centered and reader-centered approaches	☐
79	**9:**	**Understand the major characteristics of literatures from around the world**	☐
	9.1:	Demonstrating knowledge of major literary genres, styles, and trends associated with literature from around the world	☐
	9.2:	Demonstrating knowledge of the formal, stylistic, and thematic characteristics of major works and writers of literatures from around the world	☐
	9.3:	Demonstrating knowledge of the formal, stylistic, and thematic characteristics of major movements and periods in literatures from around the world	☐
	9.4:	Demonstrating knowledge of the formal, stylistic, and thematic characteristics of major literary genres and works from the oral tradition	☐

LITERATURE

PERSONALIZED STUDY PLAN

PAGE	COMPETENCY AND SKILL	KNOWN MATERIAL/ SKIP IT
97	**10: Understand the major historical, social, cultural, and political aspects of literatures from around the world**	☐
	10.1: Examining in literary works references to major historical events and to major social, cultural, and political movements and institutions	☐
	10.2: Examining in literary works the expression of diverse values, attitudes, and ideas of people from various regional, ethnic, and cultural groups	☐
	10.3: Examining how writers from diverse cultural backgrounds and various historical periods have commented on major historical events and influenced public opinion	☐
	10.4: Examining how social, cultural, and political issues, such as issues relating to age, gender, ethnicity, and human rights, are explored in classical and contemporary literary works	☐

COMPETENCY 7
UNDERSTAND STRATEGIES FOR ANALYZING AND INTERPRETING VARIOUS FORMS OF LITERARY NONFICTION, FICTION, AND DRAMA

SKILL 7.1 Recognizing the characteristics of various forms of literary nonfiction, fiction, and drama *(e.g., critical biography, historical novel, morality play)*

Prose is divided into two main genres: nonfiction and fiction. Nonfiction is based on factual information, and fiction is based on an author's imagination.

The major literary genres include those listed below.

Nonfiction
Nonfiction has many subgenres. Students should be introduced to these as writings that can be informative as well as enjoyable.

Biography
A BIOGRAPHY is a portrait of the life of an individual other than the author. Biographical prose is a subcategory of nonfiction. The earliest biographical writings were probably funeral speeches and inscriptions, usually praising the life and example of the deceased. Early biographies evolved from this and were almost invariably uncritical, even distorted, and always laudatory.

BIOGRAPHY: a portrait of the life of an individual other than the author

Autobiography
An AUTOBIOGRAPHY is a form of the biography written by the subject himself or herself. Autobiographies can range from very formal works to intimate journals and diaries in the course of a life, without a conscious eye toward publication.

AUTOBIOGRAPHY: a form of biography written by the subject himself or herself

Informational books and articles
INFORMATIONAL BOOKS AND ARTICLES make up much of the reading of modern Americans. Magazines began to be popular in the nineteenth century in this country, and although many of the contributors to those publications intended to influence the political/social/religious convictions of their readers, many also simply intended to pass on information. A book or article whose purpose is simply

INFORMATIONAL BOOKS AND ARTICLES: writings, such as in books or magazines, that are meant to pursuade or to provide information

to be informative—that is, not to persuade—is called exposition. An example of an expository book is the MLA Style Manual. The writers do not intend to persuade their readers to use the recommended stylistic features in their writing; they simply make them available in case a reader needs such a guide.

Newspaper accounts of events

A newspaper account of events is expository in nature, of course—a reporting of a happening. That happening might be a school board meeting, an automobile accident that sent several people to a hospital and left one passenger dead, or the election of the mayor. Although presented within the mannerisms of the objective viewpoint, newspaper accounts invariably contain the biases of the reporter and of the periodical or newspaper in which they appear. Even news stories headline some facts and omit others; by so doing they slant their stories to emphasize certain aspects of the truth over others. Today, with digital photography and computer-generated graphics, the story in the pictorial layout also influences the audience and is the choice of the paper's editorial board. Reporters are expected to be unbiased in their coverage, and most of them defend their disinterest fiercely; but what a writer sees in an event is inevitably shaped to some extent by his or her beliefs and experiences.

Types of nonfiction include, but are not limited to:

- Almanac
- Autobiography
- Biography
- Blueprint
- Book report
- Diary
- Dictionary
- Documentary film
- Encyclopedia
- Essay
- History
- Journal
- Letter
- Philosophy book
- Science book
- Textbook
- User manual

Fiction

Fiction is the opposite of fact, and, simple as that may seem, it's the major distinction between fictional works and nonfictional works.

A work of fiction typically has a central character, called the protagonist, and a character that stands in opposition to the protagonist, called the antagonist. The antagonist might be something other than a person. In Stephen Crane's short story "The Open Boat," for example, the antagonist is a hostile environment—a stormy sea.

Learn more about writing fiction:

crofsblogs.typepad.com
/fiction/2003/07
/narrative_voice.html

Elements of fiction:
- *Protagonist*
- *Antagonist*
- *Conflicts*
- *Plot*
- *Characterization*

UNDERSTAND STRATEGIES FOR INTERPRETING LITERATURE

Conflicts between protagonist and antagonist are typical of a work of fiction, and climax is the turning point at which those conflicts are resolved. The plot is the sequence of events during which the conflicts occur as the characters and plot move toward resolution.

A fiction writer artistically uses devices labeled characterization to reveal character. Characterization can depend on dialogue, description, or the attitude or attitudes of one or more characters toward another.

Enjoying fiction depends upon the ability of the readers to suspend disbelief. Readers make a deal with the writer that, for the time the readers take to read the story, the readers will replace their own beliefs with the convictions expressed by the writer and will accept the reality created by the writer.

This is not true in nonfiction. The writer of nonfiction must stick to verifiable facts. Thus, a writer of nonfiction is not free to create a character, no matter how realistic the author makes that character seem. All nonfiction characters have actually lived. The writer of nonfiction declares in the choice of that genre that the work is based upon reality.

Types of fiction:
- *Novel*
- *Short story*
- *Drama*
- *Poetry*

Types of fiction include, but are not limited to:

- Action-adventure
- Crime
- Detective
- Fantasy
- Horror
- Mystery
- Romance
- Science fiction
- Thriller
- Western

A *Bildungsroman* (from the German) means "novel of education" or "novel of formation" and is a novel that traces the spiritual, moral, psychological, or social development and growth of the main character from childhood to maturity.

Dickens' *David Copperfield* (1850) represents this genre, as does Thomas Wolfe's *Look Homeward, Angel* (1929).

Learn more about elements of the short story:
www.yale.edu/ynhti/curriculum/units/1983/3/83.03.09.x.html

Novel

A NOVEL is the longest form of fictional prose, containing a variety of characterizations, settings, local color, and regionalism. Most novels have complex plots, expanded description, and attention to detail. Some of the great novelists include Austen, Twain, Tolstoy, Hugo, Hardy, Dickens, Hawthorne, Forster, and Flaubert.

NOVEL: the longest form of fictional prose

Short Story

A SHORT STORY, typically, is a terse narrative with less developmental background than a novel. Short stories may include description, author's point of view, and

SHORT STORY: a terse narrative with less developmental background than a novel

LITERATURE

tone. Poe emphasized that a successful short story should create one focused impact. Considered to be great short story writers are Hemingway, Faulkner, Twain, Joyce, Shirley Jackson, Flannery O'Connor, de Maupasssant, Saki, Poe, and Pushkin.

Drama

A **DRAMA** is a play—comedy or tragedy—typically in five acts. Traditionalists and neoclassicists adhere to Aristotle's unities of time, place, and action. Modern playwrights have taken the form and broken it up as they please. Plot development is advanced via dialogue. Common dramatic devices include asides, soliloquies, and a chorus representing public opinion. Among the greatest of all dramatists/playwrights is Shakespeare. Other greats include Ibsen, Williams, Miller, Shaw, Stoppard, Racine, Moliére, Sophocles, Aeschylus, Euripides, and Aristophanes.

> **DRAMA:** a play, typically in five acts

Comedy

Comedy is a form of dramatic literature that is meant to amuse and often ends happily. It uses techniques such as satire or parody and can take many forms, from farce to burlesque.

Tragedy

Tragedy is comedy's other half. It is defined as a work of drama written in either prose or poetry, telling the story of a brave, noble hero who, because of some tragic character flaw, brings ruin upon himself. It is characterized by serious, poetic language that evokes pity and fear. In modern times, dramatists have tried to update tragedy's image by drawing its main characters from the middle class and showing their nobility through their nature instead of their standing.

> *Read more about Greek tragedy:*
>
> depthome.brooklyn.cuny.edu/classics/dunkle/studyguide/tragedy.htm

Dramatic monologue

A dramatic monologue is a speech given by an actor, usually intended for himself or herself, but with the intended audience in mind. It reveals key aspects of the character's psyche and sheds light on the situation at hand. The audience takes the part of the silent listener, passing judgment and giving sympathy at the same time. This form was invented and used predominantly by Victorian poet Robert Browning.

> *Types of poetry:*
> - Narrative
> - Epic
> - Ballad
> - Sonnet
> - Limerick
> - Cinquain
> - Haiku

Poetry

POETRY is a type of fiction, the only requirement of which is rhythm. Poetry evolved from oral literature and folk tale as a written form with set patterns, which in English literature include the sonnet, elegy, ode, pastoral, and villanelle. Unfixed variations on traditional forms have trickled through blank verse and the dramatic monologue. From Modernism to the modern day, poets

> **POETRY:** a type of fiction, the only requirement of which is rhythm

have transversed experiments with typography (Imagism) and self-revelatory themes (confessional poetry).

Narrative

The greatest difficulty in analyzing narrative poetry is that it partakes of many genres. It can have all the features of poetry, such as meter, rhyme, verses, and stanzas, but it can have all the features of fiction and nonfiction prose. It can have a protagonist, characters, conflicts, action, plot, climax, theme, and tone. It can also be a persuasive discourse and have a thesis (real or derived) and supporting points. The arrangement of an analysis depends largely upon the peculiarities of the poem itself.

Narrative poetry has been very much a part of the output of modern American writers, totally apart from attempts to write epics. Many of Dickinson's poems are narrative in form and retain the features that we look for in the finest of American poetry.

The first two verses of "A Narrow Fellow in the Grass" illustrate the use of narrative in a poem:

> A narrow fellow in the grass
> Occasionally rides;
> You may have met him—did you not?
> His notice sudden is.
> The grass divides as with a comb,
>
> A spotted shaft is seen;
> And then it closes at your feet
> And opens further on. . . .

This is certainly narrative in nature and has many of the aspects of prose narrative. At the same time, it is a poem with rhyme, meter, verses, and stanzas and can be analyzed as such.

Epic

An epic is a long poem, usually of book length, reflecting values inherent in the generative culture. Devices include the invocation of a muse for inspiration, prologue expounding a purpose in writing, universal setting, protagonist and antagonist who possess supernatural strength and acumen, and interventions of a God or the gods. Understandably, there are very few epics: Homer's *Iliad* and *Odyssey*, Virgil's *Aeneid*, Milton's *Paradise Lost*, Spenser's *The Fairie Queene*, Barrett Browning's *Aurora Leigh*, and Pope's mock-epic, *The Rape of the Lock*, are some examples.

LITERATURE

Ballad
A ballad is an *in medias res* story told or sung, usually in verse, and accompanied by music. Literary devices found in ballads include the refrain, or repeated section, and anaphora, or incremental repetition, for effect. The earliest forms were anonymous folk ballads.

Sonnet
The sonnet is a fixed-verse form of Italian origin, which consists of fourteen lines that are typically five-foot iambics rhyming according to a prescribed scheme. Popular since its creation in the thirteenth century in Sicily, the sonnet spread first to Tuscany, where it was adopted by Petrarch.

The Petrarchan sonnet generally has a two-part theme. The first eight lines, the octave, state a problem, ask a question, or express an emotional tension. The last six lines, the sestet, resolve the problem, answer the question, or relieve the tension. The rhyme scheme of the octave is abbaabba; that of the sestet varies.

Sir Thomas Wyatt and Henry Howard, Earl of Surrey, introduced this form into England in the sixteenth century. It played an important role in the development of Elizabethan lyric poetry, and a distinctive English sonnet developed, which was composed of three quatrains, each with an independent rhyme scheme, and it ended with a rhymed couplet.

A form of the English sonnet created by Edmund Spenser combines the English Italian forms. The Spenserian sonnet follows the English quatrain and couplet pattern but resembles the Italian in its rhyme scheme, which is linked: *abab bcbc cdcd ee*. Many poets wrote sonnet sequences where several sonnets were linked together, usually to tell a story. Considered the greatest of all sonnet sequences is one of Shakespeare's, which is addressed to a young man and a "dark lady" wherein the love story is overshadowed by the underlying reflections on time and art, growth and decay, and fame and fortune.

The sonnet continued to develop, more in theme than in form. After John Donne in the seventeenth century married the form with religious themes, some of which are almost sermons, or personal reflections ("When I consider how my light is spent"), there were no longer any boundaries on the themes the sonnet could encompass.

The flexibility of form is demonstrated by the wide range of themes and purposes for which the sonnet has been used—from frivolous concerns to statements about time and death. Wordsworth, Keats, and Elizabeth Barrett Browning used the Petrarchan form of the sonnet. A well-known example is Wordsworth's "The World Is Too Much With Us." Rainer Maria Rilke's *Die Sonette an Orpheus* (1922) is a well-known twentieth-century sonnet cycle.

> *Learn more about poetry's many forms:*
> poetry.suite101.com/article.cfm/lyric_poetry

Analysis of a sonnet should focus on the form. Does it fit a traditional pattern or does it break from tradition? If it breaks from tradition, why did the poet choose to make that break? Does it reflect the purpose of the poem? What is the theme? What is the purpose? Is it narrative? If so, what story does it tell, and is there an underlying meaning? Is the sonnet appropriate for the subject matter?

Limerick

The limerick probably originated in County Limerick, Ireland, in the eighteenth century. It is a form of short, humorous verse, often nonsensical and often ribald. Its five lines rhyme *aabba*, with three feet in all lines except the third and fourth, which have only two. Rarely presented as serious poetry, this form is popular because almost anyone can write it.

In the nineteenth century, Edward Lear popularized the limerick in *A Book of Nonsense*. Here's an example:

> There was an Old Man with a beard,
> Who said, "It is just as I feared!
> Two Owls and a Hen,
> Four Larks and a Wren,
> Have all built their nests in my beard!"

Analysis of a limerick should focus on its form. Does it conform to a traditional pattern, or does it break from the tradition? If it breaks from tradition, what impact does that have on the meaning? Is the poem serious or frivolous? Is it funny? Does it try to be funny but not achieve its purpose? Is there a serious meaning underlying the frivolity?

Cinquain

A cinquain is a poem with one five-line stanza. Adelaide Crapsey (1878–1914) called a five-line verse form a cinquain and invented a particular meter for it. Similar to the haiku, there is a fixed syllabic scheme: two syllables in the first and last lines and four, six, and eight in the middle three lines. It has a mostly iambic cadence. Crapsey's poem, "November Night," is an example:

> Listen...
> Like steps of passing ghosts,
> the leaves, frost-crisp'd,
> break from the trees
> And fall.

Haiku

Haiku is a popular unrhymed form that is limited to seventeen syllables arranged in three lines thus: five, seven, and five syllables. This verse form originated in Japan in the seventeenth century, where it is still the country's most popular form.

While haikus originally dealt with the seasons, the time of day, and the landscape, the form has come into more common use and the subjects have become less restricted. The imagist poets and other English writers used the form or imitated it. It's a form frequently used in classrooms to introduce students to the writing of poetry.

Here's an example by Japanese poet Kobaayashi Issa, translated by American poet Robert Haas:

> *New Year's morning—*
> *everything is in blossom!*
> *I feel about average.*

Analysis of cinquain and haiku poems should focus on form first. For a cinquain, does it have only five lines? For a haiku, does it conform to the seventeen-syllable requirement, and are the lines arranged in a five, seven, and five pattern? Does the poem distill the words so as much meaning as possible can be conveyed? Does it treat a serious subject? Is the theme discernable? Short forms like these seem simple to dash off; however, they are not effective unless the words are chosen and pared so the intended meaning is conveyed. The impact should be forceful, and that often takes more effort, skill, and creativity than for longer forms. Students should consider all this in their analyses.

The form of poetry

When we speak of form with regard to poetry, we usually mean one of three things.

The pattern of the sound and rhythm

Knowing the background of these characteristics is helpful. History was passed down in oral form almost exclusively until the invention of the printing press and was often set to music. A rhymed story is much easier to commit to memory than one that is not rhymed. Adding a tune makes it even easier to remember, so many of the earliest pieces of literature and the like were rhymed and were probably sung.

When we speak of "the pattern of sound and rhythm," we are referring to verse form and stanza form. The verse form is the rhythmic pattern of a single verse. An example would be any meter: blank verse, for instance, is iambic pentameter. A stanza is a group of a certain number of verses, having a rhyme scheme. If the poem is written, there is usually white space between the verses, although a short poem may be only one stanza long. If the poem is spoken, there is a pause between stanzas.

The visible shape it takes

In the seventeenth century, some poets shaped their poems to reflect the theme, called concrete poetry. A good example is George Herbert's "Easter Wings." Since that time, poets have occasionally played with this device; it is, however, generally viewed as nothing more than a demonstration of ingenuity. The rhythm, effect, and meaning are often sacrificed to the forcing of the shape.

Rhyme and free verse

Poets also use devices to establish form that will underscore the meanings of their poems. A very common one is alliteration, which is the repetition of initial sounds. When the poem is read aloud (which poetry is usually intended to be), the repetition of a sound may not only underscore the meaning, but also add pleasure to the reading. Following a strict rhyming pattern can add intensity to the meaning of the poem in the hands of a skilled and creative poet. When not used effectively, though, the meaning can be drowned out by the steady beat-beat-beat of it.

Shakespeare very skillfully used the regularity of rhyme in his poetry, breaking the rhythm in certain places to underscore a point very effectively. For example, in Sonnet 130: "My mistress' eyes are nothing like the sun," the rhythm is primarily iambic pentameter. It lulls the reader (or listener) to accept that this poet is following the standard conventions for love poetry, which in that day reliably used rhyme and, more often, than not iambic pentameter to express feelings of romantic love along conventional lines. However, the last two lines of Sonnet 130 sharply break from the monotonous pattern, forcing the reader or speaker to pause:

> And yet, by heaven, I think my love as rare
> As any she belied with false compare.

Shakespeare's purpose is clear: He is not writing a conventional love poem; the object of his love is not the red-and-white conventional woman written about in other poems of the period. This is a good example of a poet using form to underscore meaning.

Poets eventually began to feel constricted by the rhyming conventions and began to break away and make new rules for poetry. When poetry was only rhymed, it was easy to define. When free verse, or poetry written in a flexible form, came upon the scene in France in the 1880s, it quickly began to influence English-language poets such as T. S. Eliot, whose memorable poem "The Waste Land" had an alarming and desolate message for the modern world. It's impossible to imagine that it could have been written in the soothing, lulling, rhymed verse of previous periods. Those who first began writing in free verse in English were responding to the influence of the French *vers libre*.

However, free verse could be applied loosely to the poetry of Walt Whitman written in the mid-nineteenth century, as can be seen in the first stanza of "Song of Myself":

> *I celebrate myself, and sing myself,*
> *And what I assume you shall assume,*
> *For every atom belonging to me as good belongs to you.*

When poetry was no longer defined as a piece of writing arranged in verses that had a rhyme scheme of some sort, distinguishing poetry from prose became a point of discussion. Merriam Webster's current edition of the Encyclopedia of Literature defines poetry as "writing that formulates a concentrated imaginative awareness of experience in language chosen and arranged to create a specific emotional response through its meaning, sound and rhythm."

A poet chooses the form of poetry deliberately, based upon the emotional response being evoked and the meaning being conveyed. Robert Frost, a twentieth-century poet who chose to use conventional rhyming verse to make his point, is a memorable and often-quoted modern poet. Who can forget his closing lines in "Stopping by Woods"?

> *And miles to go before I sleep,*
> *And miles to go before I sleep.*

Would they be as memorable if the poem had been written in free verse? This is an example of the type of questions that critics explore when dealing with poetry.

SKILL 7.2 Recognizing the structural elements of literary prose (e.g., prologue, climax, denouement)

Students will develop critical thinking skills by learning to identify literary elements and analyzing how they help authors develop themes in their works.

Character development is a commonly studied story element. In stories, we often find heroes, villains, comedic characters, dark characters, and the like. When we examine the characters of a story, we look at who they are and how their traits contribute to the story. Often, because of the characters' traits, plot elements become more interesting. For example, authors may pair unlikely characters together to create specific conflict.

UNDERSTAND STRATEGIES FOR INTERPRETING LITERATURE

The SETTING of a story is the place or location where the action occurs. Often, the specific place is not as important as some of the details about it. For example, the location of *The Great Gatsby*, New York, is not as significant as the fact that the story takes place amongst incredible wealth. Conversely, *The Grapes of Wrath*, although it takes place in Oklahoma and California, is set amidst extreme poverty. In fact, as the story takes place around other migrant workers, the setting is even more significant. In a way, the setting serves as a reason for various conflicts to occur.

> **SETTING:** the time and place in which a work of literature takes place

The MOOD of a story is the atmosphere or attitude the writer conveys through descriptive language. Often, mood fits nicely with theme and setting. For example, Edgar Allan Poe's stories often reveal a mood of horror and darkness. Mood helps readers better understand the writer's theme and intentions through descriptive, stylistic language, characterization, setting, and specific plot elements.

> **MOOD:** the atmosphere or attitude the writer conveys through descriptive language

Stories are narrated from a particular POINT OF VIEW, or perspective. First-person narration means that the story is being told by a character in the story. Such a narrator uses first-person pronouns (I, me, we, us, our, my, mine, ours). Third-person narration means that the story is being told by someone not in the story and uses third-person pronouns (such as he, she, it, they, theirs, them). This general distinction is further modified by third-person omniscient or third-person limited narration, meaning that the narrator seems to know everything that is going on inside every character's head or seems to know only about one character's perspective.

> **POINT OF VIEW:** who is narrating a work of literarature

FORESHADOWING, giving clues about future developments, is a technique authors use to build cohesion into their stories and to promote readers' engagement with them. Readers' mindsets are guided in ways that promote subtle expectations about future events. A skillful writer rewards or otherwise manipulates those expectations for purposes of keeping the reader engaged in the narration.

> **FORESHADOWING:** giving clues about future developments

DICTION pertains to the distinctive vocabulary choices a writer makes and to the characteristic ways a writer structures words and phrases. The hallmark of a great writer is precise, unusual, and memorable diction the use of the right word(s) in the right place for the right purpose.

> **DICTION:** the distinctive vocabulary choices a writer makes

IMAGERY can be described as a word or sequence of words that refers to any sensory experience—that is, anything that can be seen, tasted, smelled, heard, or felt on the skin or fingers. Although prose writers may also use these devices, they are most distinctive of poetry. The poet appeals to one of the senses in order to make an experience available to the reader. The poet deliberately paints a scene in such a way that the reader can visualize it.

> **IMAGERY:** use of a word or sequence of words to refer to a sensory experience

LITERATURE

Learn more about teaching imagery:
students.ed.uiuc.edu/vallicel/Teaching_imagery.html

However, the purpose is not simply to stir the visceral feeling but also to stir the emotions. A good example of imagery can be found in "The Piercing Chill" by Taniguchi Buson (1715–1783):

> The piercing chill I feel:
> My dead wife's comb, in our bedroom,
> Under my heel . . .

In only a few short words, the reader can feel many things: the shock that might come from touching the comb, a literal sense of death, the contrast between her death and the memories he has of her when she was alive. Imagery might be defined as speaking of the abstract in concrete terms—a powerful device in the hands of a skillful poet.

SYMBOLISM: using an object or action that can be observed with the senses to suggest or represent something else

SYMBOLISM is using an object or action that can be observed with the senses to suggest or represent something else. The lion is a symbol of courage; the cross is a symbol of Christianity; the swastika was a symbol of Nazi Germany.

Symbols used in literature are usually a different sort. Their significance is only evident in the context of the work where they are used. A good example is the huge pair of spectacles on a signboard in Fitzgerald's *The Great Gatsby*. It is interesting as a part of the landscape, but it also symbolizes divine myopia. A symbol can certainly have more than one meaning. Occasionally, the meaning may be as personal as the memories and experiences of the particular reader.

When analyzing a poem or a story, students should identify the symbols and their possible meanings. Looking for symbols is often challenging, especially for novice poetry readers. However, these suggestions may be useful:

1. First, pick out all the references to concrete objects such as a newspaper, black cats, or other nouns. Note any that the poet emphasizes by describing in detail, by repeating, or by placing at the very beginning or ending of a poem. Ask: what is the poem about? What does it add up to? Paraphrase the poem and determine whether the meaning depends upon certain concrete objects. Then ponder what the concrete object symbolizes in this particular poem.

2. Look for a character with the name of a prophet who does little but utter prophecy or a trio of women who resemble the Three Fates. A symbol may be a part of a person's body, such as the eye of the murder victim in Poe's story "The Tell-Tale Heart," or a look, a voice, or a mannerism.

3. A symbol is not an abstraction such as truth, death, and love; in narrative, a well-developed character who is not at all mysterious; or the second term in a metaphor. In Emily Dickenson's "The Lightning Is a Yellow Fork," the symbol is the lightning, not the fork.

UNDERSTAND STRATEGIES FOR INTERPRETING LITERATURE

Figurative language is also called figures of speech. If all figures of speech that have ever been identified were listed, the list would be very long. However, for purposes of analyzing literature, a handful will suffice.

Alliteration is the repetition of consonant sounds in two or more neighboring words or syllables. In its simplest form, it reinforces one or two consonant sounds. One example comes from Shakespeare's Sonnet 12:

> When I do count the clock that tells the time

Some poets have used more complex patterns of alliteration by creating consonants both at the beginning of words and at the beginning of stressed syllables within words. Shelley's "Stanzas Written in Dejection Near Naples" provides such an example:

> The City's voice itself is soft like Solitude's

Bathos is a ludicrous attempt to portray pathos (that is, to evoke pity, sympathy, or sorrow). It may result from inappropriately dignifying the commonplace, using elevated language to describe something trivial, or greatly exaggerated pathos.

The Climax is a number of phrases or sentences that are arranged in ascending order of rhetorical forcefulness. An example is from Melville's *Moby Dick*:

> All that most maddens and torments; all that stirs up the lees of things; all truth with malice in it; all that cracks the sinews and cakes the brain; all the subtle demonisms of life and thought; all evil, to crazy Ahab, were visibly personified and made practically assailable in Moby Dick.

Euphemism is the substitution of an agreeable or inoffensive term for one that might offend or suggest something unpleasant. For example, to avoid using the word "death," you might use a euphemism such as "passed away," "crossed over," or "passed."

Hyperbole is the deliberate exaggeration for effect or comic effect. An example is from Shakespeare's *The Merchant of Venice*:

> Why, if two gods should play some heavenly match
> And on the wager lay two earthly women,
> And Portia one, there must be something else
> Pawned with the other, for the poor rude world
> Hath not her fellow.

Irony is expressing something other than and particularly opposite to the literal meaning, such as words of praise when blame is intended. In poetry, irony is often used as a sophisticated or resigned awareness of contrast between what is and what ought to be and expresses a controlled pathos without sentimentality. It is a form of indirection that avoids overt praise or censure. An early example is the Greek comic character Eiron, a clever underdog who by his wit repeatedly triumphs over the boastful character Alazon.

Malapropism is a verbal blunder in which one word is replaced by another similar in sound but different in meaning. This derives from Sheridan's Mrs. Malaprop in *The Rivals* (1775). Thinking of the geography of contiguous countries, she speaks of the "geometry" of "contagious countries." Meaning the "pinnacle of perfection," she describes someone as "the pineapple of perfection."

Metaphor is indirect comparison between two things. It is the use of a word or phrase denoting one kind of object or action in place of another to suggest a comparison between them. While poets use metaphors extensively, they are also integral to everyday speech. For example, chairs are said to have "legs" and "arms" although we know that humans and other animals have these appendages.

Parallelism is the arrangement of ideas in phrases, sentences, and paragraphs that balance one element with another of equal importance and similar wording. An example is from Francis Bacon's *Of Studies*:

> Reading maketh a full man, conference a ready man, and writing an exact man.

Personification is when human characteristics are attributed to an inanimate object, an abstract quality, or an animal. For example, John Bunyan wrote characters named Death, Knowledge, Giant Despair, Sloth, and Piety in his *Pilgrim's Progress*. Carl Sandburg, in his poem "Fog," writes:

> The fog comes
> on little cat feet.
>
> It sits looking
> over harbor and city
> on silent haunches
> and then moves on.

Onomatopoeia is the naming of a thing or action by a vocal imitation of the sound associated with it, such as *buzz* or *hiss* or the use of words whose sound suggests the sense. A good example is from "The Brook" by Tennyson:

> I chatter over stony ways,
> In little sharps and trebles,
> I bubble into eddying bays,
> I babble on the pebbles.

UNDERSTAND STRATEGIES FOR INTERPRETING LITERATURE

Oxymoron is a contradiction in terms deliberately employed for effect. It is usually seen in a qualifying adjective whose meaning is contrary to that of the noun it modifies, such as "wise folly" or "jumbo shrimp."

Simile is a direct comparison between two things using "like," "as," or "such as." An example is Robert Burns's poem "My love is like a red, red rose."

Poets use figures of speech to sharpen the effect and meaning of their poems and to help readers see things in ways they have never seen them before. Marianne Moore observed that a fir tree has "an emerald turkey-foot at the top." Her poem makes us aware of something we probably had never noticed before. The sudden recognition of the likeness yields pleasure in the reading.

Figures of speech add many dimensions of richness to our reading and understanding of a poem; they also allow many opportunities for worthwhile analysis. The approach to take in analyzing a poem on the basis of its figures of speech is to ask several questions: What does a particular figure of speech do for the poem? Does it underscore meaning? Does it aid understanding? Does it increase the intensity of my response?

Figurative language allows for the statement of truths that more literal language cannot. Skillfully used, a figure of speech helps the reader better understand a text and focus upon particulars.

SKILL 7.3 Analyzing the use of rhetorical, dramatic, and literary devices and techniques in a work of literary prose (e.g., analogy, foreshadowing)

See Skill 7.2

SKILL 7.4 Analyzing the diction or choice of words in a work of literary prose

See Skill 5.7

Transitions

As writers transition from one paragraph to another—or from one sentence to another—they will usually provide transitional phrases that give signposts to readers about what is coming next. Words like "however," "furthermore," "although," "likewise," etc., are good ways of communicating intention to readers. When ideas are thrown together on a page, it is hard to tell what the writer is actually doing with those ideas. Therefore, students need to become familiar with using transitional phrases.

Concluding sentences

Concluding sentences can often be unnecessary, but when written correctly, they provide a nice "farewell," or closing, to a piece of writing. Students do not always need to use concluding sentences in paragraphs; however, they should be alerted to their potential benefits.

Appropriate vocabulary

When writers use appropriate vocabulary, they are sensitive to the audience and purpose of what they are writing. For example, if someone were writing an essay on a scientific concept to a group of nonscientists, he would not use specialized vocabulary to explain concepts. However, if he was writing for a group of scientists, not using that vocabulary may seem unprofessional. It depends on what the writer intends with the piece of writing. Therefore, students need to learn early on that all writing has a purpose and that good writers will make conscious decisions about how to arrange their texts, which words to use, and which examples and metaphors to include.

Sufficient context

Finally, when writers provide sufficient context, they ensure that readers do not have to question the text extensively to figure out what is going on. Again, this has a lot to do with knowing the audience. Using the scientific concept example from above, the author would need to provide more context if the audience were a group of nonscientists than he would if the audience was composed of scientists. In other words, the author would have to provide more background so that the nonscientists could understand the concepts.

SKILL 7.5 **Analyzing the plot, setting, and characterization in a work of literary prose**

See Skill 7.2

UNDERSTAND STRATEGIES FOR INTERPRETING LITERATURE

> **SKILL 7.6** Interpreting the point of view, tone, and mood in a work of literary prose using critical theories and text-centered and reader-centered approaches

Tone and Point of View

The tone of a written passage is the author's attitude toward the subject matter. The tone (mood, feeling) is revealed through the qualities of the writing itself and is a direct product of such stylistic elements as language and sentence structure. The tone of the written passage is much like a speaker's voice; instead of being spoken, however, it is the product of words on a page.

Reason for tone

Often, writers have an emotional stake in the subject, and their purpose, either explicitly or implicitly, is to convey those feelings to the reader. In such cases, the writing is generally subjective; that is, it stems from opinions, judgments, values, ideas, and feelings. Both sentence structure (syntax) and word choice (diction) are instrumental tools in creating tone.

Types of tone

Neutral tone

Tone may be thought of generally as positive, negative, or neutral. Below is a statement about snakes that demonstrates neutral tone.

> Many species of snakes live in Florida. Some of those species, both poisonous and nonpoisonous, have habitats that coincide with those of human residents of the state.

The voice of the writer in this statement is neutral. The sentences are declarative (not exclamations or fragments or questions). The adjectives are few and nondescript—*many, some, poisonous* (balanced with *nonpoisonous*). Nothing in this brief paragraph would alert the reader to the feelings of the writer about snakes. The paragraph has a neutral, objective, detached, impartial tone.

Positive tone

Then again, if the writer's attitude towards snakes involves admiration, or even affection, the tone would generally be positive.

> Florida's snakes are a tenacious bunch. When they find their habitats invaded by humans, they cling to their home territories as long as they can, as if vainly attempting to fight off the onslaught of the human hordes.

LITERATURE

An additional message emerges in this paragraph—the writer quite clearly favors snakes over people. The writer uses adjectives such as *tenacious* to describe his or her feelings about snakes. The writer also humanizes the reptiles, making them brave, beleaguered creatures. Obviously, the writer is more sympathetic to snakes than to people in this paragraph.

Negative tone

If the writer's attitude toward snakes involves active dislike and fear, then the tone would also reflect that attitude by being negative.

> Countless species of snakes, some more dangerous than others, still lurk on the urban fringes of Florida's towns and cities. They will often invade domestic spaces, terrorizing people and their pets.

Here, obviously, the snakes are the villains. They *lurk*, they *invade*, and they *terrorize*. The tone of this paragraph might be said to be distressed about snakes.

In the same manner, a writer can use language to portray characters as good or bad. A writer uses positive and negative adjectives, as seen above, to convey the manner of a character.

SKILL 7.7 Interpreting central ideas or themes in a work of literary prose using critical theories and text-centered and reader-centered approaches

See Skill 7.2

COMPETENCY 8
UNDERSTAND STRATEGIES FOR ANALYZING AND INTERPRETING VARIOUS FORMS OF POETRY

SKILL 8.1 Recognizing the characteristics of various forms of poetry

See Skill 7.1

SKILL 8.2 Recognizing stanzaic and metrical structures and verse forms in a work of poetry (e.g., quatrain, iambic pentameter, free verse)

Essential terminology and literary devices germane to literary analysis include alliteration, allusion, antithesis, aphorism, apostrophe, assonance, blank verse, caesura, conceit, connotation, consonance, couplet, denotation, diction, epiphany, exposition, figurative language, free verse, hyperbole, iambic pentameter, inversion, irony, kenning, metaphor, metaphysical poetry, metonymy, motif, onomatopoeia, ottavo rima, oxymoron, paradox, parallelism, personification, quatrain, scansion, simile, soliloquy, Spenserian stanza, sprung rhythm, stream of consciousness, synecdoche, terza rima, tone, and wit. Some of these devices are further defined below.

For more information, consult this glossary of poetry terms:
www.infoplease.com/spot/pmglossary1.html

Share this Web site with your students—Newshour extra: poetry:
www.pbs.org/newshour/extra/poetry/#

	LITERARY DEVICES
Antithesis	Balanced writing about conflicting ideas, usually expressed in sentence form. Some examples are "expanding from the center," "shedding old habits," and "searching never finding."
Aphorism	A focused, succinct expression about life from a sagacious viewpoint. Writings by Ben Franklin, Sir Francis Bacon, and Alexander Pope contain many aphorisms. "Whatever is begun in anger ends in shame" is an aphorism.

Continued on next page

LITERATURE

Apostrophe	Literary device addressing an absent or dead person, an abstract idea, or an inanimate object. Sonneteers, such as Sir Thomas Wyatt, John Keats, and William Wordsworth, address the moon, stars, and the dead Milton. For example, in William Shakespeare's *Julius Caesar*, Mark Antony addresses the corpse of Caesar in the speech that begins: "O, pardon me, thou bleeding piece of earth / That I am meek and gentle with these butchers! / Thou art the ruins of the noblest man / That ever lived in the tide of times."
Blank Verse	Poetry written in unrhymed iambic pentameter. Works by Shakespeare and Milton are epitomes of blank verse. Milton's *Paradise Lost* states, "Illumine, what is low raise and support, / That to the highth of this great argument/ I may assert Eternal Providence / And justify the ways of God to men."
Caesura	A pause, usually signaled by punctuation, in a line of poetry. The earliest usage occurs in *Beowulf*, the first English epic dating from the Anglo-Saxon era. Pope uses a caesura in the line, "To err is human, // to forgive, divine."
Conceit	A comparison, usually in verse, between seemingly disparate objects or concepts. John Donne's metaphysical poetry contains many clever conceits. "The Flea" (1633), for example, compares a flea bite to the act of love.
Connotation	The ripple effect surrounding the implications and associations of a given word, distinct from the denotative or literal meaning. For example, the word "rest" in "Good night, sweet prince, and flights of angels sing thee to thy rest," refers to a burial.
Consonance	The repeated usage of similar consonant sounds, most often used in poetry. "Sally sat sifting seashells by the seashore" is a familiar example.
Couplet	Two rhyming lines of poetry. Shakespeare's sonnets end in heroic couplets, written in iambic pentameter. Pope is also a master of the couplet. His *The Rape of the Lock* is written entirely in heroic couplets.
Denotation	What a word literally means, as opposed to its connotative meaning.
Diction	The right word in the right place for the right purpose. The hallmark of a great writer is precise, unusual, and memorable diction.
Epiphany	The moment of realization and comprehension. James Joyce used this device in his short story collection *Dubliners*.
Exposition	Background information about characters meant to clarify and add to the narrative; the initial plot element that precedes the buildup of conflict.
Figurative Language	Language that is not literal but is meant to be interpreted through symbolism. Figurative language is made up of such literary devices as hyperbole, metonymy, synecdoche, and oxymoron. A synecdoche is a figure of speech in which the word for part of something is used to mean the whole; for example, "sail" for "boat," or vice versa.

Continued on next page

UNDERSTAND STRATEGIES FOR ANALYZING AND INTERPRETING VARIOUS FORMS OF POETRY

Free Verse	Poetry that does not have any predictable meter or rhyme. Margaret Atwood, e.e. cummings, and Ted Hughes write in this form.
Hyperbole	Exaggeration for a specific effect. For example, "I'm so hungry that I could eat a million of these."
Iambic Pentameter	The two elements in a set five-foot line of poetry. An iamb has two syllables, unaccented and accented, per foot or measure. Pentameter means that five feet appear in each line of poetry.
Inversion	An atypical sentence order to create a given effect or interest. Bacon and Milton's work use inversion successfully. Emily Dickinson also was fond of arranging words outside of their familiar order. In "Chartless," for example, she writes "Yet know I how the heather looks" and "Yet certain am I of the spot." Instead of saying "Yet I know" and "Yet I am certain," she reverses the usual order and shifts the emphasis to the more important words.
Irony	An unexpected disparity between what is written or stated and what is really meant or implied by the author. Verbal, dramatic and situational are the three literary ironies. Verbal irony occurs when an author says one thing and means something else. Dramatic irony occurs when an audience perceives something that a character in the literature does not know. Situational irony is a discrepancy between expected results and actual results. Shakespeare's plays contain numerous and highly effective uses of irony. O. Henry's short stories frequently have ironic endings.
Kenning	Another way to describe a person, place, or thing so as to avoid prosaic repetition. The earliest examples can be found in Anglo-Saxon literature such as *Beowulf* and "The Seafarer." Instead of writing King Hrothgar, the anonymous monk wrote "great Ring-Giver," or "Father of his people." A lake becomes the swans' way, and the ocean or sea becomes the great whale's way. In ancient Greek literature, this device was called an "epithet."
Metaphysical Poetry	Verse characterization by ingenious wit, unparalleled imagery, and clever conceits. The greatest metaphysical poet is John Donne. Henry Vaughn and other seventeenth-century British poets contributed to this movement as in Words: "I saw eternity the other night, like a great being of pure and endless light."
Metonymy	Use of an object or idea closely identified with another object or idea to represent the second. Washington, D.C. refers to the U.S. government, and the White House means the U.S. president.
Motif	A key, oft-repeated phrase, name, or idea in a literary work. Dorset/Wessex in Hardy's novels and the moors and the harsh weather in the Bronte sisters' novels are effective use of motifs. Shakespeare's *Romeo and Juliet* represents the ill-fated young lovers' motif.
Onomatopoeia	Word used to evoke the sound in its meaning. The early Batman series used "pow," "zap," "whop," "zonk," and "eek" in an onomatopoetic way.
Ottavo Rima	An eight-line stanza of poetry whose rhyme scheme is *abababcc*. Lord Byron's mock epic, *Don Juan*, is written in this form.

Continued on next page

LITERATURE

Oxymoron	A contradictory form of speech, such as jumbo shrimp, unkindly kind, or singer John Mellencamp's "It hurts so good."
Paradox	Seemingly untrue statement which, when examined more closely, proves to be true. John Donne's sonnet "Death Be Not Proud" postulates that death shall die and humans will triumph over death. At first thought not true, Donne's sonnet ultimately explains and proves this paradox.
Parallelism	A type of close repetition of clauses or phrases that emphasize key topics or ideas in writing. The psalms in the King James Version of the Bible contain many examples.
Personification	Giving human characteristics to inanimate objects or concepts. Great writers, with few exceptions, are masters of this literary device.
Quatrain	A poetic stanza composed of four lines. A Shakespearean or Elizabethan sonnet is made up of three quatrains and a heroic couplet.
Scansion	The analysis of a poetic line. Count the number of syllables per line and determine where the accents fall. Divide the line into metric feet. Name the meter by the type and number of feet. Much is written about scanning poetry. Try not to inundate your students with this jargon; rather allow them to feel the power of the poets' words, ideas, and images.
Soliloquy	A highlighted speech in drama, usually delivered by a major character and expounding on the author's philosophy or expressing universal truths. Soliloquies are delivered with the character alone on the stage, as in Hamlet's famous "To be or not to be" soliloquy.
Spenserian Stanza	Stanza invented by Sir Edmund Spenser for use in *The Faerie Queene*, his epic poem honoring Queen Elizabeth I. Each stanza consists of nine lines, eight of which are in iambic parameter. The ninth line, called an "alexandrine," has two extra syllables or one additional foot.
Sprung Rhythm	Invented and used extensively by the poet Gerard Manley Hopkins. Sprung rhythm consists of variable meter, which combines stressed and unstressed syllables fashioned by the author. See "Pied Beauty" or "God's Grandeur."
Stream of Consciousness	A style of writing which reflects the mental processes of the characters, and expressing, at times, jumbled memories, feelings, and dreams. James Joyce, Virginia Woolf, and William Faulkner use stream of consciousness in their writings.
Terza Rima	A series of poetic stanzas that use the recurrent rhyme scheme of aba, bcb, cdc, ded, and so forth. The second-generation Romantic poets—Keats, Byron, Shelley, and, to a lesser degree, Yeats—used this Italian verse form, especially in their odes. Dante used this stanza in *The Divine Comedy*.
Tone	The discernible attitude inherent in an author's work regarding the subject, readership, or characters. Swift or Pope's tone is satirical. Boswell's tone toward Johnson is admiring.
Wit	Writing of genius, keenness, and sagacity expressed through clever use of language. Alexander Pope and the Augustans wrote about and were said to possess wit.

UNDERSTAND STRATEGIES FOR ANALYZING AND INTERPRETING VARIOUS FORMS OF POETRY

SKILL 8.3 Analyzing formal rhyme schemes and sound devices in a work of poetry (e.g., assonance, alliteration)

See Skill 8.2

SKILL 8.4 Analyzing the use of figures of speech in a work of poetry (e.g., simile, metonymy, apostrophe)

See Skill 8.2

SKILL 8.5 Analyzing the use of poetic and literary devices in a work of poetry (e.g., imagery, allusion)

Style can be thought of as those characteristics of writing that reveal the voice or individuality of the writer. Voice is part of what might be called the rhetorical stance a writer assumes as he or she undertakes a creative project. Aspects of style seldom can be separated from one another. Sentence structure, paragraph patterns, and diction are all elements of style; style is the particular combination of choices among these elements made by a writer. The choices are governed especially by what has been called the writer's "stance," the position taken for a particular writing task. The writer moves out of himself or herself, communicating through a voice, adopting a tone and a point of view.

Vocabulary

The vocabulary peculiar to an author is often the writer's most identifiable characteristic. Mark Twain, who was a master at rendering colloquial speech, is a case in point. His early life on the Mississippi River furnished him with a unique vocabulary that distinguishes his writings from that of others. A writer's vocabulary usually reflects his or her experiences, particularly early ones. While an author may alter the vocabulary that has emerged from earlier experiences to achieve a particular purpose, traces can usually be identified by a careful observer.

Sentence Structure

Another characteristic of style that may distinguish a particular writer is the patterning of sentences. Ernest Hemingway is well known for the short, clipped speech of many of his characters. Meanwhile, William Faulkner's long sentences are a distinguishing feature of *his* style. If a writer typically writes in a particular sentence pattern, e.g., complex sentences that open with an adverbial clause, then his work will be recognizable for that characteristic.

Imagery

A writer's use of imagery also may be the author's most identifiable characteristic. Flannery O' Connor's writing is characterized by her images of the South, where she lived out her short life. She created characters that could have emerged from no other place on earth than the southern United States of America.

Learn more about teaching imagery— from the brain to the paper:

students.ed.uiuc.edu/vallicel/Teaching_imagery.html

Symbolism

Another feature that often distinguishes a writer is the use of symbols. Defining symbolism as a literary device that allows for the broader applicability of prose to meanings beyond what may be literally described, many writers—in fact, most or all authors of fiction—make the symbolic use of concepts and objects central to the meaning of their works. Joseph Conrad and James Joyce, for example, use symbolism extensively to represent themes that applied to greater contexts in their contemporary politics and society.

Allusion

Writers of fiction rely very heavily on allusions to achieve overtones of meaning, to wring the most meaning possible out of as few words as possible. The most common kind of allusion is biblical. Because most Western writers have grown up in a milieu steeped in Christianity and because most writers know that they can count on readers to have a similar background, biblical allusions occur frequently in English and American literature.

The modern American author who usually comes to mind with regard to biblical allusion is William Faulkner. His novel *Absalom, Absalom* is a retelling of the story of King David and his son. Even so, the story has impact on the literal level without the strongly biblical tint of the story as told by Faulkner. Knowing the biblical story adds depth and understanding to Faulkner's novel.

UNDERSTAND STRATEGIES FOR ANALYZING AND INTERPRETING VARIOUS FORMS OF POETRY

SKILL 8.6 Interpreting the point of view, tone, and mood in a work of poetry using critical theories and text-centered and reader-centered approaches

See Skills 7.2 and 8.2

Literary Elements

The elements of fiction vary in importance and development from story to story. Some stories are mainly plot-driven, while others are character studies. Some stories are so tightly constructed that all elements work together to develop the theme and entertain the reader. Although readers can certainly enjoy a story without an in-depth understanding of its literary elements, understanding these elements can help readers develop a deeper appreciation for an author's talent and writing skill.

Read more about tone and style:
www.delmar.edu/engl/wrtctr/handouts/ToneStyle.pdf

Plot

PLOT is sometimes called action, or the sequence of the events. If the plot does not *move*, the story quickly dies. Therefore, the successful writer of stories uses a wide variety of active verbs in creative and unusual ways. If a reader is kept interested by the movement of the story, the experience of reading it will be pleasurable. The reader will probably want to read more of this author's work. Careful, unique, and unusual choices of active verbs will bring about that effect.

PLOT: the action or the sequence of events in a story

William Faulkner is a good example of a successful writer whose stories are lively and memorable because of his use of unusual active verbs. In analyzing the development of plot, analytical readers will look at the verbs. However, the development of believable conflicts is also vital. If there is no conflict, there is no story. In critical thinking readers should ask: What devices does a writer use to develop the conflicts, and are they real and believable?

Character

Character is portrayed in many ways: description of physical characteristics, dialogue, interior monologue, the attitudes of other characters toward the character in question, and so on.

A good portrayal of a character includes:
- *Description of physical characteristics*
- *Speech patterns/dialogue*
- *Interior monologue*
- *Other characters' opinions of the character in question*

If the description of a character's appearance is a visual one, then the reader must be able to *see* the character. What is the shape of the character's nose? What color are his or her eyes? How tall or how short is this character? Is he or she thin or chubby? How does the character move? How does the character walk? Writers choose terms that will create a picture for the reader. It's not enough to say that the character's eyes are blue, for example. What kind of blue? Often the color of eyes is compared to something else to enhance the readers' ability to visualize the character.

A good test of characterization is the level of emotional involvement of the reader in the character. If the reader is to become involved, the description must provide an actual experience—seeing, smelling, hearing, tasting, or feeling. In the following example, Isaac Asimov deftly describes a character both directly and indirectly.

> Undersecretary Albert Minnim was a small, compact man, ruddy of skin, and graying, with the angles of his body smoothed down and softened. He exuded an air of cleanliness and smelled faintly of tonic. It all spoke of the good things of life that came with the liberal rations obtained by those high in Administration.
>
> –Isaac Asimov, The Robot Series: The Naked Sun

Dialogue will also reflect characteristics. Is it clipped? Is it highly dialectal? Does a character rely on colloquialisms (*y'all*, *bling*)? The ability to portray the speech of a character can make or break a story.

The kind of person the character is in the mind of the reader is dependent on impressions created by description and dialogue. How do other characters feel about this character as revealed by their treatment of him or her, their discussions of him or her with each other, or their overt descriptions of the character? For example, the line "John, of course, can't be trusted with another person's possessions" reveals another character's impression of John. In analyzing a story, it's useful to discuss the devices used to produce character.

Setting

Setting may be visual, temporal, psychological, or social. In Edgar Allan Poe's description of the house in "The Fall of the House of Usher," as the protagonist/narrator approaches the house, the air of dread and gloom that pervades the story is caught in the setting and sets the stage for the story. A setting may also be symbolic, as it is in Poe's story, where the house is a symbol of the family that lives in it. As the house disintegrates, so does the family.

The language used in all of aspects of a story—plot, character, and setting—creates the MOOD of a story. Poe's first sentence in "The Fall of the House of Usher" establishes the mood of the story:

> During the whole of a dull, dark, and soundless day in the autumn of the year, when the clouds hung oppressively low in the heavens, I had been passing alone, on horseback, through a singularly dreary tract of country; and at length found myself, as the shades of the evening drew on, within view of the melancholy House of Usher.

MOOD: the "feeling" of a story evoked by the language used to describe plot, character, and setting

Why did the author write this story? This question will lead to the THEME—the underlying main idea. Whether a story is escapist or interpretive, it will have a controlling idea that is integral to its development. This idea is more than a topic (love, anger, guilt, jealousy); it is the author's view of the topic.

> **THEME:** the underlying main idea of a story

Sometimes the title of a story will help reveal the theme. For example, in "The Tell-Tale Heart," Poe tells us a story about guilt and the effect it has on one's conscience. The title foreshadows the outcome and helps the reader understand the theme.

> **SKILL 8.7** Interpreting central ideas or themes in a work of poetry using critical theories and text-centered and reader-centered approaches

See Skill 8.6

COMPETENCY 9
UNDERSTAND THE MAJOR CHARACTERISTICS OF LITERATURES FROM AROUND THE WORLD

> **SKILL 9.1** Demonstrating knowledge of major literary genres, styles, and trends associated with literature from around the world

Prior to twentieth-century research on child development and child/adolescent literature's relationship to that development, books for adolescents were primarily *didactic*. They were designed to address history, manners, and morals.

Middle Ages

As early as the eleventh century, Anselm, the Archbishop of Canterbury, wrote an encyclopedia designed to instill in children the beliefs and principles of conduct acceptable to adults in medieval society. Early monastic translations of the Bible and other religious writings were written in Latin for the edification of the upper class.

LITERATURE

Fifteenth-century hornbooks were designed to teach reading and religious lessons. William Claxton printed English versions of *Aesop's Fables*, Malory's *Le Morte d'Arthur*, and stories from Greek and Roman mythology. Though printed for adults, tales of the adventures of Odysseus and the Arthurian knights were also popular with literate adolescents.

Renaissance

The Renaissance saw the introduction of inexpensive chapbooks, small in size and 16–64 pages in length. Chapbooks were condensed versions of mythology and fairy tales. Designed for the common people, chapbooks were imperfect grammatically but immensely popular because of their adventurous contents. Though most of the serious, educated adults frowned on the sometimes vulgar little books, chapbooks received praise from Richard Steele (of *Tattler* fame) for inspiring his grandson's interest in reading and in pursuing his other studies.

Meanwhile, the Puritans' most popular reads were the Bible, John Foe's *Book of Martyrs*, and John Bunyan's *The Pilgrim's Progress*. Though venerating religious martyrs and preaching the moral propriety that was to lead to eternal happiness, the stories of the *Book of Martyrs* were often lurid in their descriptions of the fate of the damned. In contrast, *The Pilgrim's Progress*, not written for children and difficult reading even for adults, was as attractive to adolescents for its adventurous plot as for its moral outcome.

In Puritan America, the *New England Primer* set forth the prayers, catechisms, Bible verses, and illustrations meant to instruct children in the Puritan ethic.

The seventeenth-century French used fables and fairy tales to entertain adults, but children found them enjoyable as well.

Late Seventeenth Century

The late seventeenth century brought the first concern with providing literature specifically targeting the young. Pierre Peril's *Fairy Tales*, Jean de la Fontaine's retellings of famous fables, Mme. d'Aulnoy's novels based on old folktales, and Mme de Beaumont's *Beauty and the Beast* were written to delight as well as instruct young people.

In England, publisher John Newbury was the first to publish a line of books for children. These included a translation of Perrault's *Tales of Mother Goose*; *A Little Pretty Pocket-Book*, "intended for instruction and amusement" but decidedly moralistic and bland in comparison to the previous century's chapbooks; and *The Renowned History of Little Goody Two Shoes*, allegedly written by Oliver Goldsmith for a juvenile audience.

Eighteenth Century

Largely, eighteenth-century adolescents were finding their reading pleasure in adult books: Daniel Defoe's *Robinson Crusoe*, Jonathan Swift's *Gulliver's Travels*, and Johann Wyss's *Swiss Family Robinson*. More books were being written for children, and moral didacticism, though less religious, was nevertheless present. The short stories of Maria Edgeworth, the four-volume *The History of Sandford and Merton* by Thomas Day, and Martha Farquharson's twenty-six volume *Elsie Dinsmore* series dealt with pious protagonists who learned restraint, repentance, and rehabilitation from sin.

Two bright spots in this period of didacticism were Jean Jacques Rousseau's *Emile* and *The Tales of Shakespeare*, and May and Charles Lamb's simplified versions of Shakespeare's plays. Rousseau believed that a child's abilities were enhanced by a free, happy life, and the Lambs subscribed to the notion that children were entitled to entertaining literature written in language comprehensible to them.

Nineteenth Century

Child/adolescent literature truly began its modern rise in nineteenth-century Europe. Hans Christian Andersen's *Fairy Tales* were fanciful adaptations of the Grimm brothers' somber revisions in the previous century. Andrew Lang's series of colorful fairy books contain the folklores of many nations and are still part of the collections of many modern libraries. Clement Moore's "A Visit from St. Nicholas" is a cheery, non-threatening child's view of the night before Christmas. The humor of Lewis Carroll's books about Alice's adventures, Edward Lear's poems with caricatures, and Lucretia Nole's stories of the Philadelphia Peterkin family are full of fancy and not a smidgen of morality.

For more information, read "Introductory lecture on children's & adolescent literature":

homepages.wmich.edu/~tarboxg/Introductory_Lecture_on_Children's_&_Adol_Lit.html

Other popular Victorian novels introduced the modern fantasy and science fiction genres: William Makepeace Thackeray's *The Rose and the Ring*, Charles Dickens' *The Magic Fishbone*, and Jules Verne's *Twenty Thousand Leagues Under the Sea*. Adventure to exotic places became a popular topic: Rudyard Kipling's *Jungle Books*, Jules Verne's *Around the World in Eighty Days*, and Robert Louis Stevenson's *Treasure Island* and *Kidnapped*. In 1884, the first English translation of Johanna Spyri's *Heidi* appeared.

North America was also finding its voices for adolescent readers. American Louisa May Alcott's *Little Women* and Canadian L. M. Montgomery's *Anne of Green Gables* ushered in the modern age of realistic fiction. American youth were enjoying the adventures of Mark Twain's mischievous heroes Tom Sawyer and Huckleberry Finn. For the first time, children were able to read books about real people just like themselves.

LITERATURE

Twentieth Century

The literature of the twentieth century was extensive and diverse and, as in previous centuries, much influenced by the adults who wrote, edited, and selected books for youth consumption. In the first third of the century, suitable adolescent literature dealt with children from good homes with large families. These books projected an image of a peaceful, rural existence.

Though the characters and plots were more realistic, the stories maintained focused on topics that were considered emotionally and intellectually proper. Popular at this time were Laura Ingalls Wilder's *Little House on the Prairie* series and Carl Sandburg's biography *Abe Lincoln Grows Up*. English author J.R.R. Tolkein's fantasy, *The Hobbit*, prefaced modern adolescent readers' fascination with the works of Piers Antony, Madelaine L'Engle, and Anne McCaffery.

> **SKILL 9.2** Demonstrating knowledge of the formal, stylistic, and thematic characteristics of major works and writers of literatures from around the world

Literary studies expanded beyond the borders of America and Britain to include writing from other cultures.

North American Literature

North American literature is divided between the United States, Canada, and Mexico. Canadian writers of note include feminist Margaret Atwood (*The Hand Maiden's Tale*); Alice Munro, a remarkable short story writer; and W. P. Kinsella, another short story writer whose two major subjects are North American Indians and baseball. Mexican writers include 1990 Nobel Prize– winning poet Octavio Paz (*The Labyrinth of Solitude*) and feminist Rosario Castillanos (*The Nine Guardians*).

Caribbean/Central American Literature

The Caribbean and Central America encompass a vast area and cultures that reflect oppression and colonialism by England, Spain, Portugal, France, and the Netherlands. Caribbean writers include Samuel Selvon from Trinidad and Armando Valladares of Cuba. Central American authors include dramatist Carlos Solorzano from Guatemala, whose plays include *Dona Beatriz*, *The Hapless*, *The Magician*, and *The Hands of God*.

UNDERSTAND THE MAJOR CHARACTERISTICS OF LITERATURES FROM AROUND THE WORLD

South American Literature

Chilean Gabriela Mistral was the first Latin American writer to win the Nobel Prize for literature. She is best known for her collection of poetry, *Desolation and Feeling*.

Chile was also home to Pablo Neruda, who also won the Nobel Prize for literature for his poetry. His twenty-nine volumes of poetry have been translated into more than sixty languages, attesting to his universal appeal. His works *Twenty Love Poems* and *Song of Despair* are justly famous. Isabel Allende is carrying on the Chilean literary tradition with her acclaimed novel, *House of Spirits*.

Many literary critics consider Argentine Jorge Luis Borges to be the most important writer of his century from South America. His collections of short stories, *Ficciones*, brought him universal recognition. Also from Argentina, Silvina Ocampo is famed for her poetry and short story collections, which include *The Fury* and *The Days of the Night*.

Noncontinental European Literature

Horacio Quiroga represents Uruguay, and Brazil has Joao Guimaraes Rosa, whose novel *The Devil to Pay*, is considered first-rank world literature.

Germany

German poet and playwright Friedrich von Schiller is best known for his history plays *William Tell* and *The Maid of Orleans*. He is a leading literary figure in Germany's Golden Age of Literature. Rainer Maria Rilke, the great lyric poet, is also one of the poets of the unconscious, or stream of consciousness. Germany also has given the world Herman Hesse (*Siddartha*), Gunter Grass (*The Tin Drum*), and the greatest of all German writers, Johann Wolfgang von Goethe.

Scandinavia

Scandinavian literature includes the work of Hans Christian Andersen of Denmark, who advanced the fairy tale genre with such wistful tales as "The Little Mermaid" and "Thumbelina." The social commentary of Henrik Ibsen in Norway startled the world through drama exploring such issues as feminism (*The Doll's House* and *Hedda Gabler*) and the effects of sexually transmitted diseases (*The Wild Duck* and *Ghosts*). Sweden's Selma Lagerlof is the first woman to win the Nobel Prize for literature. Her novels include *Gosta Berling's Saga* and the world-renowned *The Wonderful Adventures of Nils*, a children's work.

LITERATURE

Russia

Russian literature is vast and monumental. Who has not heard of Fyodor Dostoyevski's *Crime and Punishment* and *The Brothers Karamazov* or of Count Leo Tolstoy's *War and Peace*?

Dostoyevski's influence on modern writers cannot be overstressed. Tolstoy's *War and Peace* is the sweeping account of Napoleon's invasion of Russia and taking of Moscow. This novel is called the national novel of Russia. Tolstoy's ability to create realistic and unforgettable female characters, especially Natasha in *War and Peace* and Anna in *Anna Karenina* further advances Tolstoy's greatness.

Aleksandr Pushkin is famous for great short stories; Anton Chekhov for drama (*Uncle Vanya, The Three Sisters, The Cherry Orchard*); and Yvgeny Yvteshenko for poetry (*Babi Yar*). Boris Pasternak won the Nobel Prize (*Dr. Zhivago*). Aleksandr Solzhenitsyn (*The Gulag Archipelago*) returned to Russia after years of expatriation in Vermont. Ilya Varshavsky, who creates fictional dystopias, represents the genre of science fiction.

France

France has a multifaceted canon of great literature that is broad in scope and almost always champions some social cause, including:

- The poignant short stories of Guy de Maupassant
- The fantastic poetry of Charles Baudelaire (*Fleurs du Mal*)
- The groundbreaking lyrical poetry of Jean Nicolas Arthur Rimbaud and Paul Verlaine
- The existentialism of Jean-Paul Sartre (*No Exit, The Flies, Nausea*), Andre Malraux (*The Fall*), and Albert Camus (*The Stranger* and *The Plague*), the recipient of the 1957 Nobel Prize for literature

Drama in France is best represented by Edmond Rostand's *Cyrano de Bergerac* and the neoclassical dramas of Jean Baptiste Racine and Pierre Corneille (*El Cid*). Feminist writers include Simone de Beauvoir and Sidonie-Gabrielle Colette, known for her short stories and novels. The great French novelists include André Gide, Honoré de Balzac (*Cousin Bette*), Stendhal (*The Red and the Black*), and Alexandre Dumas (*The Three Musketeers* and *The Man in the Iron Mask*). Victor Hugo is the Charles Dickens of French literature, having penned the masterpieces *The Hunchback of Notre Dame* and *Les Miserables*. The stream of consciousness of Marcel Proust's *Remembrance of Things Past* and the Absurdist theatre of Samuel Beckett and

---

Learn more about Jean Paul Sartre:

www.users.muohio.edu
/shermalw/honors_2001
_fall/honors_papers_2001
/detwilerj_Sartre.htm

UNDERSTAND THE MAJOR CHARACTERISTICS OF LITERATURES FROM AROUND THE WORLD

Eugène Ionesco (*The Rhinoceros*) attest to the groundbreaking genius of the French writers.

Slavic Nations

Austrian writer Franz Kafka (*The Metamorphosis*, *The Trial*, and *The Castle*) is considered by many to be the literary voice of the first half of the twentieth century. Poet Vaclav Havel represents the Czech Republic. Slovakia has dramatist Karel Capek (R.U.R.). Romania is represented by Elie Weisel (*Night*), a Nobel Prize winner.

Spain

Spain's great writers include Miguel de Cervantes (*Don Quixote*) and Juan Ramon Jimenez. The anonymous national epic, *El Cid*, has been translated into many languages.

Italy

Italy's greatest writers include Virgil (*The Aeneid*); Giovanni Boccaccio (*The Decameron*); Dante Alighieri (*The Divine Comedy*); and the more contemporary Alberto Moravia.

Ancient Greece

Greece is the cradle not only of democracy, but of literature as well. Greece will always be prominent in literary stature due to Homer's epics, *The Iliad* and *The Odyssey*. Aside from Shakespeare, no secular writer is more often cited. The works of Plato and Aristotle in philosophy; of Aeschylus, Euripides, and Sophocles in tragedy; and of Aristophanes in comedy further solidify Greece's preeminence.

Africa

African literary greats include South Africans Nadine Gordimer (Nobel Prize for literature) and Peter Abrahams (*Tell Freedom: Memories of Africa*). Chinua Achebe (*Things Fall Apart*) and the poet Wole Soyinka hail from Nigeria. Mark Mathabane wrote an autobiography, *Kaffir Boy*, about growing up in South Africa. Egyptian writer Naguib Mahfouz and Doris Lessing from Rhodesia (now Zimbabwe) write about race relations in their respective countries. Lessing won the 2007 Nobel Prize for literature. Because of her radical

Learn more about postcolonial literature in English:

www.thecore.nus.edu.sg/post/misc/africov.html
no page

politics, Lessing was once banned from her homeland and the Union of South Africa; so was Alan Paton, whose seemingly simple story *Cry, the Beloved Country* brought the plight of Africans and the whites' fear of Africans under apartheid to the rest of the world.

Far East Literature

Asia has many modern writers who are being translated for the western reading public. India's Krishan Chandar has authored more than 300 stories. Rabindranath Tagore won the Nobel Prize for literature in 1913 (*Song Offerings*). R. K. Narayan, India's most famous writer (*The Guide*), is interested in mythology and legends of India. Santha Rama Rau's work *Gifts of Passage* is her true story of life in a British school where she tries to preserve her Indian culture and traditional home.

Revered as Japan's most famous female author, Fumiko Hayashi (*Drifting Clouds*) had written more than 270 literary works by the time of her death.

The 1968 Nobel Prize for literature was awarded to Yasunari Kawabata (*The Sound of the Mountain, The Snow Country*). His "Palm-of-the-Hand Stories" take the essentials of Haiku poetry and transform them into the short story genre.

Katai Tayama (*The Quilt*) is touted as the father of the Japanese confessional novel. His works, characterized as naturalism, are definitely not for the squeamish. The "slice of life" psychological writings of Ryunosuke Akutagawa gained him acclaim in the western world. His short stories, especially "Rashamon" and "In a Grove," are greatly praised for their style and content.

China, too, has contributed to the literary world. Li Po, the T'ang dynasty poet from China's Golden Age, revealed his interest in folklore by preserving the folk songs and mythology of China. Po further allows his readers to explore the Chinese philosophy of Taoism and to understand feelings against expansionism during the T'ang dynastic rule. The T'ang dynasty, which was one of great diversity in the arts, saw Jiang Fang help create the Chinese version of a short story. His themes often express love between a man and a woman.

Modern feminist and political concerns are written eloquently by Ting Ling, under the pseudonym Chiang Ping-Chih. Her stories reflect her concerns about social injustice and her commitment to the women's movement.

UNDERSTAND THE MAJOR CHARACTERISTICS OF LITERATURES FROM AROUND THE WORLD

SKILL 9.3 Demonstrating knowledge of the formal, stylistic, and thematic characteristics of major movements and periods in literatures from around the world

Sumeria

Between 7000 BCE and 3000 BCE, the domestication of animals, the development of agriculture, and the establishment of an agricultural surplus led to the invention of writing, thus making possible the emergence of literature and the development of human civilization.

These three developments allowed the small, nomadic groups of hunters and gatherers who had until then existed in pockets all over the world to evolve into larger, stationary communities. The first of these communities developed in an area in the Middle East called Mesopotamia, meaning "Land Between Two Rivers," the Tigris and the Euphrates. This ancestor to civilization as we know it was called Sumer, and the Sumerians created the wheel and the first written language.

Perhaps the Sumerians were the first to create so much of what is fundamental to civilization because of their ability to create an agricultural surplus. With their position between two flowing rivers, the Sumerians developed an extensive irrigation system that allowed them to create an abundant surplus. This surplus meant greater economic stability, security, and the ability to support a much larger population within the walls of their cities.

The growing population stimulated the development of governance and specialization. Artisans, governors, builders, regulators, merchants, and priests flourished. Keeping track of all this activity required the development of some kind of record keeping. At first, pictographs (images directly representing concrete objects) were etched into soft clay tablets and allowed to dry.

The scope of record keeping eventually grew from recording how many sacks of barley a farmer brought to the temple to describing in great detail and enthusiasm the exploits of the kings. Thus, with the evolution of the city-state and then the nation, pictographs quickly became insufficient to meet the needs of this new societal structure. Eventually, the Sumerians developed symbols to represent abstract qualities such as courage and love.

Check out Sumerian art and architecture at:

www.crystalinks.com/sumerart.html

Dark Ages

With the destruction of the Roman Empire in the fifth century CE, the Roman Catholic Church became the dominant and unifying source in Europe. With the ascendancy of the church and the demise of Rome, the social, political, and

LITERATURE

artistic achievements of the classical age were effectively "lost" for centuries, and Western civilizations entered a time known as the Dark, or Middle, Ages.

Fifteenth and Sixteenth Centuries

By the fifteenth century, however, the lot of the individual had improved dramatically, and the overwhelming influence of the Catholic Church was challenged. This period is known as the Renaissance, which started in Italy in the mid fourteenth century. The Renaissance is associated with the rediscovery and revival of classical Greek and Latin philosophy, literature, and art.

In the fifteenth and early sixteenth centuries, the invention of the printing press (around 1450) and the revolt of Martin Luther, a German Catholic monk, helped to fuel the revival of classical thought and to fuel challenges to the supremacy of the Catholic Church.

The development of paper gave rise to the invention of the printing press. Prior to the development of paper, parchment made from the skin of farm animals was used for writing. Considering that one animal generally produced about four leaves or sheets of parchment, reprinting a book the size of the Bible required the slaughter of at least 300 sheep or calves, making it a very expensive process reserved for the very elite in society.

Learn more about Martin Luther at:

www.educ.msu.edu/homepages/laurence/reformation/Luther/Luther.htm

With the development of paper from rags and the invention of the printing press, printing books and pamphlets became very cheap. In addition, books began to be printed not only in Greek and Latin (the language of scholars and diplomats) but also in the vernacular (the language of the common people). This was very important to the revolutionary success of Martin Luther, who in 1517 nailed his famous *Ninety-Five Theses* to the door of the castle church of Wittenberg.

His *Ninety-Five Theses* amounted to objections (protestations) regarding the then-pervasive sale of indulgences (pardons for sins) by the Catholic Church throughout Europe, especially in Germany.

Without the printing press, few would have known of or followed Luther's challenge to Roman Catholic authority. The German monk and his supporters turned immediately to the printing press, though, and sent out hundreds of pamphlets explaining his protests against Rome, gaining the support of the German people at all levels of society. As a result, when Luther was excommunicated by the Church in Rome, he and his followers became known as Lutherans, and the first of the Protestant or "protesting" religions was born.

UNDERSTAND THE MAJOR CHARACTERISTICS OF LITERATURES FROM AROUND THE WORLD

The study of classical texts and advances in science and astronomy aided this break with the Roman Catholic Church by challenging the traditional thinking that had been endorsed and enforced by the Church for generations.

The Renaissance

While the Renaissance revived the classics, the subsequent Age of Reason (also known as The Enlightenment) extolled and emulated the clarity and rational thinking of the great classical writers, thinkers, and artists especially of the Romans. This focus on reason is evident in the writings of John Dryden (1631–1700), in the mathematically exact music of the harpsichord, and in the classical ionic and doric architecture exhibited in palaces and stately homes of this period.

The Romantics

By the late 1700s, however, the Romantics began to challenge this exclusive admiration for the purely intellectual and logical thinking of the neo classicists. Instead of looking to science and rational thought for answers and inspiration, the Romantics celebrated the emotions and the imagination. Romantic poet William Blake (1757–1827) considered science and mathematics to be soulless disciplines that shackled the imagination and inhibited free expression of thought and feelings.

The Romantics also preferred nature to the city and distrusted most established institutions, especially the church and the government. In England, people were finding these institutions more and more oppressive. In "The Masque of Anarchy," English poet Percy Bysshe Shelley (1792–1822) encouraged the people of England to stand up against the enslaving establishment:

> Rise like Lions after slumber
> In unvanquishable number —
> Shake your chains to earth like dew
> Which in sleep had fallen on you —
> Ye are many — they are few.

For more information on Percy Bysshe Shelley:

www.wam.umd.edu/~djb/shelley/home.htm

Sentiments such as Shelley's finally led to reforms in England which, among other changes, eliminated seats in Parliament that had been purchased by wealthy families. Still, it would be fifty years before England passed a reform that allowed men from all economic and social classes to vote, and another fifty years before women were granted the same right.

LITERATURE

Nineteenth Century

The nineteenth century is considered by many to be the century of greatest change for Western civilization. Fueled in large part by the Industrial Revolution, this century introduced factories, railroads, and the automobile to civilization.

The Industrial Revolution radically changed the way people lived, allowing them greater and faster mobility and more economic possibilities. Although the growing urbanization created slums and a class of working poor, it also gave rise to a powerful middle class, with surplus wealth and free time in which to spend it.

These developments also created a new deity—"progress"—understood as holding out unlimited hope for the future and for the advancement of human civilization. Religious institutions, which had played such a fundamental role in the public and private lives of peoples in many countries, were forced to take a back seat at this time. The impact of discoveries in astronomy, geology, evolutionary biology, and archeology pushed religion out of the public limelight and into a personal and private sphere.

The Realists

A majority of the literature of this period highlighted contemporary life and manners. By the 1850s, it was known as the literature of reality, or Realism. The novelist was likened to the scientist, who creates and directs the experiment, but is not part of it. The writer is objective and observational, recording the truth of the reality around him or her.

Writers of the Realism movement include:

- Gustave Flaubert (1821–1880) of France (*Madame Bovary*)
- Fyodor Dostoevsky (1821–1881) of Russia (*Crime and Punishment*)
- Henry James (1843–1916) of America (*The Aspen Papers, The Turn of the Screw, Daisy Miller,* and *The Bostonians*)

During the first half of the twentieth century, technological advancements and breakthroughs continued. Henry Ford started the world's first automated assembly line in Detroit in 1908, mass producing the famous Model T Ford. The success of this ubiquitous black car was evident, because over 26 million Model T Fords were registered in the United States by 1929.

Radio transmission, telephones, movies, and airplanes all made their debut in the early twentieth century. In the midst of these early advances, the literature produced in these early decades was didactic or instructive in tone. Writers took on issues of the day, such as the function of social classes and professions, female suffrage, the justification of armaments and war, and the morality of empire.

UNDERSTAND THE MAJOR CHARACTERISTICS OF LITERATURES FROM AROUND THE WORLD

The first half of the twentieth century also witnessed the end of the supremacy of the British Empire, the onset of the Great Depression, and the beginnings of the First World War.

The Modernists

MODERNISM is the term used to describe the literary movement up to the First World War. Considered radical and utopian in nature, this movement was inspired by new ideas in anthropology, psychoanalysis, philosophy, and political science. Rejecting styles and forms of the post-Romantic period, writers of this movement include:

- D. H. Lawrence (1885–1930) of England (*The Rainbow* and *Women in Love*)
- James Joyce (1882–1941) of Ireland (*A Portrait of the Artist as a Young Man* and *Finnegans Wake*)

Lawrence's innovative novels reject traditional narrative styles and use myth and symbols to denounce the horrors of war and the dehumanizing effects of mass industrialization on the individual. Joyce's novels also use symbols, myth, and stream-of-consciousness writing to explore the universality of the human condition and the relationship between the conscious and the unconscious.

The cynicism that followed the horrors of World War I gave rise to a literature that was pessimistic regarding the human potential to survive the horrors and the conveniences of the modern world. In this vein, Aldous Huxley wrote his inventive, dystopian novel *Brave New World*.

The onset of World War II in 1939 in Europe halted for a time the great literary movements and inventiveness of the century's first half. The horrors of this second great war, ending with the use of atomic bombs over Japan, so profoundly affected the human spirit that writer William Golding noted, "We have discovered a limit to literature."

The post–World War II era found the United States and Russia as the new world superpowers. Britain was deeply indebted to America and definitely diminished as a world power. Along with this new world order, styles in literature shifted from Modernism to Postmodernism.

Postmodern Literature

Referred to as a shift, rather than a break, in style, POSTMODERN LITERATURE is seen as an extension of the Modernist mode of subjective literature—of looking inward, of examining and exploring the inner consciousness of the individual and

> **MODERNISM:** the term used to describe the literary movement up to the First World War

> **POSTMODERN LITERATURE:** a movement in literature seen as an extension of the Modernist mode of subjective literature—an inward examination of self

its connection to the whole. During the last half of the twentieth century, the assassinations of political and social leaders, the Cold War, civil rights movements, the feminist movement, the Space Age, the Internet, and all forms of mass media stimulated and heightened the intensity of this inward examination and exploration of self.

In an age of mass information and instant messaging, postmodern literature is still evolving and exploring realities. This literature focuses not only on the reality of the inner self and its relation to the exterior world, but also of multiple realities constructed in time and space at points all over the globe. In spite of the seeming randomness and chaotic nature of such vast and starkly different realties, they remain knowable. Making them so remains the task of the postmodern writer.

American Indian Literature

The foundation of American Indian writing is found in story telling, oratory, autobiographical and historical accounts of tribal village life, reverence for the environment, and the postulation that the earth was given in trust, to be cared for and passed on to future generations.

Early American Indian writers include:

- Hal Barland, *When the Legends Die*
- S. M. Barrett, Editor, *Geronimo: His Own Story (Apache)*
- C. Eastman and E. Eastman, *Wigwam Evenings: Sioux Folktales Retold*
- L. Riggs, *Cherokee Night* (drama)

Twentieth-century American Indian writers include:

- V. Deloria, *Custer Died for Your Sins* (Sioux)
- M. Dorris, *The Broken Cord* (Modoc)
- L. Hogan, *Mean Spirited* (Chickasaw)
- C. F. Taylor, *Native American Myths and Legends*

Female Writers

Willa Cather's work moves the reader to the prairies of Nebraska and the harsh existence eked out by the immigrant families who choose to stay there to farm. Her most acclaimed works include *My Antonia* and *Death Comes for the Archbishop*.

UNDERSTAND THE MAJOR CHARACTERISTICS OF LITERATURES FROM AROUND THE WORLD

Kate Chopin's regionalism and local color takes her readers to the upper-crust Creole society of New Orleans and resort isles off the Louisiana coast. "The Story of an Hour" is lauded as one of the greatest of all short stories. Her feminist liberation novel *The Awakening* is still hotly debated.

Eudora Welty's regionalism and dialect shine in her short stories of rural Mississippi, especially in "The Worn Path."

Modern black female writers

Modern black female writers have explored the world of feminist/gender issues as well as class prohibitions. They include:

- Alice Walker, *The Color Purple*
- Zora Neale Hurston, *Their Eyes Were Watching God*
- Toni Morrison, *Beloved, Jazz,* and *Song of Solomon*

Feminists

- Louisa May Alcott, *Little Women*
- Betty Friedan, *The Feminine Mystique* and *The Second Stage*
- Elizabeth Janeway, *Man's World, Woman's Place: A Study in Social Mythology*
- Adrienne Rich, *Of Woman Born: Motherhood As Experience and Institution* and *Driving into the Wreck*

Social, Cultural, and Political Issues

American literature is marked by a number of clearly identifiable periods. Although these stand alone, they can also be useful as histories across the curriculum.

Civil Rights

Many of the abolitionists were also early crusaders for civil rights. However, the 1960s civil rights movement focused attention on the plight of the people who had been "freed" by the Civil War in ways that brought about long-overdue changes in the opportunities and rights of African-Americans.

David Halberstam, who had been a reporter in Nashville at the time of the sit-ins by eight young African-American college students, wrote *The Children*, published in 1998 by Random House, for the purpose of reminding Americans of the courage, suffering, and achievements of those eight students. Congressman

---

Check out the brief timeline of American literature:

www.wsu.edu/~campbelld/amlit/timefram.html

Learn more about civil rights literature of the 1960s:

www.lib.virginia.edu/small/exhibits/sixties/civil.html

Some clearly identifiable topics in U.S. history that have influenced literature:
- *Civil rights*
- *Immigration*

LITERATURE

John Lewis, Fifth District, Georgia, who has gone on to a life of public service, was one of those eight young men. Halberstam records that when older African-American ministers tried to persuade these young people not to pursue their protest, John Lewis responded: "If not us, then who? If not now, then when?"

Examples of civil rights protest literature include:

- James Baldwin, *Blues for Mister Charlie*
- Martin Luther King, *Where Do We Go from Here?*
- Langston Hughes, *Fight for Freedom: The Story of the NAACP*
- Eldridge Cleaver, *Soul on Ice*
- Malcolm X, *The Autobiography of Malcolm X*
- Stokely Carmichael and Charles V. Hamilton, *Black Power*
- Leroi Jones, *Home*

Immigration

Immigration has been a popular topic for literature from the time of the Louisiana Purchase in 1804. The recent novel *Undaunted Courage* by Stephen E. Ambrose is ostensibly the autobiography of Meriwether Lewis but is actually a recounting of the Lewis and Clark expedition. Presented as a scientific expedition by President Jefferson, the expedition actually was intended to provide maps and information for the opening up of the West. A well-known novel about the settling of the West by immigrants from other countries is *Giants in the Earth* by Ole Edvart Rolvaag, himself a descendant of immigrants.

John Steinbeck's *Cannery Row* and *Tortilla Flats* glorify the lives of Mexican migrants in California. Amy Tan's *The Joy Luck Club* deals with the problems faced by Chinese immigrants.

Leon Uris's *Exodus* deals with the social history that led to the founding of the modern state of Israel. It was published in 1958, only a short time after the Holocaust. It also deals with attempts of concentration camp survivors to get to the land that has become the new Israel. In many ways, it is the quintessential work on the causes and effects of immigration.

UNDERSTAND THE MAJOR CHARACTERISTICS OF LITERATURES FROM AROUND THE WORLD

> **SKILL 9.4** Demonstrating knowledge of the formal, stylistic, and thematic characteristics of major literary genres and works from the oral tradition

Tales recounting the adventures, exploits, triumphs, and struggles of kings and warriors, as well as stories of creation and the meaning of life, constitute the major themes in ancient world literature.

Although ancient literature began with the Sumerians writing and transcribing their epic tales of heroism and of the all-too-human relationship between themselves and their deities, the body of ancient literature most relevant to the modern world was written between 800 BCE and 400 CE. Ancient Hebrew, Greek, and Latin laid the foundation for most of Western secular and religious thought and for the major themes of Western literature.

The concept of a single, all-powerful God is, perhaps, chief among the foundations of Western thought. A wildly revolutionary idea at the time, monotheism set the ancient Israelites apart from the rest of the ancient world.

Two masterpieces of ancient Greek literature, the *Iliad* and the *Odyssey*, are attributed to Homer and first existed as part of an oral tradition. War is the graphic subject of the *Iliad*. In this poem, Homer evokes two strong, contradictory, and timeless human emotions: revulsion for war and fascination with violence. In the *Iliad*, Achilles is the ultimate warrior who lives to fight and to die on the battlefield.

The *Odyssey* covers the years after the war described in the *Iliad* and instructs that battles are fought not only on the battlefield but also on the journey home, or on the journey toward a just and honorable life. It is the story of the temptations and obstacles that the soldier Odysseus must overcome before returning to his faithful wife and peaceful home.

The Romans chose first to conquer and then to write. In all matters, the Romans paid highest allegiance not to emotions or to questions of right or wrong, but to what was practical, functional, stable, and lasting. A disciplined and highly organized people, the Romans built a great empire; but for their literary inspirations, they turned to the Greeks.

Although inspired by the Greeks, the Roman poets created distinctly Roman works. In the Latin manuscripts of the Romans, the highest virtues are those that promote adherence to duty and to discipline, as best expressed in the *Aeneid* by Virgil. In this poem, Aeneas is the ideal Roman ruler, devoted to duty above all else. His god-given mission is to found the city that in time will become the seat

LITERATURE

of the great Roman Empire. To do this, he sacrifices his one and only love and then his life.

Ancient Literary Genres

The major genres employed in ancient literary works include prose, epic poetry, comedic and tragic plays, and satire.

Major genres employed in ancient literary works:
- *Prose*
- *Epic poetry*
- *Comedic plays*
- *Tragic plays*
- *Satire*

Prose

Although ancient novels did exist, the novel as a form of literary expression would not come into its own until the Victorian era. The prose that did exist consisted of historical records (such as Thucydides's account of the Peloponnesian Wars) and the works of philosophers and orators (the speeches of the Greek philosopher Socrates as recorded by his famous student Plato and of the Roman philosopher and orator Cicero).

Epic poetry

The popularity of the epic poem in the ancient world stems from its roots in the oral tradition, in which stories and accounts of wars, kings, warriors, and the gods were shared with the public. Whereas some of the greatest epic poetry is attributed to Homer and Virgil, the Sumerian epic poem Gilgamesh provides the earliest example of this literary genre.

Comedic and tragic plays

Absent in ancient Hebrew and Roman literature, drama had its birth in the fifth century in Athens. Early Greek plays include tragedies by Aeschylus (*Agamemnon*) and Sophocles (*Oedipus Tyrannus*) and comedies by Aristophanes (*Lysistrata*). These Greek dramas grew out of an ancient ritual, a dance to the god Dionysus. The ritual involved a chorus of dancers who sang the familiar songs of their epic heroes in order to honor and please Dionysus and to ensure a bountiful spring.

After the seventh century BCE, a Greek poet, Thespis, decided to add an "actor" into the chorus. The actor Thespian would stand apart from and answer to the chorus. Thus drama, which in Greek means "thing done," was born.

Satire

Whereas the play was unique to the Greeks, satire was unique to Rome. "Satire" was the term the Roman poet Juvenal gave to his poems criticizing the vices and follies of imperial Rome. Chief among these follies was blind ambition, because it caused those afflicted to pray for anything except "a sound mind in a sound body."

COMPETENCY 10

UNDERSTAND THE MAJOR HISTORICAL, SOCIAL, CULTURAL, AND POLITICAL ASPECTS OF LITERATURES FROM AROUND THE WORLD

> **SKILL 10.1** Examining in literary works references to major historical events and to major social, cultural, and political movements and institutions that have influenced the development of literatures from around the world

American Literature

When compared to other countries, America has a relatively brief history and thus a comparatively smaller canon of literature. Nevertheless, its fiction and nonfiction have the depth and breadth to tell the story of its people. To study American literature is to study American history. Students will discover the importance of writing as a reflection of the historical, social, ethnic, political, and economic environment of the times.

American literature is defined by a number of clearly identifiable periods.

Native American works from various tribes

These works were originally part of a vast oral tradition that spanned most of continental America, dating as far back as before the fifteenth century.

Characteristics of Native American literature include:

- Reverence for and awe of nature
- The interconnectedness of the elements in the life cycle

Themes of Native American literature include:

- The hardiness of the native body and soul
- Remorse for the destruction of the native way of life
- The genocide of many tribes by the encroaching settlement and Manifest Destiny policies of the U.S. government

LITERATURE

The Colonial period

Stylistically, early colonists' writings were neoclassical, emphasizing order, balance, clarity, and reason. Because the colonists had been schooled in England, their writing and speaking remained decidedly British, even as their thinking became entirely American.

Early American literature reveals the lives and experiences of the New England expatriates who left England to find religious freedom. William Bradford's excerpts from *The Mayflower Compact* relate vividly the hardships of crossing the Atlantic in a tiny vessel, the misery and suffering of the first winter, the approaches of the American Indians, the decimation of the colonists' ranks, and the establishment of the Bay Colony of Massachusetts.

Anne Bradstreet's poetry describes colonial New England life. From her journals, modern readers learn about the everyday life of the early settlers, the hardships of travel, and the responsibilities of different groups and individuals in the community. Early American literature also reveals the commercial and political adventures of the Cavaliers, who came to the New World with King George's blessing.

William Byrd's journal *A History of the Dividing Line*, concerning his trek into the Dismal Swamp separating the Carolinian territories from Virginia and Maryland, makes quite lively reading. A privileged insider to the English Royal Court, Byrd, like other Southern Cavaliers, was given grants to pursue business ventures.

The Revolutionary period

The Revolutionary period of American literature contains nonfiction genres: essay, pamphlet, speech, famous document, and epistle. There are many important writers and works of the Revolutionary Period.

Thomas Paine's pamphlet *Common Sense*, though written by a recently transplanted Englishman, spoke to the American patriots' common sense in dealing with issues in the cause of freedom.

Other contributions to Revolutionary literature are Benjamin Franklin's essays from *Poor Richard's Almanac* and satires such as "How to Reduce a Great Empire to a Small One" and "A Letter to Madame Gout."

The Revolutionary period produced great orations such as Patrick Henry's "Speech to the Virginia House of Burgesses" (the "Give me liberty or give me death" speech) and George Washington's "Farewell to the Army of the Potomac." Less memorable are Washington's inaugural addresses, which often strike modern readers as lacking sufficient focus.

"If ever two were one, then surely we. If ever man were loved by wife, then thee."

Read more about Anne Bradstreet:

www.annebradstreet.com/Default.htm

The **Revolutionary Period** of American literature contains nonfiction genres: essay, pamphlet, speech, famous document, and epistle.

The *Declaration of Independence*, the brainchild predominantly of Thomas Jefferson (along with some prudent editing by Ben Franklin), is a prime example of neoclassical writing—balanced, well crafted, and focused.

Epistles include the exquisitely written, moving correspondence between John Adams and Abigail Adams. The poignancy of their separation—she in Boston, he in Philadelphia—is palpable and real.

The Romantic period

Early American folk tales and the emergence of a distinctly American style of writing constitute the next period, called the Romantic period.

Washington Irving's characters Ichabod Crane and Rip Van Winkle represent a uniquely American folklore devoid of English influences. The characters are indelibly marked by their environment and the superstitions of the New Englander. The early writings of James Fenimore Cooper, including his *Leatherstocking Tales*, provide readers a window into their uniquely American world through stirring accounts of drums along the Mohawk Trail, the French and Indian Wars, the futile British defense of Fort William Henry, and the brutalities of this period. Natty Bumppo, Chingachgook, Uncas, and Magua are unforgettable characters who reflect the American spirit in thought and action.

The poetry of the "Fireside Poets"—James Russell Lowell, Oliver Wendell Holmes, Henry Wadsworth Longfellow, and John Greenleaf Whittier—was recited by American families and read during the long New England winters. In "The Courtin'," Lowell used Yankee dialect to tell a story. Spellbinding epics by Longfellow (such as *Hiawatha*, *The Courtship of Miles Standish*, and *Evangeline*) told of adversity, sorrow, and ultimate happiness in a uniquely American fashion. The poem "Snowbound" by Whittier relates the story of a captive family isolated by a blizzard and stresses family closeness.

Nathaniel Hawthorne and Herman Melville are the preeminent early American novelists, writing on subjects definitely regional, specific, and American, yet sharing insights about human foibles, fears, loves, doubts, and triumphs.

Hawthorne's writings range from children's stories, such as *The Cricket on the Hearth* series, to adult fare that includes dark, brooding short stories such as "Dr. Heidegger's Experiment," "The Devil and Tom Walker," and "Rapuccini's Daughter." Hawthorne's masterpiece *The Scarlet Letter* criticizes the society of hypocritical Puritan New Englanders, who ostensibly left England to establish religious freedom but who became entrenched in judgmental finger-wagging. The Puritans in the novel ostracize Hester Prynne and condemn her child, Pearl,

> Nathaniel Hawthorne and Herman Melville are the preeminent early American novelists, writing on subjects definitely regional, specific, and American, yet sharing insights about human foibles, fears, loves, doubts, and triumphs.

LITERATURE

as a child of Satan. Great love, sacrifice, loyalty, suffering, and related epiphanies add universality to this tale. *The House of the Seven Gables* deals with kept secrets, loneliness, societal pariahs, and the triumph of love over horrible wrongs.

Herman Melville's great opus *Moby Dick* follows a crazed Captain Ahab on his Homeric odyssey to conquer the great white whale that has outwitted him and his whaling crews time and again. The whale has even taken Ahab's leg and, according to Ahab, wants all of him. Melville paints in painstaking detail and with insider knowledge the harsh life of a whaler out of New Bedford by way of Nantucket.

> *Read about the life and works of Herman Melville:*
> www.melville.org

For those readers who don't want to learn about every detail of the whaler's rigging, Melville offers up the succinct tale of *Billy Budd* and his Christ-like sacrifice to the black-and-white maritime laws on the high seas. In *Billy Budd*, an accident results in the death of one of the ship's officers, a slug of a fellow who had taken a dislike to the young, affable, shy Billy. Captain Vere must hang Billy for the death of Claggert but knows that his punishment is not just. However, an example must be given to the rest of the crew so that discipline can be maintained.

Edgar Allan Poe creates a distinctly American version of romanticism with his 16-syllable lines in "The Raven," the classical "To Helen," and his Gothic "Annabelle Lee." The horror short story can be said to originate from Poe's pen. "The Tell-Tale Heart," "The Cask of Amontillado," "The Fall of the House of Usher," and "The Masque of the Red Death" are exemplary short stories. In addition, the genre of detective story emerges with Poe's "Murders in the Rue Morgue."

> *American Romanticism has its own offshoot in the Transcendentalism of Ralph Waldo Emerson and Henry David Thoreau.*

American Romanticism has its own offshoot in the Transcendentalism of Ralph Waldo Emerson and Henry David Thoreau. Emerson wrote about transcending the complexities of life; Thoreau, who wanted to get to the marrow of life, immersed himself in nature at Walden Pond and wrote an inspiring autobiographical account of his sojourn, aptly titled *On Walden Pond*. Thoreau also wrote passionately regarding his objections to the interference of government in the life of the individual in "On the Duty of Civil Disobedience."

Emerson's elegantly-crafted essays and war poetry still validate several important universal truths. Probably most remembered for his address to Thoreau's Harvard graduating class, "The American Scholar," Emerson defined the qualities of hard work and intellectual spirit required of Americans in their growing nation.

The transition between Romanticism and Realism

The Civil War period ushered in the poignant poetry of Walt Whitman and his homage to all who suffered from the ripple effects of war and presidential assassination. His "Come Up from the Fields, Father," about a Civil War soldier's death and his family's reaction, and "When Lilacs Last in the Courtyard Bloom'd," about the effects of Abraham Lincoln's death on the poet and the nation, should

> *Find more sites about American literature:*
> www.wsu.edu/~campbelld/amlit/sites.htm

be required reading in any American literature course. Further, his *Leaves of Grass* gave America its first truly unique poetry form.

Emily Dickinson, like Walt Whitman, left her literary fingerprints on a vast array of poems, all but three of which were never published in her lifetime. Her themes of introspection and attention to nature's details and wonders are, by any measurement, world-class works. Her posthumous recognition reveals the timeliness of her work. American writing had most certainly arrived!

Mark Twain also left giant footprints on the American literary landscape with his unique blend of tall tale and fable. "The Celebrated Jumping Frog of Calaveras County" and "The Man who Stole Hadleyburg" are epitomes of short story writing. With regard to the novel, Twain again rose above others by his bold, still-disputed, oft-banned *The Adventures of Huckleberry Finn*, which examines such taboo subjects as a white person's love of a slave, the issue of leaving children with abusive parents, and the outcomes of family feuds. Written partly in dialect and southern vernacular, *The Adventures of Huckleberry Finn* is touted by some as the greatest American novel.

The Realistic period

The late nineteenth century saw a reaction against the tendency of Romantic writers to look at the world through rose-colored glasses. Writers like Frank Norris (*The Pit*) and Upton Sinclair (*The Jungle*) used their novels to decry deplorable working conditions in slaughterhouses and wheat mills.

In *The Red Badge of Courage*, Stephen Crane wrote of the daily sufferings of the common soldier in the Civil War. Realistic writers wrote of common, ordinary people and events using realistic detail to reveal the harsh realities of life. They broached taboos by creating protagonists whose environments often destroyed them. In contrast, Romantic writers created protagonists whose indomitable wills helped them rise above adversity. Crane's *Maggie: A Girl of the Streets* deals with a young woman forced into prostitution to survive. In "The Occurrence at Owl Creek Bridge," Ambrose Bierce relates the unfortunate hanging of a Confederate soldier.

Short stories such as Bret Harte's "The Outcasts of Poker Flat" and Jack London's "To Build a Fire" deal with unfortunate people whose luck in life has run out. Many writers, subclassified as naturalists, believed that man was subject to a fate over which he had no control.

Contemporary American literature

Twentieth-century American writing can be divided into the following three genres: drama, fiction, and poetry.

Read more about Upton Sinclair:
www.online-literature.com/upton_sinclair/

Realistic writers *wrote of common, ordinary people and events using realistic detail to reveal the harsh realities of life. They broached taboos by creating protagonists whose environments often destroyed them.*

Romantic writers *created protagonists whose indomitable wills helped them rise above adversity.*

LITERATURE

American drama
The greatest and most prolific of American playwrights include the following:

- Eugene O'Neill, who wrote *Long Day's Journey into Night, Mourning Becomes Electra,* and *Desire Under the Elms*
- Arthur Miller, author of *The Crucible, All My Sons,* and *Death of a Salesman*
- Tennessee Williams, author of *Cat on a Hot Tin Roof, The Glass Menagerie,* and *A Streetcar Named Desire*
- Edward Albee, who wrote *Who's Afraid of Virginia Woolf?, Three Tall Women,* and *A Delicate Balance*

American fiction
The renowned American novelists include the following authors, who wrote the works listed:

- Eudora Welty, *The Optimist's Daughter*
- John Updike, *Rabbit Run* and *Rabbit Redux*
- Sinclair Lewis, *Babbit* and *Elmer Gantry*
- F. Scott Fitzgerald, *The Great Gatsby* and *Tender Is the Night*
- Ernest Hemingway, *A Farewell to Arms* and *For Whom the Bell Tolls*
- William Faulkner, *The Sound and the Fury* and *Absalom, Absalom!*
- Bernard Malamud, *The Fixer* and *The Natural*

American poetry
The poetry of the twentieth century is multifaceted, as represented by Edna St. Vincent Millay, Marianne Moore, Richard Wilbur, Langston Hughes, Maya Angelou, and Rita Dove. One of the most well-loved twentieth-century American poets is Robert Frost. His New England motifs of snowy evenings, birches, apple picking, stone-wall mending, hired hands, and nature relate universal truths through exquisite diction, polysyllabic words, and rare allusions to either mythology or the Bible.

Review a timeline of British literature:
www.studyguide.org/brit_lit_timeline.htm

British Literature

Anglo-Saxon period
The Anglo-Saxon period spans six centuries but produced only a smattering of literature. The first British epic is *Beowulf,* anonymously written by Christian monks many years after the events in the narrative supposedly occurred. This Teutonic saga relates the triumph over monsters by the hero, Beowulf. A shorter

poem titled "The Seafarer," along with some history and riddles, comprises the rest of the Anglo-Saxon canon.

Medieval period

The medieval period introduced Geoffrey Chaucer, the father of English literature, whose *Canterbury Tales* are written in the vernacular, or street language, of England rather than in Latin. Thus the tales are said to be the first true work of British literature.

Next, Thomas Malory's *Le Morte d'Arthur* brought together extant tales from Europe concerning the legendary King Arthur, Merlin, Guinevere, and the Knights of the Round Table. This work is the generative work that gave rise to the many Arthurian legends that stir the chivalric imagination.

Renaissance and Elizabethan periods

The Renaissance period, synonymous with William Shakespeare, begins with the introduction of the Petrarchan or Italian sonnet into England. Sir Thomas Wyatt and Sir Philip Sydney wrote English versions of this form. Next, Sir Edmund Spenser invented a variation of the Italian sonnet form, aptly called the Spenserian sonnet. His masterpiece is the epic *The Faerie Queene*, honoring Queen Elizabeth I's reign. He also wrote books on the Red Cross Knight and St. George and the Dragon and wrote a series of Arthurian adventures. Spenser was dubbed the "poet's poet." He created a nine-line stanza—eight lines iambic pentameter and an extra-footed ninth line—called an *alexandrine*.

The Renaissance period of British literature is synonymous with William Shakespeare.

William Shakespeare, often called the Bard of Avon, wrote 154 sonnets, 39 plays, and two long narrative poems. The sonnets are justifiably called the greatest sonnet sequence in all of literature. Shakespeare dispensed with the octave/sestet format of the Italian sonnet and invented his three quatrains, one heroic couplet format.

William Shakespeare, often called the Bard of Avon, wrote 154 sonnets, 39 plays, and two long narrative poems.

Shakespeare's plays are divided into comedies, history plays, and tragedies. Great lines from these plays are more often quoted than those of any other author. The Big Four tragedies—*Hamlet, Macbeth, Othello,* and *King Lear*—are acknowledged to be the most brilliant examples of this genre.

Seventeenth century

John Milton's devout Puritanism was the wellspring of his creative genius, which marked the close of the remarkable productivity of the English Renaissance. His social commentary in such works as *Aereopagitica* and *Samson Agonistes*, along with his elegant sonnets, would be enough to solidify his stature as a great writer. But it is his masterpiece *Paradise Lost*, based in part on the book of Genesis, that places Milton in the company of a handful of the most renowned writers of all

*John Milton's masterpiece **Paradise Lost**, based in part on the book of Genesis, places him among a handful of the most renowned writers of all time.*

LITERATURE

time. Many feel that *Paradise Lost*, written in balanced, elegant neoclassic form, truly does justify the ways of God to man.

The greatest allegory about man's journey to the Celestial City (Heaven) is found in *The Pilgrim's Progress*, written at the end of the English Renaissance by John Bunyan. *The Pilgrim's Progress* describes virtues and vices personified. This work was for a long time second only to the Bible in numbers of copies printed and sold.

The Jacobean Age gave us the marvelously witty and cleverly constructed conceits of John Donne's metaphysical sonnets as well as his insightful meditations and his version of sermons or homilies. "Ask not for whom the bell tolls" and "No man is an island unto himself" are famous epigrams from Donne's *Meditations*. His most famous conceit is that which compares lovers to a footed compass, traveling seemingly separately but always leaning toward one another and conjoined, in "A Valediction: Forbidding Mourning."

Eighteenth century

The Restoration and Enlightenment periods of the eighteenth century reflected the political turmoil brought about by the regicide of Charles I, the Interregnum Puritan government of Oliver Cromwell, and the restoration of the monarchy to England by the coronation of Charles II, who had been given refuge by the French King Louis XIV. During this time Neoclassicism became the preferred writing style, especially for Alexander Pope. New genres, evidenced in works such as *The Diary of Samuel Pepys*, the novels of Daniel Defoe, the periodical essays and editorials of Joseph Addison and Richard Steele, and Alexander Pope's mock epic *The Rape of the Lock*, demonstrate the diversity of expression during this time.

Writers who followed were contemporaries of Dr. Samuel Johnson, the lexicographer of *The Dictionary of the English Language*. Fittingly, this Age of Johnson, which encompasses James Boswell's biography of Dr. Johnson, Robert Burns' Scottish dialect and regionalism in his evocative poetry, and the mystical pre-Romantic poetry of William Blake, ushered in the Romantic age and its revolution against neoclassicism.

Romantic period

The Romantic age encompasses what is known as the First Generation Romantics, William Wordsworth and Samuel Taylor Coleridge, who collaborated on *Lyrical Ballads,* which defines and exemplifies the tenets of the Romantic style of writing. The Second Generation includes George Gordon, Lord Byron, Percy Bysshe Shelley, and John Keats. These poets wrote sonnets, odes, epics, and narrative poems, most dealing with homage to nature.

Read more about the Romantic period:
www.wwnorton.com/college/english/nael/romantic/welcome.htm

Other famous works by Wordsworth include "Intimations on Immortality" and "The Prelude." Byron's satirical epic *Don Juan* and his autobiographical *Childe Harold's Pilgrimage* are irreverent, witty, self-deprecating, and cuttingly critical of other writers and critics.

Shelley's odes and sonnets are remarkable for their sensory imagery. Keats' sonnets, odes, and longer narrative poem *The Eve of St. Agnes* are remarkable for their introspection considering the tender age of the poet, who died when he was only twenty-five. In fact, all of the Second Generation writers died before their time. Wordsworth, who lived to be eighty, outlived them all, including Coleridge, his friend and collaborator.

Others who wrote during the Romantic age are the essayist Charles Lamb and the novelist Jane Austen. The Brontë sisters, Charlotte and Emily, wrote one novel each. Their two novels are noted as two of the finest ever written: *Jane Eyre* and *Wuthering Heights*. Mary Anne Evans, also known as George Eliot, wrote several important novels: her masterpiece *Middlemarch*, *Silas Marner*, *Adam Bede*, and *Mill on the Floss*.

Jane Austen, the Brontë sisters, and George Eliot are important writers from the Romantic Age.

Nineteenth century

The Victorian period is remarkable for the diversity and proliferation of work. Poets who are typified as Victorians include Alfred, Lord Tennyson, who wrote *Idylls of the King*, twelve narrative poems about the Arthurian legend; and Robert Browning, who wrote chilling, dramatic monologues such as "My Last Duchess" as well as long poetic narratives such as *The Pied Piper of Hamlin*. Browning's wife Elizabeth wrote two major works, the epic feminist poem *Aurora Leigh* and the deeply moving and provocative *Sonnets from the Portuguese,* in which she details her deep love for Robert and his startling, to her, reciprocation.

Read more about the Victorian era:
www.victorianweb.org/

Gerard Manley Hopkins, a Catholic priest, wrote poetry using sprung rhythm. A.E. Housmann, Matthew Arnold, and the Pre-Raphaelites, especially the brother-and-sister duo Dante Gabriel Rosetti and Christina Rosetti, contributed much to the Victorian era poetic scene. The Pre-Raphaelites, a group of nineteenth-century English painters, poets, and critics, reacted against Victorian materialism and the neoclassical conventions of academic art by producing earnest, quasi-religious works. Medieval and early Renaissance painters up to the time of the Italian painter Raphael inspired the group.

During the Victorian Period, Robert Louis Stevenson, the great Scottish novelist, wrote his adventure/history lessons for young adults. Victorian prose ranges from the incomparable, keenly woven plot structures of Charles Dickens to the deeply moving Dorset/Wessex novels of Thomas Hardy, in which women are repressed and life is more struggle than euphoria. Rudyard Kipling wrote about colonialism

During the Victorian period, Robert Louis Stevenson, the great Scottish novelist, wrote his adventure/history lessons for young adults.

in India in works such as *Kim* and *The Jungle Book*, which recreate exotic locales and dissect the Raj, the British colonial government during Queen Victoria's reign. Victorian drama is a product mainly of Oscar Wilde, whose satirical masterpiece *The Importance of Being Earnest* farcically details and lampoons Victorian social mores.

Twentieth century

The early twentieth century is represented mainly by the towering achievements of George Bernard Shaw's dramas: *St. Joan*, *Man and Superman*, *Major Barbara*, and *Arms and the Man*, to name a few. Twentieth-century novelists are too numerous to list, but some of the greatest include Joseph Conrad, E. M. Forster, Virginia Woolf, James Joyce, Nadine Gordimer, Graham Greene, George Orwell, and D.H. Lawrence.

Twentieth-century poets of renown and merit include W. H. Auden, Robert Graves, T. S. Eliot, Edith Sitwell, Stephen Spender, Dylan Thomas, Philip Larkin, Ted Hughes, Sylvia Plath, and Hugh MacDiarmid. This list is by no means complete.

See also Skills 9.1, 9.2, and 9.4

Suggested Reading for Fifth and Sixth Grades

The following classic and contemporary works combine the characteristics of multiple learning theories. Functioning at the concrete operations stage (Piaget), being of the "good person" orientation (Kohlberg), still highly dependent on external rewards (Bandura), and exhibiting all five needs from Maslow's hierarchy, most 11- to 12-year-olds should appreciate the following titles, grouped by reading level. These titles are also cited for interest at that grade level and are not necessarily high-interest titles for older readers who read below grade level. Some high-interest titles for older readers will be cited later.

SUGGESTED TITLES FOR READING LEVELS 6.0 TO 6.9
Barrett, William. *Lilies of the Field*
Cormier, Robert. *Other Bells for Us to Ring*
Dahl, Roald. *Danny, Champion of the World; Charlie and the Chocolate Factory*
Lindgren, Astrid. *Pippi Longstocking*

Continued on next page

UNDERSTAND THE MAJOR ASPECTS OF WORLD LITERATURES

Lindbergh, Anne. *Three Lives to Live*
Lowry, Lois. *Rabble Starkey*
Naylor, Phyllis. *The Year of the Gopher; Reluctantly Alice*
Peck, Robert Newton. *Arly*
Speare, Elizabeth. *The Witch of Blackbird Pond*
Sleator, William. *The Boy Who Reversed Himself*

Suggested Reading for Seventh and Eighth Grades

Most seventh- and eighth-grade students, according to learning theory, are still functioning cognitively, psychologically, and morally as sixth graders. As these are not inflexible standards, some twelve- and thirteen-year-olds are much more mature socially, intellectually, and physically than the younger children who share the same school. Seventh and eighth graders are becoming concerned with establishing individual and peer group identities, which often presents conflicts with authority and the rigidity of rules. Some students at this age are still tied firmly to the family and its expectations, while others identify more with those their own age or older.

Check out these online resources for K–12 Teachers: Children's and Adolescent Literature:

www.indiana.edu/~reading /ieo/digests/d149.html

Enrichment reading for this group must help them cope with life's rapid changes or provide escape and thus must be either realistic or fantastic, depending on the child's needs. Adventures and mysteries are still popular today. Preteens also become more interested in biographies of contemporary figures than in biographies of legendary figures of the past.

SUGGESTED TITLES FOR READING LEVELS 7.0 TO 7.9
Armstrong, William. *Sounder*
Bagnold, Enid. *National Velvet*
Barrie, James. *Peter Pan*
London, Jack. *White Fang; Call of the Wild*
Lowry, Lois. *Taking Care of Terrific*
McCaffrey, Anne. *The Dragonsinger* series

Continued on next page

LITERATURE

Montgomery, L. M. *Anne of Green Gables* and sequels
Steinbeck, John. *The Pearl*
Tolkien, J. R. R. *The Hobbit*
Zindel, Paul. *The Pigman*

SUGGESTED TITLES FOR READING LEVELS 8.0 TO 8.9
Cormier, Robert. *I Am the Cheese*
McCullers, Carson. *The Member of the Wedding*
North, Sterling. *Rascal*
Twain, Mark. *The Adventures of Tom Sawyer*
Zindel, Paul. *My Darling, My Hamburger*

Suggested Reading for Ninth Grade

Depending on the school environment, ninth graders may rank as the highest class in a middle school or the lowest in a high school. Much of their social development and thus their reading interests become motivated by peer associations. They are technically adolescents, operating at the early stages of formal operations in cognitive development. Their perceptions of their own identities are becoming well-defined, and they are fully aware of the ethics required by society. Ninth graders are more receptive to the challenges of classic literature but still enjoy popular teen novels.

SUGGESTED TITLES FOR READING LEVELS 9.0 TO 9.9
Brown, Dee. *Bury My Heart at Wounded Knee*
Defoe, Daniel. *Robinson Crusoe*
Dickens, Charles. *David Copperfield*
Greenberg, Joanne. *I Never Promised You a Rose Garden*

Continued on next page

Kipling, Rudyard. *Captains Courageous*
Mathabane, Mark. *Kaffir Boy*
Nordhoff, Charles. *Mutiny on the Bounty*
Shelley, Mary. *Frankenstein*
Washington, Booker T. *Up from Slavery*

Suggested Reading for Tenth to Twelfth Grades

Most high school sophomores, juniors, and seniors can handle almost any type of literature, except for a few of the most difficult titles such as *Moby Dick* or *Vanity Fair*. However, since many high school students do not progress to the eleventh- or twelfth-grade reading level, they will still have their favorites among authors whose writings they can understand. Many will struggle with assigned novels but still read high-interest books for pleasure. A few high-interest titles are listed below without reading level designations, although most are level 6.0 to 7.9.

HIGH-INTEREST TITLES
Bauer, Joan. *Squashed*
Borland, Hal. *When the Legends Die*
Danzinger, Paula. *Remember Me to Harold Square*
Duncan, Lois. *Stranger with My Face*
Hamilton, Virginia. *The Planet of Junior Brown*
Hinton, S. E. *The Outsiders*
Paterson, Katherine. *The Great Gilly Hopkins*

Teaching Challenges

Teachers of students at all levels must be familiar with the materials offered by the libraries in their own schools. Only then can they guide their students into appropriate selections for their social age and reading level.

Adolescent literature, because of the age range of its readers, is extremely diverse. Fiction for the middle group, usually ages ten to fifteen, deals with issues of

LITERATURE

coping with internal and external changes in their lives. Because children's writers in the twentieth century have produced increasingly realistic fiction, adolescents can now find problems dealt with honestly in novels.

Teachers of middle school students see the greatest change in interests and reading abilities. Fifth and sixth graders, included in elementary grades in many schools, are viewed as older children, while seventh and eighth graders are viewed as preadolescent.

Ninth graders, included sometimes as upper tier in middle school and sometimes as underlings in high school, definitely view themselves as teenagers. Their literature choices will often be governed more by interest than by ability—thus the wealth of high-interest, low-readability books that have flooded the market in recent years. Tenth through twelfth graders will still select high-interest books for pleasure reading but are also easily encouraged to stretch their literary muscles by reading classics.

Because of rapid social changes, topics that once did not interest young people until they reached their teens—suicide, gangs, and homosexuality—are now the subjects of books for younger readers. The plethora of high-interest books reveals how desperately schools have failed to produce on-level readers and how the market has adapted to that need.

However, these high-interest books are now accessible to younger children whose reading levels are at or above normal. No matter how tastefully written, some content is inappropriate for younger readers. The problem becomes not so much one of steering these children toward books they can handle as one of encouraging them toward books whose content is appropriate to their level of cognitive and social development. A fifth-grader may be able to read and understand V.C. Andrews' book *Flowers in the Attic* but not possess the social or moral development to handle the deviant behavior of the characters. Because of the complex societal changes affecting adolescents, the teacher must be as well versed in learning theory and child development as in the subject matter of language and literature.

> *Because of rapid social changes, topics that once did not interest young people until they reached their teens—suicide, gangs, and homosexuality—are now the subjects of books for younger readers.*

SKILL 10.2 **Examining in literary works the expression of diverse values, attitudes, and ideas of people from various regional, ethnic, and cultural groups**

See Skill 10.1

UNDERSTAND THE MAJOR ASPECTS OF WORLD LITERATURES

SKILL 10.3 **Examining how writers from diverse cultural backgrounds and various historical periods have commented on major historical events and influenced public opinion about and understanding of major social, cultural, and political issues through their literary works**

See Skill 10.1

SKILL 10.4 **Examining how social, cultural, and political issues, such as issues relating to age, gender, ethnicity, and human rights, are explored in classical and contemporary literary works**

See Skills 9.3 and 10.1

LITERATURE

DOMAIN IV
LISTENING AND SPEAKING

LISTENING AND SPEAKING

PERSONALIZED STUDY PLAN

✗ KNOWN MATERIAL/ SKIP IT

PAGE	COMPETENCY AND SKILL	
115	**11: Understand strategies for effective listening**	☐
	11.1: Demonstrating knowledge of the components of the listening process	☐
	11.2: Identifying the characteristics and purposes of various types of listening, including critical, empathetic, and deliberative	☐
	11.3: Demonstrating knowledge of the barriers to listening effectively	☐
	11.4: Applying strategies for listening actively	☐
120	**12: Understand strategies for effective speaking**	☐
	12.1: Demonstrating knowledge of a systematic approach to preparing a speech	☐
	12.2: Demonstrating knowledge of the forms of speech anxiety and apprehension and ways of managing them	☐
	12.3: Distinguishing among types of speech delivery and styles of language appropriate for various topics, purposes, audiences, and occasions	☐
	12.4: Demonstrating knowledge of rhetorical techniques used to increase clarity and interest in speeches	☐
	12.5: Recognizing the different roles that voice and body language play in speech delivery	☐
125	**13: Understand strategies for effective interpersonal communication**	☐
	13.1: Demonstrating knowledge of the types, characteristics, and purposes of interpersonal communication	☐
	13.2: Recognizing the importance of social etiquette, norms, and conventions in interpersonal communication	☐
	13.3: Demonstrating knowledge of the principles of group dynamics and factors that influence group effectiveness	☐
	13.4: Applying strategies for identifying, managing, and resolving conflict in groups	☐

COMPETENCY 11
UNDERSTAND STRATEGIES FOR EFFECTIVE LISTENING

> **SKILL 11.1** Demonstrating knowledge of the components of the listening process (e.g., focusing, decoding)

The arts of debate, discussion, and conversation are different from the basic writing forms of discourse. The ability to use language and logic to convince an audience to accept your reasoning and to side with you truly is an art. This form of writing and speaking is extremely structured and logically sequenced with supporting reasons and evidence. At its best, it is the highest form of propaganda. A position statement, evidence, reason, evaluation, and refutation are integral parts of this writing schema.

Interviewing provides opportunities for students to apply expository and informative communication techniques. It teaches them how to structure questions to evoke fact-filled responses. Compiling the information from an interview into a biographical essay or speech helps students to list, sort, and arrange details in an orderly fashion.

Speeches that encourage students to describe persons, places, or events in their own lives or oral interpretations of literature help them sense the creativity and effort used by professional writers.

Learn more about oral communication skills:
www.glencoe.com/sec/teachingtoday/weeklytips.phtml/88

Listening

Communication skills are crucial in a collaborative society. A person cannot be a successful communicator, though, without being an active listener.

Focus on what others say, rather than planning what to say next. By listening to everything another person says, you may pick up on natural cues that lead the conversation without so much added effort.

Facilitating

Using standard opening lines to facilitate a conversation is acceptable. Don't agonize over coming up with witty "one-liners," as the main obstacle in initiating conversation lies in making the first statement. After that, the real substance begins. A useful technique may be to make a comment or ask a question about a shared situation. Use an opener with which you are comfortable, because then your partner in conversation will be comfortable with it as well.

Stimulating Higher-Level Critical Thinking Through Inquiry

People often rely on questions to communicate with others. However, most people fall back on simple clarifying questions rather than open-ended inquiries. For example, if you paraphrase a response by asking, "Did you mean this…" you may receive merely a "yes" or "no" answer. In an open-ended inquiry, one would ask, "What did you mean when you said…?"

Try to ask open-ended, deeper-level questions, since those tend to have the greatest reward and lead to greater understanding. With answers to those questions, you can make more complex connections and achieve more significant information.

The successful conversationalist is a person who:

- Keeps up with and ponders the meanings of events and developments
- Reads about interesting topics, both in print and online
- Has probed certain topics in some depth
- Usually has a passionate interest in human behavior
- Is interested in and concerned about social issues, both in the immediate community and on a wider scale, and has ideas for solving some of those problems

With all of this information in mind, the most important habit you can develop as a good conversationalist is to *listen*, not just wait until the other person quits speaking so you can take the floor again. By actually listening to what the other person has to say, you can also learn more about that person. Following a gathering, you will be remembered as the person who was interested enough to listen and respond to others' ideas and opinions. You will be the person who will be remembered with the most regard.

Although you can be passionate about your convictions in polite conversation, you should not be overbearing or unwilling to consider another's point of view. Keeping your emotions under control in these circumstances is important, even if the other person does not.

Political correctness is a concept tossed around frequently in the twenty-first century. It has always existed, of course. The successful speaker of the nineteenth century understood and was sensitive to audiences. However, that person was typically a man, and the only audience that was important was a male audience, and more often than not, the only important audience was a white one.

UNDERSTAND STRATEGIES FOR EFFECTIVE LISTENING

Much has changed in discourse since the nineteenth and twentieth centuries, just as the society the speaker lives in and addresses has changed, and the speaker who disregards the existing conventions for political correctness usually finds trouble.

Rap music makes a point of ignoring those conventions, particularly with regard to gender, and is often the target of hostile attacks. On the other hand, rap performers often intend to be revolutionary and have developed their own audiences and have become outrageously wealthy by exploiting those newly developed audiences based primarily on thumbing their noses at establishment conventions.

Even so, the successful speaker must understand and be sensitive to what is current in political correctness. The "n word" is a case in point. There was a time when that term was thrown about at will by politicians and other public speakers, but no more. Nothing could spell the end of a politician's career more certainly than using that term in his or her campaign or public addresses.

References to gender have become particularly sensitive in the twentieth century as a result of the women's rights movement, and speakers who disregard these sensitivities do so at their peril. The generic "he" is no longer acceptable; this development requires that you have a strategy to deal with pronominal references without the repetitive use of "he/she," "his/her," and so on.

You can approach this situation in several ways:

- Switch to a passive construction that does not require a subject
- Switch back and forth, using the male pronoun in one reference and the female pronoun in another one, making sure to sprinkle them reasonably evenly
- Switch to the plural

The last alternative is the one most often chosen. This situation requires some care, and the speaker should spend time developing these skills before stepping in front of an audience.

Debates and panel discussions fall under the umbrella of formal speaking. The rules for formal speaking should apply, although lapsing into conversational language is acceptable. Swear words should be avoided in these situations.

A debate presents two sides of a contested thesis—pro and con. Each side posits a hypothesis, proves it, and defends it. A formal debate is much like a formal dance, with each side following a strictly defined format. However, within those guidelines, debaters are free to develop their arguments and rebuttals as they choose. The successful debater prepares by thoroughly developing both sides of the thesis: "Mexico's border with the United States must be closed" and "Mexico's border with the United States must remain open," for example. Debaters must be

LISTENING AND SPEAKING

thoroughly prepared to argue their own side, but they must also have a strategy for rebutting the opposing side's arguments.

One successful way to win an argument is to rebut the opposing side, so debaters must be prepared for opposing arguments and listen for the opportunity to counter the opponent's claims.

All aspects of critical thinking and logical argument are employed during a debate, and successful debaters use ethical appeal (their own credibility) and emotional appeal to persuade the judges who will determine the winner—that is, the side that best establishes its thesis, proves it logically, but also persuades the audience to come over to its position.

A panel is typically composed of experts who explain and defend a particular topic. Often, panels include representatives from more than one field of study and more than one position on the topic. Typically, each expert has a limited amount of time to make an opening statement that either presents explanatory material or argues a point of view. Then, the meeting is opened up to the audience for questions.

A moderator keeps order and controls the time limits on the opening statements and responses. The moderator may sometimes intervene to ask a panel member who was not the target of a particular question to elaborate or rebut the answer of the panel member who was questioned. Panels are usually limited to four or five people, although in special cases, they may be much larger.

> **SKILL 11.2** **Identifying the characteristics and purposes of various types of listening, including critical** *(e.g., listening to determine the speaker's point of view),* **empathetic** *(e.g., listening to show support or improve mutual understanding and trust),* **and deliberative** *(e.g., listening to learn information)*

There are different types of listening for different purposes. Knowing the purpose helps students be better listeners. It can also help them better understand what is being said.

Deliberative listening is listening for facts and information. The focus is to understand what is being said.

Critical listening is listening to determine the speaker's point of view and to form an opinion. The focus is to evaluate the arguments given by the speaker.

Empathetic listening is listening to understand both what the speaker is saying and how he or she feels. The focus is to identify with the speaker's situation and feelings.

SKILL 11.3: Demonstrating knowledge of the barriers to listening effectively (e.g., internal and external noise, delivery, language, perceptions)

Children who are raised in homes where English is not the first language and/or where standard English is not spoken may have difficulty hearing the difference between similar-sounding words like "send" and "sent." Any child who is not in a home, day care, or preschool environment where English phonology operates may have difficulty perceiving and demonstrating the differences between English-language phonemes. If children cannot hear the difference between words that sound the same, like "grow" and "glow," they will be confused when these words appear in a print context. This confusion will, of course, impact their comprehension.

Considerations for teaching phonological processing to ELL children include the teacher's recognition that what works for the English-language speaking child from an English-language speaking family is not necessarily effective for children from homes where other languages are primarily spoken.

Research recommends that ELL children learn to read initially in their first language. It is critical for ELL to *speak* English before being taught to *read* English. Research supports that oral language development lays the foundation for phonological awareness.

All phonological instruction programs must be tailored to the children's learning backgrounds. Rhymes and alliteration introduced to ELL children should be read or shared with them in their first language, if at all possible.

Within the classroom setting, many opportunities will present themselves for students to speak and listen, and often these may be spontaneous. Activities for speaking and listening should be integrated throughout the language arts program, but there should also be times when speaking and listening are the focus of the instruction. By incorporating speaking and listening into the language arts program, students will begin to see the connection between the two and, therefore, be able to improve their reading skills with more efficiency.

LISTENING AND SPEAKING

Some of the ways that speaking and listening can be integrated include:

- Conversations
- Small group discussions
- Brainstorming
- Interviewing
- Oral reading
- Readers' Theatre
- Choral speaking
- Storytelling
- Role playing
- Booktalks
- Oral reports
- Class debates
- Listening to guest speakers

SKILL 11.4 **Applying strategies for listening actively** (e.g., clarifying, restating, validating, building or reflecting on a speaker's message)

See Skills 11.2 and 11.3

COMPETENCY 12
UNDERSTAND STRATEGIES FOR EFFECTIVE SPEAKING

SKILL 12.1 **Demonstrating knowledge of a systematic approach to preparing a speech** (e.g., selecting a topic, adapting to the audience)

Preparing to speak on a topic should be seen as a process that has stages: discovery, organization, and editing.

Discovery

Many possible sources for information can be used to create an oral presentation.

1. The first step in the discovery process is to settle on a topic or subject. For example, the topic or subject could be immigration. In the discovery stage, one's own knowledge, experience, and beliefs should be the first source, and notes should be taken as the speaker probes this source.

Learn more about designing effective oral presentations:
www.ruf.rice.edu/~riceowl/oral_presentations.htm

2. The second source can be interviews with friends and experts.

3. The third source is research: what has been written or said publicly on the topic. This stage can get out of hand very quickly, so a plan for collecting source information should be well organized, with time limits set for each part.

Organization

At this point, several decisions need to be made. The first is to determine the *purpose* of the speech. Does the speaker want to persuade the audience to believe something or to act on something, or does the speaker simply want to present information that the audience might not have?

Once that decision is made, a *thesis* should be developed. What point does the speaker want to make? What information will support that point? In what order will that information be arranged?

Introductions and *conclusions* should be written last. The introduction draws the audience into the topic. The conclusion polishes off the speech, making sure the thesis is clear, reinforcing the thesis, or summarizing the points that have been made.

Editing

Editing is the most important stage in speech preparation. Once decisions have been made in the discovery and organization stages, allow time to let the speech rest for a while before going back to it with "fresh eyes." Objectivity is extremely important, and the speaker should be willing to make drastic changes if they are needed. Turning loose of one's own composition can be difficult, but good speechmakers are able to do so. However, this can also get out of hand, so outside comments should be limited. The speaker must recognize that at some point a commitment to the speech as it stands must be made if he or she is to deliver the message with conviction.

The concept of *recursiveness* is very useful when writing speeches. Everything must be written at the outset with full knowledge that it can be changed. The willingness to go backward, even to the discovery stage, is what makes a good speechwriter.

The content to be presented orally plays a big role in organization and delivery. For example, a literary analysis or a book report will be organized inductively, laying out the details and then presenting a conclusion. If the analysis focuses on multiple layers in a story, such a discussion will probably follow the preliminary conclusion. Keeping in mind that the speaker wants to keep the audience's attention, if the content has to do with difficult-to-follow facts and statistics, slides (or PowerPoint presentations) may be used as a guide to the presentation. The speaker can also intersperse interesting anecdotes, jokes, or humor from time to time so that the listeners don't fall asleep.

SKILL 12.2 Demonstrating knowledge of the forms of speech anxiety and apprehension (e.g., audience-specific, situational) and ways of managing them (e.g., practicing, focusing on the topic, using relaxation techniques)

Speech anxiety, or "fear of public speaking," can be mild to severe. Some students will be most fearful before speaking. For them, preparing for the speech causes a great deal of anxiety. Some students will have mild anxiety while speaking. This is normal. Some common symptoms are forgetfulness, a shaky voice, and trembling. Some students may have severe speech anxiety. These students might try to avoid public speaking entirely. Common symptoms include pounding heart beat, dizziness, sweaty palms, and dry mouth.

The following techniques can help students manage speech anxiety:

- Practice! Understand the topic, and know your speech. Practice in front of friends and mirrors.
- Breathe—slowly and deeply.
- Wear comfortable clothing and shoes. Bring a sweater in case it's chilly.
- Take a walk before your speech. It will help you relax.
- Focus on the topic. Find aspects of your speech that interest you and share your enthusiam.
- Smile when you speak.

See also Skill 12.5

SKILL 12.3 Distinguishing among types of speech delivery (e.g., memorized, extemporaneous, impromptu) and styles of language (e.g., informal, technical, regional) appropriate for various topics, purposes, audiences, and occasions

See Skill 12.1

UNDERSTAND STRATEGIES FOR EFFECTIVE SPEAKING

> **SKILL 12.4** Demonstrating knowledge of rhetorical techniques used to increase clarity and interest in speeches *(e.g., narrating, repeating key words and phrases, establishing common ground)*

See Skills 12.1, 12.2, and 12.5

> **SKILL 12.5** Recognizing the different roles that voice *(e.g., volume, rate, tone)* and body language *(e.g., hand gestures, facial expressions, eye contact)* play in speech delivery

Delivery Techniques

Instruct your students on the ways in which nonverbal communication can affect the way a presentation is understood.

	NONVERBAL COMMUNICATION TECHNIQUES
Posture	Maintain a straight but not stiff posture. Instead of shifting weight from hip to hip, point your feet directly at the audience and distribute your weight evenly. Keep your shoulders towards the audience. If you have to turn your body to use a visual aid, turn 45 degrees and continue speaking towards the audience.
Movement	Instead of staying glued to one spot or pacing back and forth, stay within four to eight feet of the front row of your audience. Take a step or half-step to the side every once in a while. If you are using a lectern, feel free to move to the front or side of it to engage your audience more. Avoid distancing yourself from the audience; you want audience members to feel involved and connected.
Gestures	Gestures can maintain a natural atmosphere when speaking publicly. Use them just as you would when speaking to a friend. They shouldn't be exaggerated, but they should be used for added emphasis. Avoid keeping your hands in your pockets or locked behind your back, wringing your hands and fidgeting nervously, or keeping your arms crossed.
Eye Contact	Many people are intimidated by using eye contact when speaking to large groups. Interestingly, eye contact usually helps the speaker overcome speech anxiety by connecting with the attentive audience and easing feelings of isolation. Instead of looking at a spot on the back wall or at your notes, scan the room and make eye contact for one to three seconds per person.

In addition to the content of your presentation, you want to use a strong delivery. As with most skills, the key is practice, practice, practice. Record and play back your presentation to hear how you sound.

LISTENING AND SPEAKING

ORAL DELIVERY TECHNIQUES	
Voice	Many people fall into one of two traps when speaking: using a monotone or talking too fast. Both phenomena result from anxiety. A monotone restricts your natural inflection but can be remedied by releasing tension in upper and lower body muscles. Subtle movement will keep you loose and natural. Talking too fast, meanwhile, is not necessarily bad if you are exceptionally articulate. If you are not a strong speaker or if you are talking about very technical items, however, the audience will easily become lost. When you talk too fast and begin tripping over your words, consciously pause after every sentence you say. Don't be afraid of brief silences. The audience needs time to absorb what you are saying.
Volume	Problems with volume, whether too soft or too loud, can be overcome with practice. If you tend to speak too softly, have someone stand in the back of the room and signal you when your volume is strong enough. If possible, have someone in the front of the room as well to make sure you're not overcompensating with excessive volume. Conversely, if you have a problem with speaking too loudly, have the person in the front of the room signal you when your voice is soft enough. Check with the person in the back to make sure it is still loud enough to be heard. In both cases, note your volume level for future reference. Don't be shy about asking your audience, "Can you hear me in the back?" Suitable volume is beneficial for both you and the audience.
Pitch	Pitch refers to the length, tension, and thickness of your vocal bands. As your voice gets higher, the pitch gets higher. In oral performance, pitch reflects the emotional arousal level. More variation in pitch typically corresponds to more emotional arousal, but it can also be used to convey sarcasm or highlight specific words.

Learn more about using your voice:

www.longview.k12.wa.us
/mmhs/wyatt/pathway
/voice.html

Although these skills are essential for you to be an effective teacher, you want your students to develop these techniques as well. By encouraging the development of proper techniques for oral presentations, you are enabling your students to develop self-confidence for higher levels of communication.

COMPETENCY 13
UNDERSTAND STRATEGIES FOR EFFECTIVE INTERPERSONAL COMMUNICATION

> **SKILL 13.1** **Demonstrating knowledge of the types** *(e.g., dyadic, small-group)*, **characteristics** *(i.e., content versus relational messages)*, **and purposes of interpersonal communication** *(e.g., interviewing, problem solving, debating, forensics)*

See Skill 11.1

> **SKILL 13.2** **Recognizing the importance of social etiquette, norms, and conventions in interpersonal communication and how these are influenced by factors such as power, intimacy, and culture**

See Skills 3.6 and 11.1

> **SKILL 13.3** **Demonstrating knowledge of the principles of group dynamics and factors that influence group effectiveness** *(e.g., group size and composition, environment, group members' roles)*

See Skill 11.1

> **SKILL 13.4** **Applying strategies for identifying, managing, and resolving conflict in groups** *(e.g., compromise, negotiation, collaboration, accommodation)*

Compromise

Sometimes it is necessary to allow a "cooling off" period before contacting someone with whom you are upset, or with whom you have an issue. Whenever

LISTENING AND SPEAKING

dealing with someone who may be confrontational, it is necessary to remember the purpose for maintaining a cordial relationship with this person. Do you need that person's support? Do you need additional information that may have bearing on a project or student?

Whenever talking with someone, it is necessary that you not be demeaning, antagonistic, or confrontational.

The Importance of Collaboration

The bridge to effective learning for students begins with a collaborative approach by all stakeholders that supports the educational needs of students. Underestimating the power and integral role of the community institutions in impacting the current and future goals of students can carry high stakes for students beyond the high school years who are competing for college access, student internships, and entry-level jobs in the community.

Researchers have shown that school involvement and connections with community institutions promote student retention rates, graduations, and higher education experiences.

Researchers have shown that school involvement and connections with community institutions promote student retention rates, graduations, and higher education experiences. The current disconnect and autonomy that has become commonplace in today's society must be reevaluated in terms of promoting tomorrow's citizens.

Students as community liaisons

When community institutions provide students and teachers with meaningful connections and input, the commitment is apparent in terms of volunteering, loyalty, and professional promotion. Providing students with placements in leadership positions such as the Associated Student Body (ASB); the Parent Teacher Student Association (PTSA); school boards; neighborhood subcommittees addressing political or social issues; or government boards that impact and influence school communities creates an avenue for students to explore ethical, participatory, collaborative, transformational leadership that can be applied to all areas of a student's educational and personal life.

Community liaisons provide students with opportunities to experience accountability and responsibility.

Community liaisons provide students with opportunities to experience accountability and responsibility. They also allow students to learn about life and how organizations work with effective communication and the ability of teams to work together to accomplish goals and objectives. Teaching students skills of inclusion and social and environmental responsibility and creating public forums that represent student voices and votes foster student interest and access in developing and reflecting on individual opinions and understanding the dynamics of the world around them.

When students see that various support systems are in place and consistently working as a team to effectively provide resources and avenues of academic promotion and accountability, they have no fear of taking risks to grow by, say, becoming a teen voice on a local committee about teen violence or volunteering in a local hospice for young children with terminal diseases. The linkages of community institutions provide role models of a world in which the student will soon become an integral and vital member, so being a part of that world as a student makes the transition easier as a young adult.

LISTENING AND SPEAKING

DOMAIN V
COMPONENTS OF WRITING

COMPONENTS OF WRITING

PERSONALIZED STUDY PLAN

✗ KNOWN MATERIAL/ SKIP IT

PAGE	COMPETENCY AND SKILL	
131	**14: Understand the conventions of standard American English and the elements of effective composition**	☐
	14.1: Demonstrating knowledge of the conventions of spelling and capitalization to use when developing text	☐
	14.2: Demonstrating knowledge of the conventions of punctuation to use when developing text	☐
	14.3: Demonstrating knowledge of proper word usage and grammatical sentence structure to use when developing text	☐
	14.4: Recognizing methods of developing an introduction to a text that draws a reader's attention, specifies a topic, and provides a thesis	☐
	14.5: Recognizing methods of developing a body of a text that presents, emphasizes, links, and contrasts ideas in a clear, concise, and coherent manner	☐
	14.6: Recognizing methods of developing a conclusion to a text that provides a summary or resolution, suggests a course of action, or offers a personal commentary	☐
159	**15: Understand the writing process**	☐
	15.1: Demonstrating knowledge of the appropriate form of writing to use for a particular purpose and audience	☐
	15.2: Recognizing methods of generating and organizing ideas for writing	☐
	15.3: Recognizing methods of drafting text to show logical development of a central idea or theme through the use of relevant supporting details	☐
	15.4: Recognizing methods of revising a text to eliminate wordiness, redundancy, distracting details, and extraneous information	☐
	15.5: Recognizing methods of editing text to generate interest and clarify meaning	☐
	15.6: Recognizing methods of proofreading and preparing text for publication	☐
170	**16: Understand the elements of effective and appropriate research**	☐
	16.1: Recognizing methods of selecting and refining a topic for research	☐
	16.2: Recognizing methods of composing specific, open-ended questions for a research topic	☐
	16.3: Recognizing methods of identifying and locating multiple and various sources of information for a research topic	☐
	16.4: Recognizing methods of assessing the credibility, objectivity, and reliability of sources of information	☐
	16.5: Recognizing methods of gathering and organizing information from sources systematically	☐
	16.6: Recognizing methods of paraphrasing, summarizing, and quoting information from sources appropriately	☐
	16.7: Recognizing methods of citing or acknowledging sources of information appropriately in a text	☐

COMPETENCY 14
UNDERSTAND THE CONVENTIONS OF STANDARD AMERICAN ENGLISH AND THE ELEMENTS OF EFFECTIVE COMPOSITION

SKILL 14.1 Demonstrating knowledge of the conventions of spelling and capitalization to use when developing text

Spelling

Spelling correctly is not always easy, because English not only utilizes an often inconsistent spelling system but also includes many words derived from other languages. Correct spelling is important because incorrect spelling alters the meaning of what is written and may puzzle the reader.

Commonly misspelled words

The following list contains words that are very often misspelled.

Commitment	Prejudice	Contemporary
Succeed	Familiar	Beneficial
Necessary	Hindrance	Attachment
Connected	Controversial	Guarantee
Opportunity	Publicity	Tropical
Embarrassed	Prescription	Misfortune
Occasionally	Height	Particular
Receive	Leisurely	Yield
Their	Shield	Possession
Accelerate	Foreign	Accumulate
Patience	Innovative	Hospitality
Obstinate	Similar	Judgment
Achievement	Proceed	Conscious
Responsibility		

COMPONENTS OF WRITING

Irregular plurals
Some nouns derived from foreign words, especially Latin, may make their plurals in two different ways—one of them Anglicized. It is always a good idea to consult a dictionary.

> Some examples include:
> Appendices, appendixes   criterion, criteria   Indexes, indices
> crisis, crises

Plurals of compound words
Make the plurals of closed (solid) compound words in the usual way except for words ending in *ful*, which make their plurals on the root word.

> Some examples include: timelines, hairpins, cupsful

Make the plurals of open or hyphenated compounds by adding the change in inflection to the word that changes in number.

> Some examples include: masters of art, doctors of medicine

Plurals of letters, numbers, and abbreviations
Make the plurals of letters, numbers, and abbreviations by adding *s*.

> Some examples include: ones and fives, PCs, 1970s, ps and qs (Note that letters are italicized.)

I before E
Here are the rules for spelling with *ei/ie* words:

- *i* before *e*   grieve, fiend, niece, friend
- except after *c*   receive, conceive, receipt
- or when sounded like "*a*"   as in reindeer, weight, and reign

> Exceptions: weird, foreign, seize, leisure

Capitalization

PROPER NOUNS: nouns that name something specific

The beginning of each new sentence must be capitalized. Some people run into problems with capitalization when using proper nouns. PROPER NOUNS are nouns that name something specific.

For example, names of people, animals and places must be capitalized.

Names of People	Names of Places	Names of Animals
Nancy	Connecticut	Buster
Jack	St. Louis	Fluffy
William	Stop and Shop	Fido

For example,

> I called Mom to see if I could go to Mike's house.

When using a common noun as a proper noun, it must be capitalized.

The word *Mom* is used as a name in this sentence, therefore it must have a capital.

> Dr. Flynn told my mom she needed a flu shot.

The abbreviation *Dr.* and the name *Flynn* both have a capital letter because they are part of the same identifying name. In this sentence, *my mom* refers to a person who is not named, therefore it does not require a capital letter.

SKILL 14.2 Demonstrating knowledge of the conventions of punctuation to use when developing text

Fragments

Fragments occur:

1. If word groups standing alone are missing either a subject or a verb.

2. If word groups containing a subject and verb and standing alone are actually made dependent because of the use of subordinating conjunctions or relative pronouns.

Error: *The teacher waiting for the class to complete the assignment.*

Problem: This sentence is not complete because an *-ing* word alone does not function as a verb. When a helping verb is added (for example, *was*), it will become a sentence.

Correction: *The teacher was waiting for the class to complete the assignment.*

COMPONENTS OF WRITING

Error: *Until the last toy was removed from the floor.*

Problem: Words such as *until, because, although, when,* and *if* make a clause *dependent* and thus incapable of standing alone. An *independent clause* must be added to make the sentence complete.

Correction: *Until the last toy was removed from the floor, the kids could not go outside to play.*

Error: *The city will close the public library. Because of a shortage of funds.*

Problem: The problem is the same as above. The dependent clause must be joined to the independent clause.

Correction: *The city will close the public library because of a shortage of funds.*

Error: *Anyone planning to go on the trip should bring the necessary items. Such as a backpack, boots, a canteen, and bug spray.*

Problem: The second word group is a phrase and cannot stand alone because there is neither a subject nor a verb. The fragment can be corrected by adding the phrase to the sentence.

Correction: *Anyone planning to go on the trip should bring the necessary items, such as a backpack, boots, a canteen, and bug spray.*

Fragments are tested in sentences tied to a passage. Items will be in one of two formats.

Format A
Forensics experts conclude that the residents died from chemical <u>radiation. Or</u> perhaps from a mixture of toxic substances and asphyxiation.

    A. radiation; or

    B. radiation or

    C. radiation or,

    D. No change is necessary

Format B
<u>Forensics</u> experts conclude that the residents died from chemical <u>radiation. Or</u> perhaps from a mixture of toxic substances and <u>asphyxiation</u>.

UNDERSTAND THE CONVENTIONS OF STANDARD AMERICAN ENGLISH AND THE ELEMENTS OF EFFECTIVE COMPOSITION

A. Forensics

B. radiation or

C. asphyxiation

D. No change is necessary

In each case, the punctuation between *radiation* and *or* must be considered. The punctuation decision is difficult if one does not understand that the second group of words, the one that begins with *Or,* is not a sentence. Though these questions may appear to be only about punctuation, they are also about fragments.

The answer in both formats is B. The word group "*Or perhaps from a mixture of toxic substances and asphyxiation*" lacks a subject and a complete verb. It must be joined to the preceding sentence. A comma is not necessary since the word *residents* is the subject of the verb phrase "*died from chemical radiation and of asphyxiation.*"

Run-on Sentences and Comma Splices

Comma splices appear when only a comma joins two sentences. Fused sentences appear when two sentences are run together with no punctuation at all.

Error:	*Dr. Sanders is a brilliant scientist, his research on genetic disorders won him a Nobel Prize.*
Problem:	A comma alone cannot join two independent clauses (complete sentences). The two clauses can be joined by a semicolon or they can be separated by a period.
Correction:	*Dr. Sanders is a brilliant scientist; his research on genetic disorders won him a Nobel Prize.*
OR:	*Dr. Sanders is a brilliant scientist. His research on genetic disorders won him a Nobel Prize.*
Error:	*Florida is noted for its beaches they are long, sandy, and beautiful.*
Problem:	The first sentence ends with the word beaches, and the second sentence cannot be joined with the first. The fused sentence error can be corrected in a few ways: (1) one clause may be made dependent on another with a subordinating conjunction or a relative pronoun, (2) a semicolon may be used to combine two equally important ideas, or (3) the two independent clauses may be separated by a period.

Correction: *Florida is noted for its beaches, which are long, sandy, and beautiful.*

OR: *Florida is noted for its beaches; they are long, sandy, and beautiful.*

OR: *Florida is noted for its beaches. They are long, sandy, and beautiful.*

Error: *The number of hotels has increased, however, the number of visitors has grown also.*

Problem: The first sentence ends with the word *increased*, and a comma is not strong enough to connect it to the second sentence. The adverbial transition *however* does not function the same way as a coordinating conjunction and cannot be used with commas to link two sentences. Several different corrections are available.

Correction: *The number of hotels has increased; however, the number of visitors has grown also.*

Two closely related sentences are combined by using a semicolon.

OR: *The number of hotels has increased. However, the number of visitors has grown also.*

Two separate sentences are created.

OR: *Although the number of hotels has increased, the number of visitors has grown also.*

One idea is made subordinate to the other and separated with a comma.

OR: *The number of hotels has increased, but the number of visitors has grown also.*

The comma before the coordinating conjunction but is appropriate. The adverbial transition *however* does not function the same way as the coordinating conjunction *but* does.

Commas

Commas indicate a brief pause. They are used to set off dependent clauses and long introductory word groups, to separate words in a series, to set off unimportant material that interrupts the flow of the sentence, and to separate independent clauses joined by conjunctions.

Error: *After I finish my master's thesis I plan to work in Chicago.*

UNDERSTAND THE CONVENTIONS OF STANDARD AMERICAN ENGLISH AND THE ELEMENTS OF EFFECTIVE COMPOSITION

Problem: A comma is needed after an introductory dependent word group containing a subject and verb.

Correction: *After I finish my master's thesis, I plan to work in Chicago.*

Error: *I washed waxed and vacuumed my car today.*

Problem: Commas should separate nouns, phrases, or clauses in a list, as well as two or more coordinate adjectives that modify one word. Although the word *and* is sometimes considered optional, it is often necessary to clarify the meaning.

Correction: *I washed, waxed, and vacuumed my car today.*

Error: *She was a talented dancer but she is mostly remembered for her singing ability.*

Problem: A comma is needed before a conjunction that joins two independent clauses (complete sentences).

Correction: *She was a talented dancer, but she is mostly remembered for her singing ability.*

SKILL 14.3 Demonstrating knowledge of proper word usage and grammatical sentence structure to use when developing text

Writers strive to craft sentences that convey their thoughts precisely. One of the first rules of grammar is to use complete sentences, so a review of sentence structure is a must for students.

Clauses and Phrases

CLAUSES are connected word groups that are composed of *at least* one subject and one verb. (A subject is the doer of an action or the element that is being joined. A verb conveys either the action or the link.)

> <u>Students</u> <u>are waiting</u> for the start of the assembly.
> Subject Verb
>
> At the end of the play, <u>students</u> <u>wait</u> for the curtain to come down.
>   Subject Verb

CLAUSES: connected word groups that are composed of at least one subject and one verb

COMPONENTS OF WRITING

INDEPENDENT CLAUSE: a clause that can stand alone as a sentence or be joined to another clause

Clauses can be independent or dependent. INDEPENDENT CLAUSES can stand alone or can be joined to other clauses. Connect independent clauses with the coordinating conjunctions—*and, but, or, for,* or *nor*—when their content is of equal importance. Use subordinating conjunctions—*although, because, before, if, since, though, until, when, whenever, wher*e—and relative pronouns—*that, who, whom, which*—to introduce clauses that express ideas that are subordinate to the main ideas expressed in independent clauses.

CONNECTING CLAUSES		
Comma and coordinating conjunction		
Independent clause	, for	Independent clause
	, and	Independent clause
	, nor	Independent clause
	, but	Independent clause
	, or	Independent clause
	, yet	Independent clause
	, so	Independent clause
Semicolon		
Independent clause	;	Independent clause
Subordinating conjunction, dependent clause, and comma		
Dependent clause	,	Independent clause
Independent clause followed by a subordinating conjunction that introduces a dependent clause		
Independent clause		Dependent clause

DEPENDENT CLAUSES: clauses that contain at least one subject and one verb but cannot stand alone as complete sentences

DEPENDENT CLAUSES, by definition, contain at least one subject and one verb. However, they cannot stand alone as complete sentences. They are structurally dependent on the main clause.

There are two types of dependent clauses: (1) those with a subordinating conjunction, and (2) those with a relative pronoun.

Sample subordinating conjunctions: *although, when, if, unless, because*

Unless a cure is discovered, many more people will die of the disease.
(Coordinating conjunction + dependent clause + independent clause)

Sample relative pronouns: *who, whom, which, that*

The White House has an official website, which contains press releases, news updates, and biographies of the president and vice president.
(Independent clause + relative pronoun + relative dependent clause)

Be sure to place the conjunctions so that they express the proper relationship between ideas (cause/effect, condition, time, space).

Incorrect: Because mother scolded me, I was late.

Correct: Mother scolded me because I was late.

Incorrect: The sun rose after the fog lifted.

Correct: The fog lifted after the sun rose.

Notice that placement of the conjunction can completely change the meaning of the sentence. The main emphasis is shifted by the change.

Although Jenny was pleased, the teacher was disappointed.
Although the teacher was disappointed, Jenny was pleased.
The boys who had written the essay won the contest.
The boys who won the contest had written the essay.

While not syntactically incorrect, the last sentence makes it appear that the boys won the contest for something else before they wrote the essay.

Misplaced and dangling modifiers

Misplaced modifiers occur when particular phrases are not placed near the word they modify. Dangling modifiers occur when particular phrases do not relate to the subject being modified.

Error: Returning to my favorite watering hole brought back many fond memories.

Problem: The person who returned is never indicated, and the participle phrase dangles. This problem can be corrected by creating a dependent clause from the modifying phrase.

Correction: *When I returned to my favorite watering hole, many fond memories came back to me.*

Error: *One damaged house stood only to remind townspeople of the hurricane.*

Problem: The placement of the misplaced modifier "only" suggests that the sole reason the house remained was to serve as a reminder. The faulty modifier creates ambiguity.

Correction: *Only one damaged house stood, reminding townspeople of the hurricane.*

Parallelism

Students should recognize parallel structures using phrases (prepositional, gerund, participial, and infinitive) and omissions from sentences that create a lack of parallelism. Parallelism provides balance between the grammar and the ideas.

Prepositional phrase/single modifier

Incorrect: *Coleen ate the ice cream with enthusiasm and hurriedly.*

Correct: *Coleen ate the ice cream with enthusiasm and in a hurry.*

Correct: *Coleen ate the ice cream enthusiastically and hurriedly.*

Participial phrase/infinitive phrase

Incorrect: *After hiking for hours and to sweat profusely, Joe sat down to rest and drinking water.*

Correct: *After hiking for hours and sweating profusely, Joe sat down to rest and drink water.*

Recognition of syntactical redundancy or omission

Redundancy and omission errors occur when superfluous words are added to a sentence or key words are omitted from a sentence.

Redundancy

Incorrect: *Joyce made sure that when her plane arrived that she retrieved all of her luggage.*

Correct: *Joyce made sure that when her plane arrived she retrieved all of her luggage.*

Incorrect: *He was a mere skeleton of his former self.*

Correct: *He was a skeleton of his former self.*

Learn more about parallel structure vs. faulty parallelism:

jerz.setonhill.edu/writing/grammar/parallel.html

Omission

Incorrect: *Dot opened her book, recited her textbook, and answered the teacher's subsequent question.*

Correct: *Dot opened her book, recited from the textbook, and answered the teacher's subsequent question.*

Avoidance of double negatives

A double negative occurs when two negatives cancel each other in meaning.

Incorrect: *Dot didn't have no double negatives in her paper.*

Correct: *Dot didn't have any double negatives in her paper.*

Parts of Speech

The eight parts of speech form the syntactical framework of our language. While the study of grammar can be detailed, let's review some of the basics.

- Noun: names a person, place, or thing
- Pronoun: takes the place of one or more nouns
- Verb: expresses action or state of being
- Adjective: describes or modifies a noun or pronoun
- Adverb: modifies a verb, an adjective, or another adverb
- Conjunction: is a connecting word
- Preposition: relates a noun or pronoun to another word in a sentence
- Interjection: expresses emotion

Nouns

A **NOUN** names a person, place, or thing/idea. A **COMMON NOUN** names *any* person, place, or thing/idea; a **PROPER NOUN** names a *particular* person, place, or thing/idea. A proper noun is capitalized.

	Person	Place	Thing	Idea
Common Noun	Actor	museum	ship	bravery
Proper Noun	Meryl Streep	The Smithsonian	*Titanic*	

NOUN: part of speech that names a person, place, or thing/idea

COMMON NOUN: names any person, place, or thing/idea

PROPER NOUN: names a particular person, place, or thing/idea and is capitalized

COMPONENTS OF WRITING

Possessive nouns

Make the possessives of singular nouns by adding an apostrophe followed by the letter *s* (*'s*).

> baby's bottle, father's job, elephant's eye, teacher's desk, sympathizer's protests, week's postponement

Make the possessives of singular nouns ending in *s* by adding either an apostrophe or an (*'s*), depending on common usage or sound. When the possessive sounds awkward, use a prepositional phrase instead. Even with the sibilant ending, with a few exceptions, it is advisable to use the (*'s*) construction.

> dress's color, species' characteristics or characteristics of the species, James' hat or James's hat, Delores's shirt.

Make the possessives of plural nouns ending in *s* by adding the apostrophe after the *s*.

> horses' coats, jockeys' times, four days' time

Make the possessives of plural nouns that do not end in *s* by adding *'s*, just as with singular nouns.

> children's shoes, deer's antlers, cattle's horns

Make the possessives of compound nouns by adding the inflection at the end of the word or phrase.

> the mayor of Los Angeles' campaign, the mailman's new truck, the mailmen's new trucks, my father-in-law's first wife, the keepsakes' values, several daughters-in-law's husbands

Note: Because a gerund functions as a noun, any noun preceding it and operating as a possessive adjective must reflect the necessary inflection. However, if the gerundive following the noun is a participle, no inflection is added.

> The general was perturbed by the private's sleeping on duty. (The word **sleeping** is a gerund, the object of the preposition **by**.)
>
> but
>
> The general was perturbed to see the private sleeping on duty. (The word **sleeping** is a participle modifying **private**.)

Pronouns

A **PRONOUN** takes the place of one or more nouns and must agree with that noun in case and number. The noun to which a pronoun refers is called the **ANTECEDENT**.

> **PRONOUN:** takes the place of one or more nouns and must agree with that noun in case and number
>
> **ANTECEDENT:** the noun to which a pronoun refers

Proper case forms

Pronouns, unlike nouns, change case forms. Pronouns must be in the subjective, objective, or possessive form according to their function in the sentence.

PERSONAL PRONOUNS

	SUBJECTIVE (NOMINATIVE)		POSSESSIVE		OBJECTIVE	
	Singular	Plural	Singular	Plural	Singular	Plural
1st Person	I	we	my	our	me	us
2nd Person	you	you	your	your	you	you
3rd Person	he she it	they	his her its	their	him her it	them

RELATIVE PRONOUNS

Who	Subjective/Nominative
Whom	Objective
Whose	Possessive

Rules for clearly identifying pronoun reference

Misuse of pronouns creates agreement errors and clouds the meaning of the sentence. Here are a few tips to correct this common grammatical error.

Make sure that the antecedent reference is clear and cannot refer to something else

A "distant relative" is a relative pronoun or a relative clause that has been placed too far away from the antecedent to which it refers. It is a common error to place a verb between the relative pronoun and its antecedent.

Error: *Return the books to the library that are overdue.*

Problem: The relative clause "that are overdue" refers to the "books" and should be placed immediately after the antecedent.

Correction: *Return the books that are overdue to the library.*
or
Return the overdue books to the library.

A pronoun should not refer to adjectives or possessive nouns

Adjectives, nouns, or possessive pronouns should not be used as antecedents. This will create ambiguity in sentences.

Error: *In Todd's letter he told his mom he'd broken the priceless vase.*

Problem: In this sentence the pronoun "he" seems to refer to the noun phrase "Todd's letter," though it was probably meant to refer to the possessive noun "Todd's."

Correction: *In his letter, Todd told his mom that he had broken the priceless vase.*

A pronoun should not refer to an implied idea

A pronoun must refer to a specific antecedent rather than to an implied antecedent. When an antecedent is not stated specifically, the reader has to guess or assume the meaning of a sentence. Pronouns that do not have antecedents are called expletives. "It" and "there" are the most common expletives, though other pronouns can also become expletives as well. In informal conversation, expletives allow for casual presentation of ideas without supporting evidence. However, in more formal writing, it is best to be more precise.

Error: *She said that it is important to floss every day.*

Problem: The pronoun "it" refers to an implied idea.

Correction: *She said that flossing every day is important.*

Error: *They returned the book because there were missing pages.*

Problem: The pronouns "they" and "there" do not refer to the antecedent.

Correction: *The customer returned the book with missing pages.*

UNDERSTAND THE CONVENTIONS OF STANDARD AMERICAN ENGLISH AND THE ELEMENTS OF EFFECTIVE COMPOSITION

Using who, that, and which

Who, *whom*, and *whose* refer to human beings and can introduce either essential or nonessential clauses. *That* refers to things other than humans and is used to introduce essential clauses. *Which* refers to things other than humans and is used to introduce nonessential clauses.

Error: *The doctor that performed the surgery said the man would recover fully.*

Problem: Since the relative pronoun is referring to a human, *who* should be used.

Correction: *The doctor who performed the surgery said the man would recover fully.*

Error: *That ice cream cone that you just ate looked really delicious.*

Problem: *That* has already been used, so you must use *which* to introduce the next clause, whether it is essential or nonessential.

Correction: *That ice cream cone, which you just ate, looked really delicious.*

Error: *Tom and me have reserved seats for next week's baseball game.*

Problem: The pronoun *me* is the subject of the verb *have reserved* and should be in the subjective form.

Correction: *Tom and I have reserved seats for next week's baseball game.*

Error: *Who's coat is this?*

Problem: The interrogative possessive pronoun is *whose*; *who's* is the contraction for *who is*.

Correction: *Whose coat is this?*

Error: *The voters will choose the candidate whom has the best qualifications for the job.*

Problem: The case of the relative pronoun *who* or *whom* is determined by the pronoun's function in the clause in which it appears. The word *who* is in the subjective case, and *whom* is in the objective. Analyze how the pronoun is being used within the sentence.

Correction: *The voters will choose the candidate who has the best qualifications for the job.*

COMPONENTS OF WRITING

VERB: expresses action or state of being

Verbs

A **VERB** expresses action or state of being. Most verbs show time (tense) by an inflectional ending to the word. Other irregular verbs take completely different forms.

Both regular and irregular verbs must appear in their standard forms for each tense. Note: the *-ed* or *-d* ending is added to regular verbs in the past tense and for past participles.

REGULAR VERB FORMS		
Infinitive	**Past Tense**	**Past Participle**
bake	baked	baked

IREGULAR VERB FORMS		
Infinitive	**Past Tense**	**Past Participle**
be	was, were	been
become	became	become
break	broke	broken
bring	brought	brought
choose	chose	chosen
come	came	come
do	did	done
draw	drew	drawn
eat	ate	eaten
fall	fell	fallen
forget	forgot	forgotten
freeze	froze	frozen

Continued on next page

Infinitive	Past Tense	Past Participle
give	gave	given
go	went	gone
grow	grew	grown
have/has	had	had
hide	hid	hidden
know	knew	known
lay	laid	laid
lie	lay	lain
ride	rode	ridden
rise	rose	risen
run	ran	run
see	saw	seen
steal	stole	stolen
take	took	taken
tell	told	told
throw	threw	thrown
wear	wore	worn
write	wrote	written

Error: *She should have went to her doctor's appointment at the scheduled time.*

Problem: The past participle of the verb *to go* is *gone*. *Went* expresses the simple past tense.

Correction: *She should have gone to her doctor's appointment at the scheduled time.*

COMPONENTS OF WRITING

Error: *My train is suppose to arrive before two o'clock.*

Problem: The verb following *train* is a present tense passive construction, which requires the present tense verb *to be* and the past participle.

Correction: *My train is supposed to arrive before two o'clock.*

Error: *Linda should of known that the car wouldn't start after leaving it out in the cold all night.*

Problem: *Should of* is a nonstandard expression. *Of* is not a verb.

Correction: *Linda should have known that the car wouldn't start after leaving it out in the cold all night.*

Use of verbs: tense

PRESENT TENSE is used to express that which is currently happening or is always true.

> Randy is playing the piano.
> Randy plays the piano like a pro.

PAST TENSE is used to express action that occurred in a past time.

> Randy learned to play the piano when he was six years old.

FUTURE TENSE is used to express action or a condition of future time.

> Randy will probably earn a music scholarship.

PRESENT PERFECT TENSE is used to express action or a condition that started in the past and is continued or completed in the present.

> Randy has practiced the piano every day for the last ten years.
> Randy has never been bored with practice.

PAST PERFECT TENSE expresses action or a condition that occurred as a precedent to some other past action or condition.

> Randy had considered playing clarinet before he discovered the piano.

PRESENT TENSE: expresses that which is currently happening or is always true

PAST TENSE: expresses action that occurred in a past time

FUTURE TENSE: expresses action or a condition of future time

PRESENT PERFECT TENSE: expresses action or a condition that started in the past and is continued or completed in the present

PAST PERFECT TENSE: expresses action or a condition that occurred as a precedent to some other past action or condition

FUTURE PERFECT TENSE expresses action that started in the past or the present and will conclude at some time in the future.

By the time he goes to college, Randy will have been an accomplished pianist for more than half of his life.

> **FUTURE PERFECT TENSE:** expresses action that started in the past or the present and will conclude at some time in the future

Use of verbs: mood

Indicative mood is used to make unconditional statements; **subjunctive mood** is used for conditional clauses or wish statements that pose conditions that are untrue. Verbs in subjunctive mood are plural with both singular and plural subjects.

If I were a bird, I would fly.

I wish I were as rich as Donald Trump.

Use of verbs: voice

A verb is in the **ACTIVE VOICE** when its subject is the doer of the action. A verb is in the **PASSIVE VOICE** when its subject is the receiver of the action.

> **ACTIVE VOICE:** when the subject of the verb is the doer of the action

> **PASSIVE VOICE:** when the subject of the verb is the receiver of the action

Active Voice	Passive Voice
The director adjourned the meeting. The subject, *director*, performs the action, *adjourned*.	**The meeting was adjourned by the director.** The subject, *meeting*, is not performing the action; instead, it is receiving the action, *was adjourned*.
The mechanic at the Shell station inspected Mrs. Johnson's automobile. The subject, *mechanic*, performed the action, *inspected*.	**Mrs. Johnson's automobile was inspected by the mechanic at the Shell station.** The subject, *automobile*, is not acting; it is receiving the action, *was inspected*.

How do you recognize passive voice? Look at the verb. A passive-voice verb has at least two parts:

1. A form of the verb to be (am, is, are, was, were, be, been)

    The computer was installed by Datacorp.

COMPONENTS OF WRITING

2. A past participle form of the main verb (thrown, driven, planted, talked)

> The computer was <u>installed</u> by Datacorp.

– Sometimes the subject is in an object position in the sentence.

> The computer was installed by <u>Datacorp</u>. (object of preposition)

– Watch for a "by" statement between the verb phrase and the object.

> The computer was installed <u>by</u> Datacorp. (preposition)

– Sometimes the doer is not even present.

> The computer was installed. (By whom?)

Verb conjugation

The conjugation of verbs follows the patterns used in the discussion of tense above. However, the most common errors in verb use stem from the improper formation of the past and past participial forms.

> Regular verb: believe, believed, (have) believed
> Irregular verbs: run, ran, run; sit, sat, sat; teach, taught, taught

Other errors stem from the use of verbs that are the same in some tenses but have different forms and different meanings in other tenses.

> *I lie on the ground. I lay on the ground yesterday. I have lain down. I lay the blanket on the bed. I laid the blanket there yesterday. I have laid the blanket down every night.*
>
> *The sun rises. The sun rose. The sun has risen.*
>
> *He raises the flag. He raised the flag. He had raised the flag.*
>
> *I sit on the porch. I sat on the porch. I have sat in the porch swing.*
>
> *I set the plate on the table. I set the plate there yesterday. I had set the table before dinner.*

Adjectives and adverbs

ADJECTIVES are words that modify or describe nouns or pronouns. Adjectives usually precede the words they modify, but not always; for example, an adjective occurs after a linking verb. Adjectives answer *what kind, how many*, or *which one*.

ADJECTIVES: words that modify or describe nouns or pronouns

ADVERBS are words that modify verbs, adjectives, or other adverbs. They cannot modify nouns. Adverbs answer such questions as *how, why, when, where, how much,* or *how often.* Many adverbs are formed by adding *-ly*.

> **ADVERBS:** words that modify verbs, adjectives, or other adverbs

Error: *The birthday cake tasted sweetly.*

Problem: *Tasted* is a linking verb; the modifier that follows should be an adjective, not an adverb.

Correction: *The birthday cake tasted sweet.*

Error: *You have done good with this project.*

Problem: *Good* is an adjective and cannot be used to modify a verb phrase such as *have done*.

Correction: *You have done well with this project.*

Error: *The coach was positive happy about the team's chance of winning.*

Problem: The adjective *positive* cannot be used to modify another adjective, *happy*. An adverb is needed instead.

Correction: *The coach was positively happy about the team's chance of winning.*

Error: *The fireman acted quick and brave to save the child from the burning building.*

Problem: *Quick* and *brave* are adjectives and cannot be used to describe a verb. Adverbs are needed instead.

Correction: *The fireman acted quickly and bravely to save the child from the burning building.*

Conjunctions

A **CONJUNCTION** connects words, phrases, or clauses. It acts as a signal, indicating when a thought is added, contrasted, or altered.

> **CONJUNCTION:** connects words, phrases, or clauses

Meet the FANBOYS! This mnemonic device will help students remember the seven coordinating conjunctions.

For, And, Nor, But, Or, Yet, So

COMPONENTS OF WRITING

COORDINATING CONJUNCTIONS: join similar elements

COORDINATING CONJUNCTIONS join similar elements.

Strong and tall (adjectives)
Easily and quickly (adverbs)
Of the people, by the people, for the people (prepositional phrases)
We disagreed, but we reached a compromise. (sentences)

SUBORDINATING CONJUNCTIONS: connect clauses (subject-verb combinations) in a sentence and signal that the clause is subordinate and cannot stand alone

SUBORDINATING CONJUNCTIONS connect clauses (subject-verb combinations) in a sentence. They signal that the clause is subordinate and cannot stand alone.

SUBORDINATING CONJUNCTIONS			
after	because	though	whenever
although	before	till	where
as	if	unless	whereas
as if	since	until	wherever
as though	than	when	while

Check out this guide to grammar and writing:

grammar.ccc.commnet.edu/grammar/

I will be grateful **if you will work on this project with me**.
Because I am running late, you will need to cover for me.

PREPOSITION: relates a noun or pronoun to another word in a sentence

Prepositions

A PREPOSITION relates a noun or pronoun to another word in a sentence. Think of prepositions as words that show relationships. Below is a partial list.

about	above	according to	across	after	against
along	along with	among	apart from	around	as/as for
at	because of	before	behind	below	beneath
beside	between	beyond	by	by means of	concerning
despite	down	during	except	except for	excepting

Continued on next page

152

MINNESOTA COMMUNICATION ARTS/LITERATURE (5–1

UNDERSTAND THE CONVENTIONS OF STANDARD AMERICAN ENGLISH AND THE ELEMENTS OF EFFECTIVE COMPOSITION

for	from	in	in addition to	in back of	in case of
in front of	in place of	inside	in spite of	instead of	into
like	near	next	of	off	on
onto	on top of	out/out of	outside	over	past
regarding	round	since	through	throughout	till
to	toward	under	underneath	unlike	until
up/upon	up to	with	within	without	

PREPOSITION GUIDELINES	
Include necessary prepositions	*I graduated from high school. (not I graduated high school.)*
Omit unnecessary prepositions	*Both printers work well. (not Both of the printers work well.)* *Where are the printers? (not Where are the printers at?)*
Avoid the overuse of prepositions	*Error: We have received your application for credit at our branch in the Fresno area.* *Correction: We have received your credit application at our Fresno branch.*

Interjections

An **INTERJECTION** is a word or group of words that express emotion, surprise, or disbelief. An interjection has no grammatical connection to other words in a sentence.

INTERJECTION: a word or group of words that express emotion, surprise, or disbelief

SOME COMMON INTERJECTIONS			
aha	great	my	ouch
alas	ha	no	well
gee	hey	oh	wow
good grief	hooray	oops	yes

COMPONENTS OF WRITING

INTERJECTION GUIDELINES	
When an interjection expresses strong emotion, it usually stands alone. It begins with a capital letter and ends with an exclamation point.	*Ouch!* That paper cut really hurts. *Good grief!* My favorite store has closed.
When an interjection expresses mild feeling, it is written as part of the sentence and is set off with commas.	*Yes,* we will comply with your request.

SKILL 14.4 Recognizing methods of developing an introduction to a text that draws a reader's attention, specifies a topic, and provides a thesis

Structuring an Essay

Forming a thesis and topic

A good thesis gives structure to an essay and helps focus the writer's thoughts. When forming a thesis, look at the prewriting strategy—clustering, questioning, or brainstorming. Then decide quickly which two or three major areas will be discussed. Remember, the scope of the paper must be limited because of the time factor.

OUTLINE: lists those main areas or points as topics for each paragraph

The OUTLINE lists those main areas or points as topics for each paragraph. Looking at the prewriting cluster on computers, one might choose several areas in which computers help us, for example in science and medicine, business, and education. Also, consider people's reliance on this "wonder" and include at least one paragraph about this reliance. A formal outline for this essay might look like the one below:

I. Introduction and thesis

II. Computers used in science and medicine

III. Computers used in business

IV. Computers used in education

V. People's reliance on computers

VI. Conclusion

UNDERSTAND THE CONVENTIONS OF STANDARD AMERICAN ENGLISH AND THE ELEMENTS OF EFFECTIVE COMPOSITION

Under the pressure of time, however, one may use a shorter organizational plan, such as abbreviated key words in a list. For example

1. intro: wonders of the computer -OR-	a. intro: wonders of computers—science
2. science	b. in the space industry
3. med	c. in medical technology
4. schools	d. conclusion
5. business	
6. conclusion	

After focusing on the topic and generating ideas, form a thesis, the controlling idea of the essay. The **THESIS** is the general statement to the reader that expresses a point of view and guides the essay's purpose and scope. The thesis should allow one either to explain the subject or to take an arguable position about it. A strong thesis statement is neither too narrow nor too broad.

> **THESIS:** the general statement to the reader that expresses a point of view and guides the essay's purpose and scope

> *A strong thesis statement is neither too narrow nor too broad.*

Subject and assertion of the thesis

From the analysis of the general topic, it is possible to see the topic in terms of its two parts—*subject* and *assertion*. On the exam, a thesis or viewpoint on a particular topic is stated in two important points:

1. The subject of the essay
2. The assertion about the subject

The **SUBJECT OF THE THESIS** relates directly to the topic prompt and expresses the specific area that has been chosen to be discussed. (Remember, the exam topic will be general and will allow the writer to choose a particular subject related to the topic). For example, *the computer is one modern invention.*

The **ASSERTION OF THE THESIS** is a viewpoint, or opinion, about the subject. The assertion provides the motive or purpose for the essay, and it may be an arguable point or one that explains or illustrates a point of view.

For example, an argument may be presented for or against a particular issue. Two people, objects, or methods may be contrasted to show that one is better than the other. A situation may be analyzed in all aspects, and recommendations can be made for improvement. The writer may assert that a law or policy should be adopted, changed, or abandoned. As in the computer example, the writer may explain to the reader that a situation or condition exists; rather than argue a viewpoint, the writer would use examples to illustrate the assertion about the essay's subject.

> **SUBJECT OF THE THESIS:** relates directly to the topic prompt and expresses the specific area that has been chosen to be discussed

> **ASSERTION OF THE THESIS:** a viewpoint, or opinion, about the subject

> *The assertion provides the motive or purpose for the essay.*

Guidelines for writing thesis statements

The following guidelines are not a formula for writing thesis statements, but rather are general strategies for making a thesis statement clearer and more effective.

1. State a particular point of view about the topic with both a *subject* and an *assertion*. The thesis should give the essay purpose and scope and thus provide the reader a guide. If the thesis is vague, the essay may be undeveloped because there is not an idea to assert or a point to explain. Weak thesis statements are often framed as facts, questions, or announcements:

    A. Avoid a fact statement as a thesis. While a fact statement may provide a subject, it generally does not include a point of view about the subject that provides the basis for an extended discussion. The *fact statement provides a detail, not a point of view.* Such a detail might be found within an essay, but it does not state a point of view.

    B. Avoid framing the thesis as a vague question. In many cases, rhetorical questions do not provide a clear point of view for an extended essay. Example: *How do people recycle?* This question neither asserts a point of view nor does it helpfully guide the reader to understand the essay's purpose and scope.

    C. Avoid the "announcer" topic sentence that merely states the topic to be discussed. Example: *I will discuss ways to recycle.* This sentence states the subject, but the scope of the essay is only suggested. Again, this statement does not assert a view that guides the essay's purpose. It merely "announces" that the writer will write about the topic.

2. Start with a workable thesis. The thesis might be revised after writing begins and a point of view is discovered.

3. If feasible and appropriate, perhaps state the thesis in multipoint form, expressing the scope of the essay. By stating the points in parallel form, the writer clearly lays out the essay's plan for the reader.

    > To improve the environment, we can recycle our trash, elect politicians who see the environment as a priority, and support lobbying groups who work for environmental protection.

4. Because of the exam time limit, place the thesis in the first paragraph to key the reader to the essay's main idea.

> **SKILL 14.5** Recognizing methods of developing a body of a text that presents, emphasizes, links, and contrasts ideas in a clear, concise, and coherent manner

Techniques for Revising Written Texts

Enhancing interest

Listed below are some strategies for enhancing interest:

- Start out with an attention-grabbing introduction; this sets an engaging tone for the entire piece and will more likely pull the reader in.

- Use dynamic vocabulary and varied sentence beginnings; keep the readers on their toes—if they can predict what is going to be said next, switch it up.

- Avoid using clichés (such as "cold as ice," "the best thing since sliced bread," "nip it in the bud"); these are easy shortcuts, but they are not interesting, memorable, or convincing.

Ensuring understanding

Listed below are some strategies for enhancing understanding:

- Avoid using the words "clearly," "obviously," and "undoubtedly"; often, things that are clear or obvious to the author are not as apparent to the reader. Instead of using these words, make the point so strongly that it is clear on its own.

- Use the word that best fits the meaning intended, even if it is longer or a little less common; try to find a balance, and go with a familiar yet precise word.

- When in doubt, explain further.

Transitions

Even if the sentences that make up a given paragraph or passage are arranged in logical order, the document as a whole can still seem choppy, and the various ideas can appear disconnected. TRANSITIONS, words that signal relationships between ideas, can help improve the flow of a document. Transitions can help achieve clear and effective presentation of information by establishing connections between sentences, paragraphs, and sections of a document. With transitions, each sentence builds on the ideas previously introduced, and each paragraph links clearly to the preceding one. As a result, the reader receives clear directions on how to piece together the writer's ideas in a logically coherent argument. By signaling how to organize, interpret, and react to information, transitions allow a writer to explain his or her ideas effectively and elegantly.

> **TRANSITIONS:** words that signal relationships between ideas

COMPONENTS OF WRITING

LOGICAL RELATIONSHIP	TRANSITIONAL EXPRESSION
Similarity	also, in the same way, just as ... so too, likewise, similarly
Exception/Contrast	but, however, in spite of, on the one hand ... on the other hand, nevertheless, nonetheless, notwithstanding, in contrast, on the contrary, still, yet
Sequence/Order	first, second, third, ... next, then, finally
Time	after, afterward, at last, before, currently, during, earlier, immediately, later, meanwhile, now, recently, simultaneously, subsequently, then
Example	for example, for instance, namely, specifically, to illustrate
Emphasis	even, indeed, in fact, of course, truly
Place/Position	above, adjacent, below, beyond, here, in front, in back, nearby, there
Cause and Effect	accordingly, consequently, hence, so, therefore, thus
Additional Support or Evidence	additionally, again, also, and, as well, besides, equally important, further, furthermore, in addition, moreover, then
Conclusion/Summary	finally, in a word, in brief, in conclusion, in the end, in the final analysis, on the whole, thus, to conclude, to summarize, in sum, in summary

Example of transitions

The following example shows good logical order and transitions. The transition words are in boldface type.

*No one really knows how Valentine's Day started. There are several legends, **however**, which are often told. The **first** attributes Valentine's Day to a Christian priest who lived in Rome during the third century, under the rule of Emperor Claudius. Rome was at war, and **apparently**, Claudius felt that married men did not fight as well as bachelors. **Consequently**, Claudius banned marriage for the duration of the war. **However**, Valentinus, the priest, risked his life to marry couples secretly in violation of Claudius' law. The **second** legend is **even more** romantic. **In this story**, Valentinus is a prisoner, having been condemned to death for refusing to worship pagan deities. **While** in jail, he fell in love with his jailer's daughter, who happened to be blind. Daily, he prayed for her sight to return, and miraculously it did. On February 14, the day that he was condemned to die, he was allowed to write the young woman a note. **In this farewell letter**, he promised eternal love, and signed at the bottom of the page the now famous words, "Your Valentine."*

SKILL 14.6
Recognizing methods of developing a conclusion to a text that provides a summary or resolution, suggests a course of action, or offers a personal commentary

See Skill 15.3

COMPETENCY 15
UNDERSTAND THE WRITING PROCESS

SKILL 15.1
Demonstrating knowledge of the appropriate form of writing to use for a particular purpose and audience

Discourse, whether in speaking or writing, falls naturally into four different forms: narrative, descriptive, expository, and persuasive. The first question to be asked when reading a written piece, listening to a presentation, or writing is, "What's the point?" This is usually called the thesis. If you are reading an essay, when you've finished, you want to be able to say, "The point of this piece is that the foster-care system in America is a disaster." If it's a play, you should also be able to say, "The point of that play is that good overcomes evil." The same is true of any written document or performance. If it doesn't make a point, the reader/listener/viewer is confused or feels that it's not worth the effort. Knowing this is very helpful when you are sitting down to write your own document, be it an essay, a poem, or a speech. What point do you want to make? We make these points in the forms that have been the structure of western thinking since the Greek rhetoricians.

Discourse, whether in speaking or writing, falls naturally into four different forms: narrative, descriptive, expository, and persuasive.

PERSUASION is a piece of writing, a poem, a play, or a speech whose purpose is to change the minds of the audience members or to get them to do something. This is achieved in many ways:

- The credibility of the writer/speaker might lead the listeners/readers to a change of mind or a recommended action.
- Reasoning is important in persuasive discourse. No one wants to believe that he accepts a new viewpoint or goes out and takes action just because he

PERSUASION: a piece of writing, a poem, a play, or a speech whose purpose is to change the minds of the audience members or to get them to do something

COMPONENTS OF WRITING

likes and trusts the person who recommended it. Logic comes into play in reasoning that is persuasive.

- The third and most powerful force that leads to acceptance or action is emotional appeal. Even if a person has been persuaded logically, reasonably, that he should believe in a different way, he is unlikely to act on it unless he is moved emotionally.

A man with resources might be convinced that people suffered in New Orleans after Katrina, but he will not be likely to do anything about it until he is moved emotionally, until he can see dead bodies floating in the dirty water or elderly people stranded in houses. Sermons are good examples of persuasive discourse.

EXPOSITION is discourse intended only to inform. Expository writing is not interested in changing anyone's mind or getting anyone to take a certain action. It exists to give information. Some examples are driving directions to a particular place or the directions for putting together a toy that arrives unassembled. The writer doesn't care whether you do or don't follow the directions. She or he wants only to be sure you have the information in case you do decide to use it.

NARRATION is discourse that is arranged chronologically: something happened, and then something else happened, and then something else happened. It is also called a story. News reports are often narrative in nature, as are records of trips, etc.

DESCRIPTION is discourse intended to make an experience available through one of the five senses: seeing, smelling, hearing, feeling (as with the fingers), and tasting. Descriptive words are used to make it possible for the reader to "see" with his or her own mind's eye, hear through his or her own mind's ear, smell through his or her own mind's nose, taste with his or her mind's tongue, and feel with his or her mind's fingers. This is how language moves people. Only by experiencing an event can the emotions become involved. Poets are experts in descriptive language.

PARAPHRASE is the rewording of a piece of writing. The result will not necessarily be shorter than the original. It will use different vocabulary and possibly different arrangement of details. Paraphrases are sometimes written to clarify a complex piece of writing. Sometimes, material is paraphrased because it cannot be borrowed as is for purposes of copyright restraints.

SUMMARY is a distilling of the elements of a piece of writing or speech. It will be much shorter than the original. To write a good summary, the writer must determine what the "bones" of the original piece are. What is its structure? What is the thesis and what are the subpoints? A summary does not make judgments about the original; it simply reports the original in condensed form.

EXPOSITION: discourse intended only to inform

NARRATION: discourse that is arranged chronologically

DESCRIPTION: discourse intended to make an experience available through one of the five senses

Persuasive writing often uses all forms of discourse. The introduction may be a history or background of the idea being presented—exposition. Details supporting some of the points may be stories—narrations. Descriptive writing will be used to make sure the point is established emotionally.

PARAPHRASE: the rewording of a piece of writing

SUMMARY: a distilling of the elements of a piece of writing or speech

Letters are often expository in nature—their purpose is to give information. However, letters are also often persuasive—the writer wants to persuade or get the recipient to do something. They are also sometimes descriptive or narrative—the writer will share an experience or tell about an event.

Research reports are a special kind of expository writing. A topic is researched—explored by some appropriate means such as searching literature, interviewing experts, or even conducting experiments—and the findings will be written up in such a way that a particular audience may know what was discovered. They can be very simple, such as delving into the history of an event, or very complex, such as a report on a scientific phenomenon that requires complicated testing and reasoning to explain. A research report often reports possible conclusions but puts forth one as the best answer to the question that inspired the research in the first place, which will become the *thesis* of the report.

SKILL 15.2 Recognizing methods of generating and organizing ideas for writing

As you instruct your students in composition, you should explain that, like all skills, writing is a skill that improves with practice. What follows is a way for you to address your students. You can use this same process as you prepare for your teacher certification essays.

What to Tell the Students

Even before you select a topic, determine what each prompt is asking you to discuss. This first decision is crucial. If you pick a topic, you don't really understand or about which you have little to say, you'll have difficulty developing your essay. Take a few moments to analyze each topic carefully *before* you begin to write.

> Topic A: A modern invention that can be considered a wonder of the world

In general, the topic prompts have two parts: the subject of the topic and an assertion about the subject.

The subject is a *modern invention*. In this prompt, the word *modern* indicates you should discuss something invented recently, at least in this century. The word *invention* indicates you're to write about something created by humans (not natural phenomena such as mountains or volcanoes). You may discuss an invention that has potential for harm, such as chemical warfare or the atomic bomb, or

COMPONENTS OF WRITING

you may discuss an invention that has the potential for good: the computer, DNA testing, television, antibiotics, and so on.

The assertion (a statement of point of view) is that *the invention has such powerful or amazing qualities that it should be considered a wonder of the world*. The assertion potentially it limits the range for discussion. In other words, you would discuss particular qualities or uses of the invention, not just discuss how it was invented or whether it should have been invented at all.

Note also that this particular topic encourages you to use examples to show the reader that a particular invention is a modern wonder. Some topic prompts lend themselves to essays with an argumentative edge, in which you take a stand on a particular issue and persuasively prove your point. Here, you could offer examples or illustrations of the many "wonders" and uses of the particular invention you chose.

Be aware that misreading or misinterpreting the topic prompt can lead to serious problems. Papers that do not address the topic occur when one reads too quickly or only half-understands the topic. Misreading can also lead to a paper that addresses only part of the topic prompt rather than the entire topic.

To develop a complete essay, spend a few minutes planning. Jot down your ideas and quickly sketch an outline. Although you may feel under pressure to begin writing, you will write more effectively if you plan out your major points.

Prewriting

Before actually writing, you'll need to generate content and to develop a writing plan. Three prewriting techniques that can be helpful are brainstorming, questioning, and clustering.

Brainstorming

When brainstorming, quickly create a list of words and ideas that are connected to the topic. Let your mind roam free to generate as many relevant ideas as possible in a few minutes. For example, on the topic of computers you may write:

> computer—modern invention
>
> types—personal computers, microchips in calculators and watches
>
> wonder—acts like an electronic brain
>
> uses—science, medicine, offices, homes, schools
>
> problems—too much reliance; the machines aren't perfect

NCTE beliefs about the teaching of writing:

1. *Everyone has the capacity to write, writing can be taught, and teachers can help students become better writers.*
2. *People learn to write by writing.*
3. *Writing is a process.*
4. *Writing is a tool for thinking.*
5. *Writing grows out of many different purposes.*
6. *Conventions of finished and edited texts are important to readers and therefore to writers.*
7. *Writing and reading are related.*
8. *Writing has a complex relationship to talk.*
9. *Literate practices are embedded in complicated social relationships.*
10. *Composing occurs in different modalities and technologies.*
11. *Assessment of writing involves complex, informed, human judgment.*

—Writing Study Group of the NCTE Executive Committee November 2004

UNDERSTAND THE WRITING PROCESS

This list could help you focus on the topic and states the points you could develop in the body paragraphs. The brainstorming list keeps you on track and is well worth the few minutes it takes to jot down the ideas. Although you haven't ordered the ideas, seeing them on paper is an important step.

Questioning

Questioning helps you focus as you mentally ask a series of exploratory questions about the topic. You may use the most basic questions: who, what, where, when, why, and how.

> "**What** is my subject?"
> [computers]
>
> "**What** types of computers are there?"
> [personal computers, microchip computers]
>
> "**Why** have computers been a positive invention?"
> [act like electronic brains in machinery and equipment; help solve complex scientific problems]
>
> "**How** have computers been a positive invention?"
> [used to make improvements in:
> science (space exploration, moon landings)
> medicine (MRIs, CAT scans, surgical tools, research models)
> business (PCs, FAX, telephone equipment)
> education (computer programs for math, languages, science, social (studies),
> personal use (family budgets, tax programs, healthy diet plans)]
>
> "**How** can I show that computers are good?"
> [citing numerous examples]
>
> "**What** problems do I see with computers?"
> [too much reliance; not yet perfect]
>
> "**What** personal experiences would help me develop examples to respond to this topic?"
> [my own experiences using computers]

Of course, you may not have time to write out the questions completely. You might just write the words *who, what, where, when, why, how* and the major points next to each. An abbreviated list might look as follows:

> **What**—computers/modern wonder/making life better
>
> **How**—through technological improvements: lasers, calculators, CAT scans.
>
> **Where**—in science and space exploration, medicine, schools, offices

In a few moments, your questions should help you to focus on the topic and to generate interesting ideas and points to make in the essay. Later in the writing process, you can look back at the list to be sure you've made the key points you intended.

COMPONENTS OF WRITING

Clustering

Some visual thinkers find clustering an effective prewriting method. When clustering, you draw a box in the center of your paper and write your topic within that box. Then you draw lines from the center box and connect it to small satellite boxes that contain related ideas. Note the cluster below on computers:

Sample Cluster

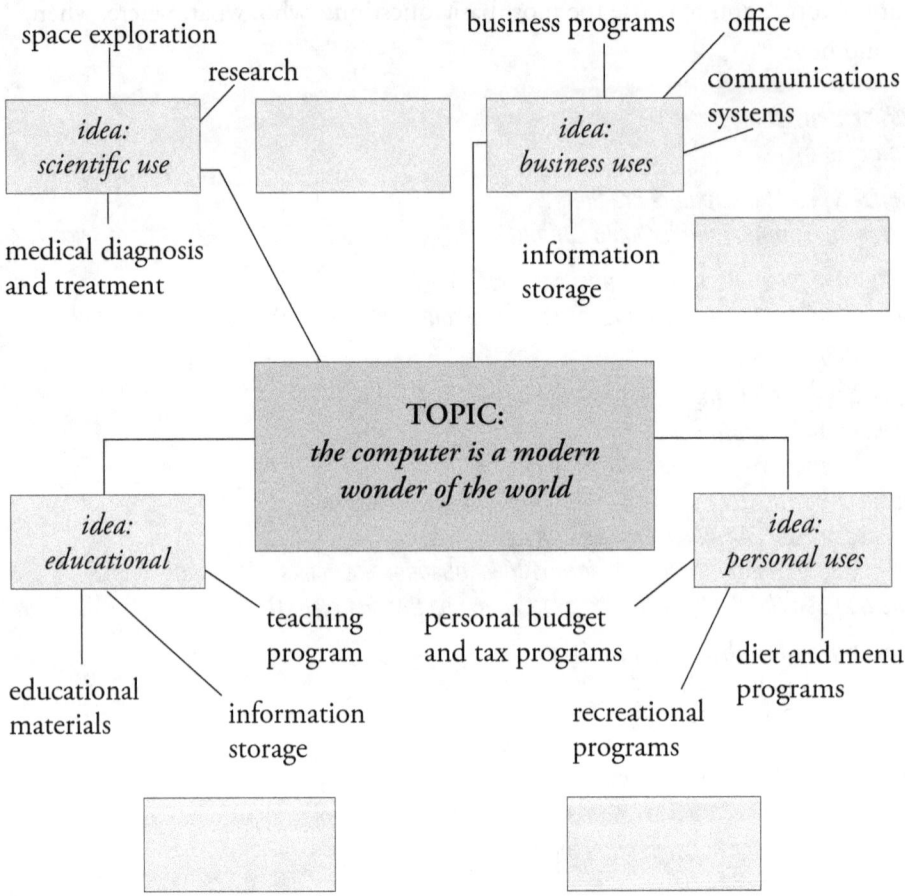

Developing the Essay

With a working thesis and an outline, you can begin writing the essay. The essay should be divided into three main sections:

I. The introduction sets up the essay and leads to the thesis statement

II. The body paragraphs are developed with concrete information leading from the topic sentences

III. The conclusion ties the essay together

Introduction

Put your thesis statement into a clear, coherent opening paragraph. One effective device is to use a funnel approach, in which you begin with a brief description of the broader issue and then move to a clearly focused, specific thesis statement.

Consider the following possible introductions to the essay on computers. The length of each is obviously different. Read each, and consider the other differences.

> *Does each introduce the subject generally?*
> *Does each lead to a stated thesis?*
> *Does each relate to the topic prompt?*

Introduction 1: *Computers are used every day. They have many uses. Some people who use them are workers, teachers, and doctors.*

Analysis: This introduction does give the general topic—computers are used every day—but it does not explain what those uses are. This introduction does not offer a point of view in a clearly stated thesis, nor does it convey the idea that computers are a modern wonder.

Introduction 2: *Computers are used just about everywhere these days. I don't think there's an office around that doesn't use computers, and we use them a lot in all kinds of jobs. Computers are great for making life easier and work better. I don't think we'd get along without the computer.*

Analysis: This introduction gives the general topic as computers and mentions one area that uses computers. The thesis states that people could not get along without computers, but it does not state the specific areas the essay will discuss. Note, too, that the meaning is not helped by vague diction, such as *a lot* and *great*.

Introduction 3: *Each day, we either use computers or see them being used around us. We wake to the sound of a digital alarm operated by a microchip. Our cars run by computerized machinery. We use computers to help us learn. We receive phone calls and letters transferred from computers across continents. Our astronauts walked on the moon and returned safely, all because of computer technology. The computer is a wonderful electronic brain that we have come to rely on, and it has changed our world through advances in science, business, and education.*

Analysis: This introduction is the most thorough and fluent because it provides interest in the general topic and offers specific information about computers as a modern wonder. It also leads to a thesis that directs the reader to the scope of the discussion—advances in science, business, and education.

Topic sentences

Just as the essay must have an overall focus reflected in the thesis statement, each paragraph must have a central idea reflected in the topic sentence. A good topic sentence provides transition from the previous paragraph and relates to the essay's thesis. Good topic sentences, therefore, provide unity throughout the essay.

Consider the following potential topic sentences. Determine whether each provides transition and clearly states the subject of the paragraph.

Topic Sentence 1: *Computers are used in science.*

Analysis: This sentence simply states the topic: Computers are used in science. It does not relate to the thesis or provide transition from the introduction. The reader still does not know how computers are used in science.

Topic Sentence 2: *Now I will talk about computers used in science.*

Analysis: Like the faulty "announcer" thesis statement, this "announcer" topic sentence is vague and merely names the topic.

Topic Sentence 3: *First, computers used in science have improved our lives.*

Analysis: The transition word *First* helps link the introduction and this paragraph. It adds unity to the essay. It does not, however, give specifics about the improvements computers have made in our lives.

Topic Sentence 4: *First used in scientific research and spaceflights, computers are now used extensively in the diagnosis and treatment of disease.*

Analysis: This sentence is the most thorough and fluent. It provides specific areas that will be discussed in the paragraph and it offers more than an announcement of the topic. The writer gives concrete information about the content of the paragraph that will follow.

SUMMARY GUIDELINES FOR WRITING TOPIC SENTENCES
Specifically relate the topic to the thesis statement
State clearly and concretely the subject of the paragraph
Provide some transition from the previous paragraph
Avoid topic sentences that are facts, questions, or announcements

See also Skill 14.4

SKILL 15.3 Recognizing methods of drafting text to show logical development of a central idea or theme through the use of relevant supporting details

If you have a good thesis and a good outline, you should be able to construct a complete essay. Your paragraphs should contain concrete, interesting information and supporting details to support your point of view. As often as possible, create images in your reader's mind. Fact statements also add weight to your opinions, especially when you are trying to convince the reader of your viewpoint.

Check out ten steps to writing an essay:

www.aucegypt.edu/academic/writers/

Supporting Details

Because every good thesis has an assertion, you should offer specifics, facts, data, anecdotes, expert opinion, and other details to prove that assertion. While you know what you mean, your reader does not. On the exam, you must explain and develop ideas as fully as possible in the time allowed.

In the following paragraph, the sentences in bold print provide a *skeleton of a paragraph that discusses the benefits of recycling*. The sentences in bold are generalizations that by themselves do not explain the need to recycle. The sentences in italics *add details to support the general points in bold*. Notice how the supporting details help you understand the necessity for recycling.

COMPONENTS OF WRITING

> *While one day recycling may become mandatory in all states, right now it is voluntary in many communities.* Those of us who participate in recycling are amazed by how much material is recycled. **For many communities, the blue-box recycling program has had an immediate effect.** By just recycling glass, aluminum cans, and plastic bottles, we have reduced the volume of disposable trash by one-third, thus extending the useful life of local landfills by over a decade. Imagine the difference if those dramatic results were achieved nationwide. **The number of reusable items we thoughtlessly dispose of is staggering.** For example, Americans dispose of enough steel every day to supply Detroit car manufacturers for three months. Additionally, we dispose of enough aluminum annually to rebuild the nation's air fleet. These statistics, available from the Environmental Protection Agency (EPA), should encourage all of us to watch what we throw away. **Clearly, recycling in our homes and in our communities directly improves the environment.**

Notice how the author's supporting examples enhance the message of the paragraph and relate to the author's thesis noted above. If you only read the boldface sentences, you have a glimpse of the topic. This paragraph of illustration, however, is developed through numerous details creating specific images: *Reduced the volume of disposable trash by one-third; extended the useful life of local landfills by over a decade; enough steel every day to supply Detroit car manufacturers for three months; enough aluminum to rebuild the nation's air fleet.* If the writer had merely written a few general sentences, as those shown in bold, you would not fully understand the vast amount of trash involved in recycling or the positive results of current recycling efforts.

Conclusion

End your essay with a brief, straightforward concluding paragraph that ties together the essay's content and leaves the reader with a sense of its completion. The conclusion should reinforce the main points, offer some insight into the topic, provide a sense of unity for the essay by relating it to the thesis, and signal clear closure of the essay.

SKILL 15.4 Recognizing methods of revising a text to eliminate wordiness, redundancy, distracting details, and extraneous information

Revising Sentences

Sometimes students see this exercise as simply catching errors in spelling or word use. Students need to reframe their thinking about revising and editing. Some questions that need to be asked:

- Is the reasoning coherent?

UNDERSTAND THE WRITING PROCESS

- Is the point established?
- Does the introduction make the reader want to read this discourse?
- What is the thesis? Is it proven?
- What is the purpose? Is it clear? Is it useful, valuable, and interesting?
- Is the style of writing so wordy that it exhausts the reader and interferes with engagement?
- Is the writing so spare that it is boring?
- Are the sentences too uniform in structure?
- Are there too many simple sentences?
- Are too many of the complex sentences the same structure?
- Are the compounds truly compounds or are they unbalanced?
- Are parallel structures truly parallel?
- If there are characters, are they believable?
- If there is dialogue, is it natural or stilted?
- Is the title appropriate?
- Does the writing show creativity or is it boring?
- Is the language appropriate? Is it too formal? Too informal? If jargon is used, is it appropriate?

Studies have clearly demonstrated that this is the most fertile area in teaching writing. If students can learn to revise their own work effectively, they are well on their way to becoming effective, mature writers. Word processing software is an important tool for teaching this stage in the writing process. Microsoft Word has tracking features that make the revision exchanges between teachers and students more effective than ever before.

SKILL 15.5 Recognizing methods of editing text to generate interest and clarify meaning *(e.g., varying sentence length and structure, maintaining parallelism, using appropriate transitions, simplifying inflated language)*

See Skills 14.5 and 15.4

SKILL 15.6 Recognizing methods of proofreading and preparing text for publication

See Skills 14.5 and 15.4

COMPETENCY 16
UNDERSTAND THE ELEMENTS OF EFFECTIVE AND APPROPRIATE RESEARCH

SKILL 16.1 Recognizing methods of selecting and refining a topic for research

See Skill 15.2

SKILL 16.2 Recognizing methods of composing specific, open-ended questions for a research topic

See Skill 15.2

SKILL 16.3 Recognizing methods of identifying and locating multiple and various sources of information for a research topic

The resources used to support a piece of writing can be divided into two major groups: primary sources and *secondary sources*.

Primary sources are works, records, and the like that were created during the period being studied or immediately after it. Secondary sources are works written significantly after the period being studied and based upon primary sources. **PRIMARY SOURCES** are the basic materials that provide raw data and information.

PRIMARY SOURCES: the basic materials that provide raw data and information

UNDERSTAND THE ELEMENTS OF EFFECTIVE AND APPROPRIATE RESEARCH

SECONDARY SOURCES are the works that contain the explications of, and judgments on, this primary material.

> **SECONDARY SOURCES:** works that contain explications of and judgments on primary material

Primary sources include the following kinds of materials:

- Documents that reflect the immediate, everyday concerns of people: memoranda, bills, deeds, charters, newspaper reports, pamphlets, graffiti, popular writings, journals or diaries, records of decision-making bodies, letters, receipts, snapshots, and others.

- Theoretical writings that reflect care and consideration in composition and an attempt to convince or persuade. The topic will generally be deeper than is the case with "immediate" documents. These may include newspaper or magazine editorials, sermons, political speeches, or philosophical writings.

- Narrative accounts of events, ideas, and trends written with intentionally by someone contemporary with the events described.

- Statistical data, although statistics may be misleading.

- Literature and nonverbal materials, novels, stories, poetry and essays from the period, as well as coins, archaeological artifacts, and art produced during the period.

Secondary sources include the following kinds of materials:

- Books written on the basis of primary materials about the time period.

- Books written on the basis of primary materials about persons who played a major role in the events under consideration.

- Books and articles written on the basis of primary materials about the culture, the social norms, the language, and the values of the period.

- Quotations from primary sources.

- Statistical data on the period.

- The conclusions and inferences of other historians.

- Multiple interpretations of the ethos of the time.

Questions for analyzing sources

To determine the authenticity or credibility of your sources, consider these questions:

- Who created the source and why? Was it created through a spur-of-the-moment act, a routine transaction, or a thoughtful, deliberate process?

- Did the recorder have firsthand knowledge of the event? Did the recorder report what others saw and heard?

Learn more about assessing the credibility of online sources:

www.webcredible.co.uk/user-friendly-resources/web-credibility/assessing-credibility-online-sources.shtml

- Was the recorder a neutral party, or did the recorder have opinions or interests that might have influenced what was recorded?
  Did the recorder produce the source for personal use, for one or more individuals, or for a large audience?

- Was the source meant to be public or private?

- Did the recorder wish to inform or persuade others? (Check the words in the source. The words may tell you whether the recorder was trying to be objective or persuasive.) Did the recorder have reasons to be honest or dishonest?

- Was the information recorded during the event, immediately after the event, or after some lapse of time?

Whether researching for your own purposes or teaching students research skills, the best place to start is usually at a library. Not only do libraries have numerous books, videos, and periodicals to use, but also librarians are always a valuable resource for information and can help retrieve information. In spite of the abundance of online sources, researchers still need librarians.

> "Those who declared librarians obsolete when the Internet rage first appeared are now red-faced. We need them more than ever. The Internet is full of 'stuff' but its value and readability is often questionable. 'Stuff' doesn't give you a competitive edge, high-quality related information does."
>
> —Patricia Schroeder, President of the Association of American Publishers

The Internet is a multifaceted goldmine of information, but you must be careful to discriminate between reliable and unreliable sources. Use sites that are associated with an academic institution, such as a university or a scholarly organization. Typical domain names end in "edu" or "org."

Keep *content* and *context* in mind when researching. Don't be so wrapped up with how you are going to apply your resource to your project that you miss the author's entire purpose or message. Remember that there are multiple ways to get the information you need. Read an encyclopedia article about your topic to get a general overview, and then focus from there. Note names of important people associated with your subject, time periods, and geographic areas. Make a list of key words and their synonyms to use while searching for information. And finally, don't forget about articles in magazines and newspapers, or even personal interviews with experts related to your field of interest.

UNDERSTAND THE ELEMENTS OF EFFECTIVE AND APPROPRIATE RESEARCH

SKILL 16.4 Recognizing methods of assessing the credibility, objectivity, and reliability of sources of information

To be sure you are using credible resources, review these guidelines for the use of secondary sources:

- Do not rely upon only a single secondary source.
- Check facts and interpretations against primary sources whenever possible.
- Do not accept the conclusions of other historians uncritically.
- Place greatest reliance on secondary sources created by the best and most respected scholars.
- Do not use the inferences of other scholars as if they were facts.
- Ensure that you recognize any bias the writer brings to his or her interpretation of history.
- Understand the primary point of the book as a basis for evaluating the relevance of the material presented in it to your questions.

Cross-checking or comparing sources not only helps you to test their validity, but also helps you to understand your sources in context. One observer of the 1939 invasion of Poland is good; two (or three or four) are even better. Each source will contribute something new to your understanding of the event and to your sense of how you might best represent or analyze it.

While bias cannot be eliminated, writers should carefully examine their resources and their own writings to avoid negative one-sidedness.

When evaluating sources, first go through this checklist to make sure the source is worth reading:

- Title (How relevant is it to your topic?)
- Date (How current is the source?)
- Organization (What institution produced this source?)
- Length (How in depth is the source?)

Check for signs of bias:

- Does the author or publisher have political ties or religious views that could affect his or her objectivity?
- Is the author or publisher associated with any special-interest groups that might only see one side of an issue, such as Greenpeace or the National Rifle Association?

- How fairly does the author treat opposing views?
- Does the language of the piece show signs of bias?

Keep an open mind while reading, and don't let opposing viewpoints prevent you from absorbing the text. Remember that you are not judging the author's work; you are examining its assumptions, assessing its evidence, and weighing its conclusions.

Further, review your own writing carefully to eliminate any conscious bias. Are you so convinced of your own viewpoint that you ignore valid opposing arguments? Have you backed every assertion with credible and reliable information?

Before accepting as fact anything that is printed in a newspaper or presented on radio, television, or the Internet, you should consider the source. Even though news reporters and editors claim to be unbiased in the presentation of news, they usually take an editorial point of view. A newspaper may avow that it is liberal or conservative and may even make recommendations at election time, but it may still claim to present the news without bias. Sometimes this is true, and sometimes it is not. For example, Fox News declares itself to be conservative and to support the Republican Party. Its presentation of news often reveals that bias.

On the other hand, CBS has tended to favor more liberal politicians although it avows that it is even-handed in its coverage. Dan Rather presented a story critical of President Bush's military service that was based on a document that could not be validated. His failure to play by the rules of certification of evidence cost him his job.

Even politicians usually play by the rules of fairness in the choices they make about going public. They usually try to be even-handed when selecting news outlets. However, some channels and networks show deference to one politician over another.

SKILL 16.5 Recognizing methods of gathering and organizing information from sources systematically

See Skill 16.3

UNDERSTAND THE ELEMENTS OF EFFECTIVE AND APPROPRIATE RESEARCH

> **SKILL 16.6** Recognizing methods of paraphrasing, summarizing, and quoting information from sources appropriately and of integrating a paraphrase, summary, or quotation effectively into a text

Synthesizing involves developing new understanding about a topic by gathering and studying information from multiple sources and perspectives, inferring significant new understanding from that study, and giving expression to the inferences. More simply, this skill captures the heart and soul of research: to yield new insights about some topic.

This skill implies an awareness of the spectrum of sources available to a modern student and an ability to assign appropriate weight to information from any given source.

Modern students should be aware, for instance, of print resources such as encyclopedias, journals, magazines, books, newspapers, legal documents, letters, and the like. In addition, they need to be able to use the Internet to access information not only for electronic versions of print resources but also for information stored in multimedia formats. Similarly, they need to be aware that they can gather information through interviewing people who hold positions or who have life experiences related to the particular topic.

Students need to be aware of the perspective underlying the information that they gather. Variations in perspective are legion, but common ones to consider would be based on age, gender, experience, education, nationality, political agenda, geographical location, economic status, and position in an organization or business. It would be important to consider, for instance, whether information on a collective bargaining issue comes from the CFO or from a union representative. Familiarity with the concepts of bias and credibility provides an important foundation for making the most sense of various perspectives.

Mastery of this skill involves developing a matrix or paradigm that does justice to the dynamic relationships among the various sources of information and perspectives gathered in the attempt to understand something new about a given topic. Then, through careful study of the matrix or paradigm, a student should be able to identify trends, connections, or insights that comprise the goal of the research—the new understanding, the synthesis. The final stage of this skill is to communicate the synthesis effectively. This skill includes having the know-how to craft a multimedia presentation that incorporates print, audio, and visual sources.

Learn more about the art of asking good questions:

www.youthlearn.org/learning/teaching/questions.asp

COMPONENTS OF WRITING

SKILL 16.7 Recognizing methods of citing or acknowledging sources of information appropriately in a text

This skill pertains to recognizing that stealing intellectual property is an academic and, in some cases, a legal crime; because it is so, students need to learn how to give credit where credit is due.

Students need to be aware of the rules that apply to borrowing ideas from various sources. Increasingly, consequences for violations of these rules (plagiarism) are becoming more severe, and students are expected to be aware of how to avoid such problems. Such consequences include failing a particular assignment, losing credit for an entire course, expulsion from a learning environment, and civil penalties.

Software exists that enables teachers and other interested individuals to determine quickly whether a given paper includes plagiarized material. As members of society in the information age, students are expected to recognize the basic justice of intellectual honesty and to conform to the systems meant to ensure it. Pleading ignorance is less and less of a defense.

There are several style guides for documenting sources. Each guide has its own particular ways of signaling that information has been directly borrowed or paraphrased; familiarity with where to find the relevant details of the major style guides is an essential for students. Many libraries publish overviews of the major style guides for students to consult, most bookstores carry full guides for the major systems, and relevant information is readily available on the Web as well.

Documentation of sources takes two main forms. The first form applies to citing sources in the text of the document or as footnotes or endnotes. In-text documentation is sometimes called parenthetical documentation and requires specific information within parentheses placed immediately after borrowed material. Footnotes or endnotes are placed either at the bottom of relevant pages or at the end of the document.

Beyond citing sources in the text, style guides also require a bibliography, a references section, or a works cited section at the end of the document. Sources for any borrowed material are to be listed according to the rules of the particular guide. In some cases, including a works consulted listing may be required even though no material is directly cited or paraphrased to the extent that an in-text citation would be required.

UNDERSTAND THE ELEMENTS OF EFFECTIVE AND APPROPRIATE RESEARCH

The major style guides to be familiar with include the *Modern Language Association Handbook (MLA)*, the *Manual of the American Psychological Association (APA)*, *The Chicago Manual of Style*, *Turabian*, and *Scientific Style and Format: The CBE Manual*.

Documentation of sources from the Internet is particularly involved and continues to evolve at a pace such that writers should visit the latest online update available for a particular style guide.

Learn more about MLA works cited documentation:

www.studyguide.org /MLAdocumentation.htm

COMPONENTS OF WRITING

DOMAIN VI
MODES OF WRITING

MODES OF WRITING

PERSONALIZED STUDY PLAN

PAGE	COMPETENCY AND SKILL	✓ KNOWN MATERIAL/ SKIP IT
183	**17: Understand strategies for expository writing**	☐
	17.1: Demonstrating knowledge of the forms and purposes of expository writing	☐
	17.2: Recognizing methods of selecting and limiting a subject for expository writing	☐
	17.3: Recognizing methods of formulating a specific question to address through expository writing and of developing a thesis statement that provides a focus for writing	☐
	17.4: Recognizing methods of selecting an effective organizational approach to use in expository writing	☐
	17.5: Recognizing methods of selecting effective and appropriate supporting details to use in expository writing	☐
	17.6: Recognizing methods of developing expository writing that is clear, concise, and coherent	☐
189	**18: Understand strategies for persuasive writing**	☐
	18.1: Demonstrating knowledge of the forms and purposes of persuasive writing	☐
	18.2: Recognizing methods of establishing a clear position or controlling idea in persuasive writing	☐
	18.3: Recognizing methods of selecting an effective organizational approach to use in persuasive writing	☐
	18.4: Recognizing methods of selecting effective and appropriate supporting details to use in persuasive writing	☐
	18.5: Recognizing methods of anticipating questions, concerns, and counterarguments for points made in persuasive writing and of incorporating effective responses to them into the writing	☐
	18.6: Recognizing methods of selecting an appropriate style, tone, voice, and diction to use in persuasive writing	☐
195	**19: Understand strategies for narrative writing**	☐
	19.1: Demonstrating knowledge of the forms and purposes of narrative writing	☐
	19.2: Recognizing methods of selecting and limiting a subject for narrative writing	☐
	19.3: Recognizing methods of selecting an effective organizational approach to use in narrative writing	☐
	19.4: Recognizing methods of developing narrative writing that employs literary devices and techniques	☐
	19.5: Recognizing methods of developing narrative writing that establishes a distinct point of view, tone, and mood	☐
	19.6: Recognizing methods of developing narrative writing that is creative, compelling, and insightful	☐

MODES OF WRITING

PERSONALIZED STUDY PLAN

KNOWN MATERIAL/ SKIP IT

PAGE	COMPETENCY AND SKILL	
203	**20: Understand strategies for critical and analytical writing**	☐
	20.1: Demonstrating knowledge of the forms and purposes of critical and analytical writing	☐
	20.2: Recognizing methods of formulating a specific question to address through critical or analytical writing and of developing a thesis statement that makes a significant claim or conveys a purpose for writing	☐
	20.3: Recognizing methods of selecting an effective organizational approach to use in critical or analytical writing	☐
	20.4: Recognizing methods of developing a convincing critique or cogent analysis of a literary work	☐
	20.5: Relating elements of one literary work to elements of other literary works	☐

COMPETENCY 17
UNDERSTAND STRATEGIES FOR EXPOSITORY WRITING

SKILL 17.1 Demonstrating knowledge of the forms and purposes of expository writing (e.g., explaining a factual subject, reporting an event)

See Skill 5.7

SKILL 17.2 Recognizing methods of selecting and limiting a subject for expository writing

The formal outline has lost favor in recent years as a way of controlling thesis statement development, but helping students develop a working sentence outline will improve their ability to write coherently. If the essay conveys a particular perspective on a subject, the form will be persuasive discourse.

The thesis will be arguable and will have two possible sides. Take the example "The best way to control illegal immigration is to build a fence." This is only one perspective on the immigration issue. Another perspective might be "The best way to control illegal immigration is to penalize companies that hire illegal immigrants." In either case, the supporting arguments should be determined ahead of time. A useful tool for students when developing this kind of essay is to ask the questions "Why?" and "How?" of the topic sentence, then use the answers as topic sentences in the development of the essay. This technique will keep the argument's development on track.

For example, if you ask why "the best way to control illegal immigration is to build a fence along the border," you have several possible answers: (1) "An adequate physical barrier will prevent the individuals and groups who are now crossing over from coming into the United States." (2) "Border guards are not sufficient to stop individuals and groups." (3) "Penalizing companies that hire illegal workers is too difficult and doesn't work." If you ask "how," then you can answer, "Instead of spending the money on more border guards, that money can be used to pay for the fence."

It's best to develop at least three points. This will not produce a formal outline, but it will provide a working outline that can be changed as each section of the essay is developed.

> **SKILL 17.3** Recognizing methods of formulating a specific question to address through expository writing and of developing a thesis statement that provides a focus for writing

See Skill 14.4

> **SKILL 17.4** Recognizing methods of selecting an effective organizational approach to use in expository writing *(e.g., cause and effect)*

The first decision a writer makes is the purpose for a particular writing project. If the purpose is expository—providing information about a particular topic—then the next question regards how to organize the information to communicate what the writer has in mind. Students need a tool kit for developing expository essays; the following tools should be in that kit.

Citing Particulars, Instances, Examples, and Illustrations

Citing examples is probably the easiest and often the best way to clarify a general statement. For example, if the point of an expository essay is, "The houses in our block represent the worst characteristics of modern tract-house architecture," then citing examples and explaining in the negative aspects of tract- house architecture by referring to particular houses is the most obvious way to develop it. This is an important form of development for students to master; it will be useful for many writing situations, including writing essay answers on exams.

Check here for eleven graphic organizers to teach cause and effect:

www.greece.k12.ny.us /instruction/ela/6-12/Tools /cause%20and%20effect .pdf

Incident and Extended Illustration

Instead of providing a series of instances, the writer might make a point by telling a story or describing a single illustration in some detail. If the point of the essay is that "running for the U.S. presidency today requires extraordinary fundraising skills," the development might include an extended account of George W. Bush or Bill Clinton, with a focus on how they raised the funds to finance their campaigns. This extended illustration will require some research, of course. However, students might also choose a topic with which they are familiar and develop it by using an incident or extended illustration from their own experience.

Cause and Effect

We use cause-and-effect reasoning regularly in our daily lives and conversations. The statement, "The beekeeping business is declining in America because the use of insecticides is killing off the bees," can be developed by exploring the causes of the excessive use of insecticides and the ways in which they are killing off bees. Students need help learning to use cause-and-effect reasoning because of the tendency to fall into the post-hoc-ergo-propter-hoc fallacy. Just because one event occurred after another does not necessarily mean that one caused the other. The connection between the two events must be established before the reasoning can be considered valid.

Analogy

Helping students develop skills to make comparisons between the unknown and the familiar will be useful in all their writing exercises. Analogy is the most common tool for this skill. In analogy, the writer draws a parallel between the point being made and an illustration that is familiar. Victor Hugo described the Battle of Waterloo as a giant letter A. Aldous Huxley said that life is like a game of chess. The similarities must be clear, or the analogy will not work.

Comparison and Contrast

Comparison-and-contrast technique is similar to analogy, but in this case, the two examples are compared example by example. A proposition like "Boston is not a small New York" calls for side-by-side comparisons of the two cities showing ways in which they are alike and ways in which they are not. Students might compare their grade school experiences with their high school experiences, or where they live now with where they lived previously.

Restatement and Amplification

Sometimes an extended restatement of the topic with amplifications makes the point clear.

MODES OF WRITING

> **SKILL 17.5** Recognizing methods of selecting effective and appropriate supporting details to use in expository writing *(e.g., statistics, examples)*

Writers and speakers use important rhetorical techniques to clarify their main ideas and to keep their audiences involved.

Parallelism

PARALLELISM gives two or more parts of a sentence a similar form so as to give the whole a definite pattern. Coordinated ideas are arranged in phrases, sentences, and paragraphs that balance one element with another of equal importance and similar wording. The repetition of sounds, meanings, and structures serves to order, emphasize, and highlight relationships. In its simplest form, parallelism consists of single words that have a slight variation in meaning: "ordain and establish" or "overtake and surpass." Sometimes three or more units are parallel, such as "Reading maketh a full man, conference a ready man, and writing an exact man" (Francis Bacon, "Of Studies").

> **PARALLELISM:** a literary device that gives two or more parts of a sentence a similar form

Lacking parallelism:
She likes cooking, jogging, and to **read**.

Parallel:
She likes cooking, jogging, and **reading**.

Lacking parallelism:
The dog ran across the yard, jumped over the fence, and **down the alley he sprinted**.

Parallel:
The dog ran across the yard, jumped over the fence, and **sprinted down the alley**.

Analogy

ANALOGIES are used to clarify an unfamiliar point by referring to the familiar. When employing the method of analogy, it should always be possible to show that the resemblances noted are relevant on the point to be established, whereas the differences are irrelevant. In many cases, it is difficult to be sure of this distinction; arguments from analogy are therefore precarious unless supported by independently establishable considerations.

> **ANALOGY:** a literary device used to clarify an unfamiliar point by referring to the familiar

Writing a book of poetry is like dropping a rose petal down the Grand Canyon and waiting for the echo. (Don Marquis)

Humor

HUMOR is the ability or quality of people, objects, or situations to evoke feelings of amusement in others. The term encompasses a form of entertainment or human communication that evokes such feelings, or which makes people laugh or feel happy. As such, humor applies to writing that makes people laugh or that amuses them. Many famous writers, such as Mark Twain, have been defined by their use of humor. Writing comedy for the stage or television has developed as an entirely new subcategory for writers.

HUMOR: a literary device used to evoke feelings of amusement in others

Humor may be achieved through the use of exaggeration, understatement, irony, words that sound funny, jokes, stereotyping, and word play, to name a few. Humor is difficult to write successfully. More often than not, student attempts fall flat because it is a writing form that simply requires more maturity than most students have achieved. Student attempts to be funny should be dealt with gently. Even if the attempt may be ridiculous or even ludicrous, approval on the part of the teacher might lead to improvement.

> Example of student humor:
> What did the people say when they hung the vassal?
> Serf's up.

Repetition

Studied repetition can be an effective rhetorical device if used skillfully. However, with students, repetition is often careless and leads to wordy and amateurish writing. Students should develop the ability to find synonyms for often-used terms in an essay that will not seem pretentious or obvious. Sometimes, a sentence needs to be rewritten to eliminate a careless repetition.

> Example
> *"Users of the library often use little care in handling books"* can become *"Users of the library are often careless in handling books."*

Illustrations

Carefully used illustrations can bring a dull piece of writing alive and make a cloudy point clear. It's wise to promote in students the tendency to illustrate. They will become better writers if they develop this tendency and skill.

Varied Language

There is always the tendency on the part of a reader, even a serious one who desires to glean the meaning of a particular written piece, to experience glazed-over eyes and drooping eyelids. There are many things a writer can do to avoid this reader reaction, and the most important one is to vary the language. There are many ways to do this.

Notice how the three sentences in the above paragraph begin with the same empty subject-verb construction (There is…There are…There are). Did your eyes glaze over? Did you have to reread the paragraph to understand it clearly? What exactly are "things" and "ways"?

The following are some proven techniques for varying your writing style:

- Avoid writing only long or only short paragraphs
- Write a variety of sentence patterns
    - Avoid writing only simple sentences, even if they are embellished with phrases and modifiers
    - Avoid writing only one form of a complex sentence
    - Having the adverbial clause appear at the beginning of a sentence frequently can become boring
    - Move the adverbial clause to the middle of the sentence sometimes and to the end sometimes
    - Avoid writing only compound sentences or only compound sentences in one form
    - Using "therefore" over and over becomes monotonous
- Paragraphs should be written in a variety of forms—topic sentence first, in the middle, or at the end, for instance

SKILL 17.6 Recognizing methods of developing expository writing that is clear, concise, and coherent

See Skill 5.5

COMPETENCY 18
UNDERSTAND STRATEGIES FOR PERSUASIVE WRITING

SKILL 18.1 Demonstrating knowledge of the forms and purposes of persuasive writing (e.g., stating an opinion, influencing beliefs)

In classical rhetoric, the Greek term translated "introduction" means "a leading into." The Latin term means "beginning a web" by mounting a woof or laying a warp. The basic function of the introduction, then, is to fill in the background and lead the reader into the discourse. Introductions inform the readers of the purpose of the discourse and dispose them to being receptive to what is written.

One way to elicit reader interest is to show that the subject is important, curious, or interesting. An introduction may show that although the points may seem improbable, they are, in fact, true. Also, the introduction may show that the subject has been neglected, misunderstood, or misrepresented. It may explain an unusual mode of development or forestall some misconception of the purpose. The introduction may also rouse interest with an anecdotal lead-in.

An important function of the beginning section of a persuasive discourse is the statement of fact, where the essential facts of the piece are presented. This can be seen easily in a court trial where the accusing lawyer, usually the prosecutor, lays out the facts in the case. A good example of statement of fact can be seen in the trial *State of Tennessee v. John Thomas Scopes* in Rhea County, Tennessee:

> That John Thomas Scopes, heretofore on the 24th of April 1925, in the county aforesaid, then and there, unlawfully did willfully teach in the public schools of Rhea County, Tennessee, which said public schools are supported in part and in whole by the public school fund of the state, a certain theory and theories that deny the story of the divine creation of man as taught in the Bible, and did teach instead thereof that man has descended from a lower order of animals, he, the said John Thomas Scopes, being at the time, and prior thereto, a teacher in the public schools of Rhea County, Tennessee, aforesaid, against the peace and dignity of the State.

MODES OF WRITING

> **SKILL 18.2** Recognizing methods of establishing a clear position or controlling idea in persuasive writing

You should differentiate between "subject" and "thesis" for your students. The subject is the topic of the discourse. For example, it is not enough to decide that "democracy" is the subject or topic one is going to write about. First, something must be predicated of the subject. The subject must be converted into a proposition. For example:

Democracy functions best when people are educated.

Now we have a thesis. Many aspects of the subject "democracy" could be developed in an essay, and many have been, but the burden lies with the writer to decide which aspect to address in this particular piece. Once that aspect has been determined, the writer must develop a thesis sentence.

For students, a cardinal principle when writing a thesis statement is that *it must be stated in a single declarative sentence*. As soon as the student writer launches into the second sentence, he or she has wandered off into development and does not clarify the thesis statement. However, experienced writers can depart from this expected formula.

The importance of having a declarative thesis statement cannot be overstated. For example, a hortatory sentence like, "Let us fight to preserve the integrity of our democracy" or interrogatory sentences like, "Is democracy a feasible form of government?" leave the subject cloudy, uncertain, and tentative, and are very difficult to develop. Therefore, the thesis will be clearly and firmly stated if the predicate asserts or denies something about the subject: "The integrity of our democracy can be preserved only if we fight to maintain it"; or "Democracy is (is not) a feasible form of government." Both of these statements lend themselves to clear supporting development.

The thesis statement forces the writers to determine at the outset what exactly they want to say about the chosen subject. It also lays the foundation for a unified, coherent discourse. The thesis statement often suggests some of the supporting statements that will occur in the body, too.

Prewriting facilitates a thesis statement. The writing teacher does well to require that students prewrite ideas about the subject before attempting to write a thesis statement. Prewriting should yield several possible thesis statements; these help students determine which one will be developed in this particular essay. Remember—the beginning of all good writing is a sharply defined thesis.

UNDERSTAND STRATEGIES FOR PERSUASIVE WRITING

SKILL 18.3 Recognizing methods of selecting an effective organizational approach to use in persuasive writing (e.g., logical order, order of importance)

Writers use a variety of organizational patterns so that a work has coherence and the relationship of ideas is clear.

The organization of a written work includes two factors: the order in which the writer has chosen to present the different parts of the discussion or argument and the relationships he or she constructs between these parts.

Written ideas need to be presented in a logical order so that a reader can follow the information easily and quickly. There are many different ways in which to order a series of ideas, but they all share one thing in common: to lead the reader along a desired path by giving a clear, strong presentation of the writer's main idea while avoiding backtracking and skipping around. Some of the ways in which a paragraph may be organized are listed in the table below.

Learn more about coherence:

www.accd.edu/sac/english/lirvin/wguides/Coherence.htm

Sequence of Events	In this type of organization, the details are presented in the order in which they have occurred. Paragraphs that describe a process or procedure, give directions, or outline a given period of time (such as a day or a month) are often arranged chronologically.
Statement Support	In this type of organization, the main idea is stated, and the rest of the paragraph explains or proves it. This organizational structure is also referred to as relative order or order of importance. This type of order can be organized in one of four ways: most to least, least to most, most-least-most, and least-most-least.
Comparison-Contrast	In this type of organization, a paragraph describes the differences between or similarities of two or more ideas, actions, events, or things. Usually, the topic sentence describes the basic relationship between the ideas or items, and the rest of the paragraph explains this relationship.
Classification	In this type of organization, the paragraph presents grouped information about a topic. The topic sentence usually states the general category, and the rest of the sentences show how various elements of the category have a common base and also how they differ from the common base.
Cause and Effect	This pattern describes how two or more events are connected. The main sentence usually states the primary cause(s) and the primary effect(s) and how they are basically connected. The rest of the sentences explain the connection—how one event caused the next.
Spatial/Place	In this type of organization, certain descriptions are organized according to the location of items in relation to each other and to a larger context. The orderly arrangement guides the reader's eye as he or she mentally envisions the scene or place being described.
Example, Clarification, and Definition	These types of organizations show, explain, or elaborate on the main idea. This can be done by showing specific cases, examining meaning multiple times, or extensively describing one term.

MODES OF WRITING

> **SKILL 18.4** **Recognizing methods of selecting effective and appropriate supporting details to use in persuasive writing** *(e.g., facts, reasons, appeals)*

The three appeals are *rational, ethical* (defined as establishing credibility), and emotional, according to the original Greek rhetoricians; these appeals have stood the tests of time. Today, even with all the multimedia tools available, there are three possibilities for persuading another person to accept a position or to take some action. How do politicians persuade large groups of people to accept their points of view? How do they persuade those people to take action? They use these three means of persuasion.

Rational Appeal

Rational appeal involves logical reasoning. If an essay is going to change anyone's mind, it must make sense. Once the thesis is established, asking the questions "How?" or "Why?" leads to possible reasons the writer can use to persuade.

For example:

> Building a strong fence on the border will solve the immigration crisis.

Why? (1) "It will stop those border crossings that the scattered border patrol officers have not been able to stop up till now." (2) "It will give the border patrol officers the tool they need to stop those who try to cross the border illegally." How? "The cost of the fence can be covered by a decrease in the number of officers now guarding the border." Any thesis should have at least three supporting points.

> *Any thesis should have at least three supporting points.*

Ethical Appeal

The rhetoricians defined ethical appeal as establishing credibility. Some people will accept a speaker's point of view just because of who he or she is. A veteran border patrol officer has credibility regarding protection of the border because that officer knows more about the issues than others do. The governor of a border state usually has credibility, too. When Governor Schwarzenegger of California addresses border issues, people listen.

There are many ways to establish credibility. The background discussion that begins an essay or speech is a good place to demonstrate that the writer/speaker knows the issue well enough to take a position on it. The credentials of the writer/speaker may persuade the audience that this person is credible.

UNDERSTAND STRATEGIES FOR PERSUASIVE WRITING

Emotional Appeal

Most people like to think that they make decisions on the basis of logic or reasoning, but the truth is that few change their minds or take action unless they have been moved emotionally. An argument that relies too heavily on emotion, though, will destroy credibility.

There are two major ways to create emotional appeal. The first way involves describing an experience in such way that the reader/listener can participate in the experience. An argument against returning illegal immigrants to Mexico often relies on heart-rending stories of families, especially children, who will suffer if they are sent back. Descriptive language is the tool to use to make an experience available through one of the senses, as in describing a scene of suffering children in such a way that the reader/listener can "see" the children in his or her mind's eye or "hear" them crying.

The second way to move a reader/listener emotionally is by using "charged" words—words that carry emotional overtones themselves such as "cruel" or "callous" or "unfeeling." Others are "murderers," "liars," and "prejudice."

SKILL 18.5 Recognizing methods of anticipating questions, concerns, and counterarguments for points made in persuasive writing and of incorporating effective responses to them into the writing

---

The two forms of reasoning used to support an argument are inductive and deductive. Inductive reasoning goes from the particular to the general. For example, I observe that all the green apples I have ever tasted are sour: (1) I have tasted some from my grandfather's orchard; (2) I have tasted the Granny Smiths that my mother buys in the grocery store and uses to make pies; (3) I tasted the green apples in my friend's kitchen. All are sour (conclusion). Then I can *generalize* that all green apples are sour. This is inductive reasoning, a prevalent aspect of the way we think and deal with each other and an essential aspect to persuasive discourse.

Deductive reasoning, on the other hand, reverses the order by going from general to particular. The generalization drawn in the previous illustration, "All green apples are sour," can be used to make a statement about a particular apple. A new variety of green apples has appeared in the grocery store. Arguing from the generalization that all green apples are sour, I may reject this new variety because I am sure that they are going to be sour. Deductive reasoning is based on the syllogism:

Learn more about deductive and inductive argument:

www.iep.utm.edu/d/ded-ind.htm

MODES OF WRITING

> *All green apples are sour.*
> *This apple is green.*
> *Therefore, this apple is sour.*

When a prosecutor presents a trial in a courtroom, he typically puts forth the statement of fact: On November 2 in an alley between Smith and Jones Street at the 400 block, Stacy Highsmith was brutally raped and murdered. The coroner has concluded that she was bludgeoned with a blunt instrument at or around midnight, and her body was found by a shopkeeper the next morning. (There may be other "knowns" presented in the statement of fact.)

Following the laying out of the facts of the case, the prosecutor will use inductive reasoning to accuse the person on trial for the crime. For example: (1) Terry Large, the accused, was seen in the neighborhood at 11:30 PM on November 2; (2) He was carrying a carpenter's toolkit, which was later recovered; (3) A hammer with evidence of blood on it was found in that toolkit; and (4) The blood was tested, and it matched the victim's DNA. Ultimately, the prosecutor will reach the generalization: Terry Large murdered Stacy Highsmith in the alley in the middle of the night on November 2.

Also see Skill 18.4

SKILL 18.6 Recognizing methods of selecting an appropriate style, tone, voice, and diction to use in persuasive writing

See Skill 7.6

COMPETENCY 19
UNDERSTAND STRATEGIES FOR NARRATIVE WRITING

> **SKILL 19.1** Demonstrating knowledge of the forms and purposes of narrative writing *(e.g., relating a personal experience, portraying a character, exploring points of view, imagining an event or situation)*

Narrative writing presents ordered events to inform or to entertain. Both in fiction and in nonfiction, the goal of narrative writing is to portray a series of events that occurred to a person or people. Narrative writing can be used in the following writing tasks:

- Anecdotes
- Personal writing or memoirs
- Creative writing
- Fiction

Learn more about teaching literature using narratives:
www.teachingliterature.org/teachingliterature/chapter7/activities.htm

An important element for good narrative writing is theme. Typically more important than most plot elements, the theme of the story represents the underlying message, moral, ideal, or lesson that the writer wants to communicate to the readers. Common literary themes include love, money, good versus evil, and jealousy. Literature does not openly state its theme. Instead, the theme is conveyed through settings, plots, and characters. Good writing will suggest the theme without directly mentioning it.

Generating ideas for themes or ideas for narratives is the first step of the writing process, but it can be a daunting task for student writers. Successful authors often offer the following advice when helping other writers to generate good ideas for their writing:

- **Freewriting:** Write nonstop for ten minutes. When you are brainstorming, just write what comes to your mind. Do not evaluate your ideas at this time. Jot down notes, thoughts, descriptions, names, events, themes ... anything that comes to mind.

- **Keep a journal:** Journals help writers record, express, organize, and explore their thoughts and ideas. Any one journal entry or event from your life could spark an idea later on for a good narrative piece. A journal also

Learn more about journal writing:
www.education-world.com/a_curr/curr144.shtml

MODES OF WRITING

allows students to consider their own experiences and how they may play into a future character or plot.

- Read: Read as much as you can. Ideas, characters, or storylines from other writers may produce ideas within a student's head for his or her own story. A character or storyline might remind students of something in their lives or inspire an original idea. Reading also provides students with examples of what makes a good story.

- Collaborate with peers: Two minds are sometimes better than one, and working with peers may provide students with that one idea or memory that may be just what the writer needs to get started.

- Short stories: Sometimes when the pressure of writing an entire, detailed story is removed, a good short story may evolve. Students and/or teachers can analyze several short stories to determine which might have the potential to be developed into a more detailed piece. Then, a more thorough story is more likely to emerge naturally during the revision process.

- Self or peer questioning: When questioned about their experiences, young writers may trigger ideas for stories that can be used or adapted as a plot for a good narrative.

- Webbing/word associations: Webbing allows students to write down their ideas in a somewhat organized way. Students are asked during both webbing and word associations to write down words that are connected, triggered from one another, or linked in some way. This quick-thinking exercise may produce ideas or thoughts that can be developed into themes or ideas for writing.

Learn more about student-centered learning:

www.wcer.wisc.edu /step/ep301/Fall2000 /Tochonites/stu_cen.html

SKILL 19.2 Recognizing methods of selecting and limiting a subject for narrative writing

Typically, the purpose of writing narratives is to entertain, and maintaining a reader's interest is often an important goal of a writer. What good is a book, a short story, or a newspaper article that doesn't get read?

Developing creative and unique storylines is a good way to maintain readers' interest, and this factor should be addressed in the planning/brainstorming process with students. Teachers should help students develop good plots for their narrative pieces. Stories with high levels of human interest often maintain readers' interest well. When a story relates to events that most people experience or face, the chance that the reader will remain interested in the story increases.

UNDERSTAND STRATEGIES FOR NARRATIVE WRITING

However, most teachers will tell you that after reading the fourth story about a lost pet or a move to a new state, their own interest begins to wane. That is not to say that these stories are not of human interest and should not be written, but students need to be guided towards finding unique ways to tell their stories by changing the perspective or thickening the plot. Suspense, adventure, mystery, love, and humor are just some of the good plot elements to keep readers reading.

Creating interesting characters is one way to maintain reader interest. Characters who seem real will help readers connect with or feel for that character. Once the readers are interested in what will happen to the character, their interest will compel them to read the story. Well-developed and thoroughly researched settings also make a story unique and interesting.

Technical elements can help maintain readers' interest, too. For example, dialogue not only helps to develop good characters, but it also helps with the pace and flow of the story. Another technical way to maintain readers' interest is by varying points of view. Sometimes, authors change the writing perspective by chapters or sections of the book to keep the reader interested in how the story will be presented. Finally, varying sentence styles and structures as well as using unique transitions and chapter openings help maintain readers' interest in the narrative.

SKILL 19.3 **Recognizing methods of selecting an effective organizational approach to use in narrative writing** *(e.g., chronological order, in medias res, flashback)*

Authors have many techniques for creating effective narrative plots, settings and characters. Teachers should expose students to a variety of these techniques within the writing process as formal or mini-lessons so that students can begin to practice and use these methods in their written work.

Transitions

Technical transitions are important elements that add to a piece of the writing's flow. However, these transitions aid more in the flow of sentences and paragraphs than in the flow of the entire narrative.

The following are examples of transitions:

another reason	in addition	first of all	besides that
furthermore	also	moreover	for example

Beside these words and phrases, transitions can be sentences or paragraphs that act as two-way indicators. They show the relationship of ideas to each other and move the reader from one point to another. Narrative transitions are transitions that provide logical and smooth connections between events in the story. These transitions are often used between chapters, sections of chapters, and as the character moves through various settings. Effective transitions are essential to keeping the flow of the story straightforward so that the reader can follow the story easily.

Flashbacks

Another device authors can use to add depth to their plots is the flashback. Flashbacks provide information about the past during the course of the current action of a story. Flashbacks can provide the reader with background information, but writers need to be sure to "lead" the reader with an effective transition. An example of a simple transition is: "Heather recalled that morning at work." After a flashback, the author must link the reader back to the current action so that it can be continued.

Suspense

Suspense is the feeling of uncertainty or that something is about to happen. Authors use suspense to maintain readers' interest, and they do so by using descriptive language, foreshadowing, and other techniques to keep the reader reading. The use of suspense/tension adds another level to the plot and compels the reader to see what the outcome will be. Suspense is an effective technique to use in thrillers, mysteries, and other dramatic narrative pieces.

Dialogue

Dialogue is an important aspect of most narrative pieces. Without conversations, readers can easily become bored with a story. Narration can become long, tedious, and uninteresting without dialogue.

When used properly, dialogue can accomplish any or all of the following:

- Keep the story moving
- Display characters' thoughts and personalities
- Create a "hook" for the opening of the story
- Condense or replace large amounts of background
- "Show, don't tell"
- Add humor

Some elements to remember when writing dialogue are:

- **Dialogue should read like natural speech:** For example, an elderly doctor would not use the term "awesome," just as an average tenth grader is unlikely to use the word "succinctly."

- **Use dialogue that serves a purpose:** Dialogue should move the story while making the characters seem real. If the dialogue doesn't accomplish this, take it out and use narration instead.

- **Keep dialogue short:** Generally, three or fewer sentences is adequate for one character to say at a time. You don't have to say everything at once; readers will recall the details.

- **Mix dialogue and action:** Physical details help to break up dialogue while keeping the story going. For example, "I can't believe it!" exclaimed Beth. She crumpled her test paper between her fists until it resembled a snowball. "I studied for three hours for that test!"

- **Vary taglines:** But don't overdo it! Writers do not need to consult a thesaurus for every version of "said," but they should be encouraged to select a tagline that adds to the purpose of the conversation.

- **Avoid stereotypes, profanity, and slang:** Seek to be objective rather than shocking or too cool.

- **Punctuate dialogue correctly:** Without correct punctuation, meaning could be misconstrued.

Some stories by Ernest Hemingway rest completely on dialogue. In "A Clean Well-Lighted Place," the taglines are not always clear, and the punctuation can be confusing. Understanding the meaning can be challenging.

Mood

The mood of a narrative is an important element in keeping the structure and purpose of a piece held together without being blatantly obvious. When writing a narrative, authors automatically develop a mood with their choices of words, plot, characters, and more. Moods can include the satirical, determined, hopeful, confused, reflective, remorseful, light, or serious. However, mood is also the essence of what the reader takes away from the piece.

Foreshadowing

Foreshadowing is a literary device authors employ to provide hints for events to come in the plot (and therefore maintain reader interest and add dimension to the narrative piece). Foreshadowing aids the author in creating suspense/tension, providing necessary information (for a future event), and more. Foreshadowing can appear anywhere in a story, but it is exceptionally useful at the end of chapters or sections, acting as a cliffhanger to keep the reader engaged. When reading novels with their classes, teachers should help students recognize foreshadowing so they may later use the same device in their own writing.

In Medias Res

Latin for "into the middle of things," *in medias res* is a literary technique authors use when they want to start the action in the middle of the story rather than at the beginning. Authors then use flashbacks and dialogue to introduce the characters, setting, and conflict to the reader.

> **SKILL 19.4** **Recognizing methods of developing narrative writing that employs literary devices and techniques** *(e.g., figurative language, symbolism)*

See Skill 19.3

> **SKILL 19.5** **Recognizing methods of developing narrative writing that establishes a distinct point of view, tone, and mood** *(e.g., creating interesting dialogue, choosing sensory details)*

Students will improve their narrative writing skills by recognizing the elements of a good story.

Plots

Effective plots are essential to narrative writing and are complemented by the narrative's characters, settings, and points of view. The best plots are driven by the characters. To develop an effective plot, the writer must incorporate and balance meaningful dialogue, necessary interior thoughts, and characters' actions and reactions.

Characters

Describing a character's physical features is only the beginning of character development. Students often feel that they develop good characters by describing the physical features, but excellent character development takes more. Physical features need to be balanced with actions, thoughts, temperament, mannerisms, and other traits. A character's action and motives are essential to the plot of the story and lead to a more well-rounded character.

Students should be given opportunities to practice developing different types of characters. One activity involves having the teacher "act out" specific traits while the students identify these traits based on the teacher's pantomime. Sad, happy, and shy are easy traits to start with, and then the teacher can encourage students to suggest more difficult traits (such as jealous, lazy, cruel, witty) to portray.

Devising a list of possible character traits is the easy part. Bringing those traits alive through writing in the narrative, though, is the challenging part. To help bridge this gap, writing classes often use an exercise called "Show, Don't Tell." The objective of this exercise and style of writing is to have students describe the character's traits without coming straight out and telling the reader what those traits are.

For example, a student should be encouraged to change a statement such as:

> *William was shy about speaking in front of the class.*

This sentence simply tells the reader that the character is shy. A more descriptive characterization would be:

> *William slowly walked to the podium at the front of the room. He lowered his eyes to his papers as he turned to face the class. A fluttering sensation filled his stomach as he inhaled to begin his speech.*

Use of more descriptive language leads to more interesting characters and a more effective plot line. In addition, such phrasing builds suspense and makes the experience more realistic to the reader—all elements that help maintain readers' interest in the story.

Settings

Effective settings enhance quality narrative pieces. When authors are thorough in their descriptions of unique settings, the reader feels more connected to the story, perhaps almost as if they are there. Even the simplest setting with which many readers would be familiar (i.e., modern-day suburbia) warrants clear description of the area, time of day, time of year, and so on. Like with character development, "show, don't tell" is an excellent exercise to create an effective setting.

For example, instead of:

> Sarah walked to the park in late autumn.

The author could write:

> A crisp breeze cooled Sarah's cheeks as she quickened her pace, hurrying along the path littered with golden leaves.

Again, these details help the reader feel as a part of the story.

Unique settings, however, require much more detailed descriptions. Research is often needed to depict accurate historical settings or settings in another country or region. For example, writers might research traditional language or slang in a region with which they are not familiar. Science fiction and fantasy require extremely in-depth description if the reader is to visualize a world that is only known in the author's mind.

Points of View

In narrative writing, the point of view is the voice of the story. A story's point of view is not necessarily that of the author. An effective point of view encourages the reader to connect with the narrator (usually the main character), not the author, of the story. The ability to use viewpoints effectively is a mark of a good writer.

Most narrative pieces are written in the first-person or the third-person point of view. In the first-person point of view, sentences are written as though the character is speaking or telling the story. The following is an example of first-person point of view:

> I woke up suddenly. Realizing I was late, I grabbed my tote bag and ran out of the door.

The benefit of writing in the first person is that all the opinions and thoughts of that one character's mind are accessible to the reader. However, the limit of this style is just the same—that this character is the only viewpoint the reader has, and we are limited to what this character knows.

Stories can also be written two ways in the third person: the third-person omniscient or the third-person limited point of view. The third-person omniscient can move among different characters' viewpoints with knowledge of everyone's thoughts, actions, and experience. The third-person limited follows one character throughout the book and does not pretend to understand everything about every character.

To maintain interest and/or to create a different reading experience, some authors switch a story's point of view among characters as they go through chapters or sections of the book. With this method, characters can take turns being read in first person or third-person limited, and the reader is eventually exposed to the thoughts and minds of more than one character.

> **SKILL 19.6** **Recognizing methods of developing narrative writing that is creative, compelling, and insightful** *(e.g., incorporating an inventive plotline and dynamic characters, explicating a significant theme, building actions around a conflict)*

See Skills 19.2 and 19.3

COMPETENCY 20
UNDERSTAND STRATEGIES FOR CRITICAL AND ANALYTICAL WRITING

> **SKILL 20.1** **Demonstrating knowledge of the forms and purposes of critical and analytical writing** *(e.g., critiquing or evaluating a literary work, interpreting a literary work)*

See Skill 8.2

> **SKILL 20.2** **Recognizing methods of formulating a specific question to address through critical or analytical writing and of developing a thesis statement that makes a significant claim or conveys a purpose for writing**

See Skill 16.2

MODES OF WRITING

> **SKILL 20.3** Recognizing methods of selecting an effective organizational approach to use in critical or analytical writing *(e.g., comparison-and-contrast)*

See Skill 15.2

> **SKILL 20.4** Recognizing methods of developing a convincing critique or cogent analysis of a literary work *(e.g., incorporating specific words and phrases from a literary work to support a claim)*

Just as you talk to different people in different ways, so do you write in different styles and levels of formality. Students should learn that writers use different writing styles to accomplish their purposes and to reach their different audiences.

Is a business letter outdated? Although much business-letter writing has been relegated to e-mail communications, letters are still a valuable form of communication. A carefully written letter can be powerful. It can convince, persuade, alienate, entice, motivate, and/or create good will.

As with any other communication, you need to know information about your receiver. If there will be more than one receiver of the message, write for the largest or most important group of readers without "writing down" to any of those who will read and be affected or influenced by the letter. Sending more than one form of the letter to the various receivers may be appropriate in some cases.

Learn more about writing a cover letter:

www.womenwork.org/career/careercenter/Getting_Hired/coverletter.htm

Purpose is the most powerful factor in writing a business letter. What is the letter expected to accomplish? Is it intended to motivate the receiver to act or to act in a specific manner? If so, you should clearly define the letter's purpose for yourself before beginning. To avoid procrastination, include a time deadline for the response.

Why should you choose a letter format as your channel of communication?

- It's easy to keep a record of the transaction.
- The message can be edited and perfected before it is transmitted.
- It facilitates the handling of details.
- It's ideal for communicating complex information.
- It's a good way to disseminate mass messages at a relatively low cost.

Because letters have external readers, they typically use formal language. They should be straightforward and courteous. The writing should be concise and complete; otherwise, more than one exchange of letters or phone calls to get the message across may be necessary.

A complaint is a different kind of business letter. Complaints can come under the classification of a "bad news" business letter, and guidelines are helpful when writing this kind of letter. A positive writing style can overcome much of the inherent negativity of a letter of complaint. No matter how right you may be, maintaining self-control and courtesy and avoiding demeaning or blaming language is more likely to be effective. Abruptness, condescension, or harshness of tone will not help achieve your purpose, particularly if you are requesting a positive response such as reimbursement for a bad product or some help in righting a wrong that may have been done to you. The goal is to solve the specific problem and to retain the good will of the receiver whenever possible.

Induction is better than deduction for this type of communication. Beginning with the details and building to the statement of the problem generally has the effect of softening the bad news. Beginning with an opening that will serve as a buffer can be useful. The same is true for the closing. Leave the reader with a favorable impression by writing a closing paragraph that will generate good will rather than bad.

E-mail has revolutionized business communications. It has most of the advantages of business letters and the added ones of immediacy, lower costs, and convenience. Even very long reports can be attached to an e-mail. At the same time, a two-line message can be sent and a response received immediately, bringing together the features of a postal system and the telephone.

E-mail has an unwritten code of behavior that includes restrictions on how informal the writing can be. The level of accepted business conversation is usually also acceptable in e-mails. Capital letters and bolding are considered shouting and are usually frowned on.

Remind students that e-mail messages, even if intended for just one reader, may eventually reach a much wider audience. In recent years, a number of e-mail writers have found themselves in embarrassing situations or legal troubles because of the circulation of their personal e-mails on the Internet. When writers need to address a sensitive, unpleasant or controversial matter, they should consult state laws to determine whether personal privacy laws protect the correspondence. If the law does protect such correspondence from being circulated by the addressee, then the writers may wish to mention this in their messages to forestall publication. Otherwise, clarity, concision, and civility in written works will protect writers.

MODES OF WRITING

Personal Letters

When writing personal notes or letters, the writer needs to keep the following key matters in mind:

- Once the topic is determined, the writer must determine the appropriate tone to introduce and express it. Is humor appropriate? Seriousness? Bluntness or subtlety? Does the situation call for formal or informal language? The answers to these questions will depend, in good part, on the writer's relationship to the reader. Plan appropriately for the situation and audience.

- Does the writer's introduction clearly explain the topic/situation to a reader who doesn't know or feel what the reader knows or feels? Don't assume that the writer and reader are of the same mindset. Use a checklist to make sure all key information is clearly and concisely expressed.

- If a note or letter involves a request, what type of response/result does the writer desire? Devise a strategy or strategies for achieving a desired outcome.

- If a note or letter involves a complaint about the reader, the writer needs to decide whether to ask for particular amends or to let the reader decide what, if anything, to do. If no amends are requested, the writer may wish to suggest ideas that would help avoid similar conflicts in the future. Asking the reader for his or her opinions is also a possibility.

- If a timely response to any note or letter is needed, the writer must mention this.

Provide students in-class opportunities to write a variety of personal notes and letters, whether involving real-life or hypothetical situations. Invitations, thank-you notes, complaints, requests for favors, or personal updates represent a few of the options available. Have students experiment with a variety of tones and strategies in a particular piece of personal correspondence. Structure in-class activities to allow for peer feedback.

SKILL 20.5 Relating elements of one literary work *(e.g., character, theme, style, point of view)* to elements of other literary works

Students should learn that characters in literature, fiction and nonfiction, reveal themselves in many ways. Authors populate their writing with a variety of personalities as a way to explore our relationships with the world.

Characterization

The choice the writer makes about the devices used to reveal character requires an understanding of human nature and the artistic skill to convey a personality to the reader. Characterization usually is accomplished subtly through dialogue, interior monologue, description, and the character's behavior. In some successful stories, the writer tells the reader directly what this character is like. However, sometimes there will be discrepancies between what the narrator tells the reader about the character and what is revealed through the character's actions. In this case, the narrator is unreliable, and that unreliability becomes an important and significant device for understanding the story.

Archetype

An archetype is an idealized model of a person, object, or concept from which similar instances are derived, copied, patterned, or emulated. In psychology, an archetype is a model of a person, personality, or behavior. Archetypes often appear in literature. An image, character, or pattern of circumstances that recurs frequently in literature can be considered an archetype. William Shakespeare, for example, is known for popularizing many archetypal characters. Although he based many of his characters on existing archetypes from fables and myths, Shakespeare's characters stand out against a complex, social literary landscape.

For example, Iago in *Othello* is the villain who masterminds plots; Polonius in *Hamlet* is the trusted adviser and doting father; Romeo and Juliet are the archetypical star-crossed lovers.

In Greek drama, *Oedipus Rex* has a structure that appears to be repeated in the lives of all men in the sense that all sons are replacements for their fathers. Faulkner, in "Barn Burning," provides an original example that calls forth this archetype.

There are many archetypes, and skillful and creative writers often rely on them to create successful literary contexts.

Examples of action archetypes:

- The search for the killer
- The search for salvation (or the Holy Grail)
- The search for the hero
- The descent into hell

Read complete books and articles on archetypes in literature:

www.questia.com
/library/literature
/literary-themes-and
-topics/archetypes-in
-literature.jsp

Examples of character archetypes:

- The double
- The scapegoat
- The prodigal son
- The Madonna and the Magdalene

The family has often been used as a recurring archetypal theme in literature, including Greek literature such as the *Medea*. Many of Shakespeare's plays also used this archetype: *Hamlet*, *Romeo and Juliet*, and *King Lear*, for example. Modern writers also use the family archetype, such as *Desire Under the Elms* by Eugene O'Neill and *A Streetcar Named Desire* by Tennessee Williams.

Toni Morrison, in her popular novel *Beloved*, uses the archetype of family by chronicling the difficulties the protagonist Sethe and her family face before, during, and after the Civil War. The result is a compelling picture of a family's response to the devastation brought on by slavery.

Genre

GENRE: a division of a particular form of art according to criteria particular to that form

A **GENRE** is a division of a particular form of art according to criteria particular to that form. Genres are formed by sets of conventions, and many works cross into multiple genres by way of borrowing and recombining these conventions. All works are recognized as either reflecting on or participating in the conventions of a particular genre. The major literary genres include poetry, fiction, and drama. However, each of these major genres may be broken down into several subgenres.

Poetry

Early attempts to define poetry focused on the uses of speech in rhetoric, drama, song, and comedy. Later, the concentration shifted to features such as repetition and rhyme and emphasized the aesthetics that distinguish poetry from prose. Since the mid-twentieth century, poetry has come to be more loosely defined as a fundamental creative act using language. Clearly, poetry is not a simple phenomenon to define, especially given the existence of numerous examples of poetic prose and of prosaic poetry. Nowadays, saying what poetry is not seems easier than saying what it is.

Poetry often uses particular forms and conventions to expand the literal meaning of words or to evoke emotional or sensual responses. Literary devices such as assonance, alliteration, and rhythm are sometimes used to achieve musical or incantatory effects. Poetry's use of ambiguity, symbolism, irony, and other stylistic elements often leaves a poem open to multiple interpretations. Similarly, metaphor and simile create a resonance between otherwise disparate images—a layering of meanings, forming connections previously not perceived.

Fiction

R. F. Dietrich and Roger H. Sundell, in *The Art of Fiction*, write the following:

> In its broadest sense, a fiction is any imaginative recreation or reconstruction of life. In this sense, not only are your daydreams fiction, but also the myths you daily create about yourself and others to help you explain life.

However, the term *fiction* is generally synonymous with literature. Fiction refers only to novels or short stories and is often divided into two categories: popular fiction (e.g., science fiction or mystery fiction) and literary fiction (e.g., works by Marcel Proust or William Faulkner). Typically, a work of fiction has a plot that eventually yields a climax, characters that carry the conflicts that lead to climax or resolution, and a discernible theme.

Drama

Drama is a literary form involving parts written for actors to perform. The term comes from the Greek word meaning "action." Dramas can be performed in various media: live performance, radio, film, or television. Drama is also often combined with music and dance, such as in opera, which is sung throughout; musicals, which include spoken dialogue and songs; or plays that have musical accompaniment, such as the Japanese Noh drama.

SAMPLE TEST

SAMPLE TEST

SAMPLE TEST

Media Literacy (Skills 1.1 – 2.5)

(Easy) (Skill 1.1)

1. What is not a characteristic of an effective editorial cartoon?

   A. It presents a message or point of view concerning people, events, or situations using caricature and symbolism to convey the cartoonist's ideas

   B. It has wit and humor, which is usually obtained by exaggeration that is slick and not used merely for comic effect

   C. It has a foundation in truth; that is, the characters must be recognizable to the viewer, and the point of the drawing must have some basis in fact even if it has a philosophical bias

   D. It seeks to reflect the editorial opinion of the newspaper that carries it

(Rigorous) (Skill 1.1)

2. What is the common advertising technique used by these advertising slogans?

   "It's everywhere you want to be."
   —Visa

   "Have it your way."
   —Burger King

   "When you care enough to send the very best."
   —Hallmark

   "Be all you can be."
   —U.S. Army

   A. Peer approval
   B. Rebelion
   C. Individuality
   D. Escape

(Average) (Skill 1.1)

3. Why are posters no longer as effective as they used to be?

   A. No one takes the time to look at them like they used to because people are too busy.

   B. Video and multimedia have taken over as a more popular method of persuading people.

   C. The cost of paper has become more than many politicians and companies can afford now that video and multimedia are more affordable.

   D. People no longer have the manpower to hang them in high-traffic locations.

(Easy) (Skill 1.2)

4. What is a positive aspect about print messages?

   A. They have longevity and are easily portable.
   B. They are understood by everyone.
   C. Print messages must be actively read.
   D. They appeal to a wider range of people.

(Rigorous) (Skill 1.2)

5. Compared with print, what is better about a graphic message?

   A. It is easier to create a graphic message.
   B. It takes less time to create a graphic message.
   C. Graphic messages convey a shorter range of information

(Average) (Skill 1.3)

6. How does the media influence consumers and their behavior?

   A. Through news and documentary programming
   B. Primarily through advertising
   C. Shows and other sitcoms
   D. By influencing body image

(Rigorous) (Skill 1.4)

7. The literary device of personification is used in which example below?

   A. "Beg me no beggary by soul or parents, whining dog!"
   B. "Happiness sped through the halls, cajoling as it went."
   C. "O wind thy horn, thou proud fellow."
   D. "And that one talent which is death to hide."

(Rigorous) (Skill 2.1)

8. In presenting a report to peers about the effects of Hurricane Katrina on New Orleans, the students wanted to use various media in their argument to persuade their peers that more needed to be done. Which of these would be the most effective?

   A. A PowerPoint presentation showing the blueprints of the levees before the flood and redesigned now for current construction
   B. A collection of music clips made by the street performers in the French Quarter before and after the flood
   C. A recent video showing the areas devastated by the floods and the current state of rebuilding
   D. A collection of recordings of interviews made by the various government officials and local citizens affected by the flooding

(Average) (Skill 2.1)

9. What is NOT included in still visual media?

   A. Speeches
   B. Pictures
   C. Drawings
   D. Charts and tables

(Rigorous) (Skill 2.3)

10. What is necessary in the development of moving visual media presentations?

    A. A storyboard must be utilized before the presentation can be developed.

    B. Capable designers must be employed at a fair rate of pay.

    C. A storyline or presentation rationale must be decided upon.

    D. An appropriate volume, pitch, voice, and rhythm must be utilized to increase the effectiveness of the presentation.

(Average) (Skill 2.4)

11. When making or preparing a presentation, what are some key aspects to keep in mind?

    A. Aesthetics, principals of communication, effective use of technology

    B. Font size, vocabulary used, and a receptive audience

    C. Whether films or filmstrips will be used

    D. The amount of audience engagement desired

Reading (Skills 3.1 – 6.4)

(Rigorous) (Skill 3.2)

12. Mr. Martin has a bag of letter tiles for every student in his class. He tells the students to make the word "cat" with their letter tiles. Next, Mr. Martin tells the students to change the word "cat" to "sat." Mr. Martin continues changing the first letter of the words to create rhyming words. This is an activity in:

    A. Phonics

    B. Fluency

    C. Phonemic awareness

    D. Comprehension

(Rigorous) (Skill 3.2)

13. A first grade student is reading a level D guided reading book aloud and his teacher is listening. The student gets stuck on one of the words and looks to the teacher for help. The teacher says, "What is the first sound?" Then she says, "Sound out the rest of the letters as you blend the sounds together." The teacher is teaching the student:

    A. Phonemic awareness

    B. Fluency

    C. Comprehension

    D. Phonics

SAMPLE TEST

(Rigorous) (Skill 3.2)

14. Mr. Miller is having his students participate in a reader's theater activity. Mr. Miller first read the short play aloud to the students in class. For the remainder of the week students read the play to themselves, with a partner, and at home for homework. The teacher is helping to develop:

    A. Phonemic awareness
    B. Phonics
    C. Fluency
    D. Comprehension

(Average) (Skill 3.6)

15. Written on the sixth-grade reading level, most of S. E. Hinton's novels (for instance, *The Outsiders*) have the greatest reader appeal with:

    A. Sixth graders
    B. Ninth graders
    C. Twelfth graders
    D. Adults

(Average) (Skill 3.6)

16. Which teaching method would best engage underachievers in the required senior English class?

    A. Assign use of glossary work and extensively footnoted excerpts of great works
    B. Have students take turns reading aloud the anthology selection
    C. Let students choose which readings they'll study and write about
    D. Use a chronologically arranged, traditional text, but also assign group work, panel presentations, and portfolio management

DIRECTIONS for Questions 17 and 18: Read the following sentences and attempt to determine the meanings of the underlined words.

(Average) (Skill 4.1)

17. Farmer John got a two-horse plow and went to work. Straight furrows stretched out behind him.

    The word <u>furrows</u> means:

    A. Long cuts made by plow
    B. Vast, open fields
    C. Rows of corn
    D. Pairs of hitched horses

(Average) (Skill 4.1)

18. The survivors struggled ahead, shambling through the terrible cold, doing their best not to fall.

    The word <u>shambling</u> means:

    A. Frozen in place
    B. Running
    C. Shivering uncontrollably
    D. Walking awkwardly

(Easy) (Skill 4.2)

19. To understand the origins of a word, one must study its:

    A. Synonyms
    B. Inflections
    C. Phonetics
    D. Etymology

(Average) (Skill 4.2)

20. The synonyms "gyro," "hero," and "submarine" reflect which influence on language usage?

    A. Social
    B. Geographical
    C. Historical
    D. Personal

(Rigorous) (Skill 4.2)

21. Which word in the following sentence is a bound morpheme: "The quick brown fox jumped over the lazy dog"?

    A. The
    B. Fox
    C. Lazy
    D. Jumped

(Rigorous) (Skill 4.8)

22. In order for someone to make an inference they must rely on:

    A. Literal comprehension
    B. Background knowledge
    C. Context clues
    D. Conclusions

(Rigorous) (Skill 5.1)

23. Factors that have caused the decline of newspaper readership include which of the following?

    A. People are now relying on the Internet for their news, causing a decline in newspaper advertising
    B. Because of environmental concerns and the high cost of paper, people are turning to the radio and television to keep current with the news
    C. Many people think newspapers are too biased in their coverage and seek their information from more credible sources
    D. Newspaper unions have negotiated tough contracts for their workers, and the profits are being negated by high salaries

(Rigorous) (Skill 5.2)

24. Which aspect of language is innate?

    A. Biological capability to articulate sounds understood by other humans
    B. Cognitive ability to create syntactical structures
    C. Capacity for using semantics to convey meaning in a social environment
    D. Ability to vary inflections and accents

(Easy) (Skill 5.4)

25. The Inca were a group of Indians who ruled an empire in South America.

    A. Fact
    B. Opinion

(Easy) (Skill 5.4)

26. The Inca were clever.

    A. Fact
    B. Opinion

(Easy) (Skill 5.4)

27. The Inca built very complex systems of bridges.

    A. Fact
    B. Opinion

(Average) (Skill 5.5)

28. What is one way to make an irrelevant sentence relevant?

    A. Add an example.
    B. Add a connotation.
    C. Make the sentence ambiguous.
    D. Take out transitions.

(Rigorous) (Skill 5.6)

29. Which of the following is not a fallacy in logic?

    A. All students in Ms. Suarez's fourth period class are bilingual.
       Beth is in Ms. Suarez's fourth period.
       Beth is bilingual.
    B. All bilingual students are in Ms. Suarez's class.
       Beth is in Ms. Suarez's fourth period.
       Beth is bilingual.
    C. Beth is bilingual.
       Beth is in Ms. Suarez's fourth period.
       All students in Ms. Suarez's fourth period are bilingual.
    D. If Beth is bilingual, then she speaks Spanish.
       Beth speaks French.
       Beth is not bilingual.

(Average) (Skill 5.7)

30. Which of the following responses to literature typically gives middle school students the most problems?

    A. Interpretive
    B. Evaluative
    C. Critical
    D. Emotional

(Average) (Skill 5.7)

31. Which of the following is not one of the four forms of discourse?

    A. Exposition
    B. Description
    C. Rhetoric
    D. Persuasion

(Rigorous) (Skill 5.7)

32. The arrangement and relationship of words in sentences or sentence structures best describes:

    A. Style
    B. Discourse
    C. Thesis
    D. Syntax

Literature (Skills 7.1 – 10.4)

(Average) (Skill 7.1)

33. Which is the best definition of free verse, or *vers libre*?

   A. Poetry that consists of an unaccented syllable followed by an unaccented sound
   B. Short, lyrical poetry written to entertain but with an instructive purpose
   C. Poetry that does not have a uniform pattern of rhythm
   D. Poetry that tells the story and has a plot

(Rigorous) (Skill 7.1)

34. Which sonnet form describes the following?

   My galley charg'd
      with forgetfulness,
   Through sharp seas, in
      winter night doth pass
   'Tween rock and rock; and
      eke mine enemy, alas,
   That is my lord steereth with
      cruelness.
   And every oar a thought with
      readiness,
   As though that death were
      light in such a case.
   An endless wind doth tear
      the sail apace
   Or forc'ed sighs and trusty
      fearfulness.
   A rain of tears, a cloud of dark
      disdain,
   Hath done the wearied
      cords great hinderance,
   Wreathed with error and eke
      with ignorance.
   The stars be hid that led me
      to this pain
   Drowned is reason that
      should me consort,
   And I remain despairing
      of the poet

   A. Petrarchan or Italian sonnet
   B. Shakespearian or Elizabethan sonnet
   C. Romantic sonnet
   D. Spenserian sonnet

(Rigorous) (Skill 7.1)

35. Which term best describes the form of the following poetic excerpt?

   And more to lulle him in his
      slumber soft,
   A trickling streake from high rock
      tumbling downe,
   And ever-drizzling raine upon
      the loft.
   Mixt with a murmuring winde,
      much like a swowne
   No other noyse, nor peoples
      troubles cryes.
   As still we wont t'annoy the
      walle'd towne,
   Might there be heard: but
      careless Quiet lyes,
   Wrapt in eternall silence farre
      from enemyes.

   A. Ballad
   B. Elegy
   C. Spenserian stanza
   D. Ottava rima

(Rigorous) (Skill 7.1)
36. Which poem is typified as a villanelle?

    A. "Do not go gentle into that good night"
    B. "Dover Beach"
    C. *Sir Gawain and the Green Knight*
    D. *The Pilgrim's Progress*

(Easy) (Skill 7.2)
37. The substitution of "went to his rest" for "died" is an example of a:

    A. Bowdlerism
    B. Jargon
    C. Euphemism
    D. Malapropism

(Average) (Skill 7.2)
38. In literature, evoking feelings of pity or compassion is to create:

    A. Colloquy
    B. Irony
    C. Pathos
    D. Paradox

(Rigorous) (Skill 8.2)
39. Which of the following is a characteristic of blank verse?

    A. Meter in iambic pentameter
    B. Clearly specified rhyme scheme
    C. Lack of figurative language
    D. Unspecified rhythm

(Average) (Skill 8.2)
40. Which is an untrue statement about a theme in literature?

    A. The theme is always stated directly somewhere in the text.
    B. The theme is the central idea in a literary work.
    C. All parts of the work (plot, setting, mood) should contribute to the theme in some way.
    D. By analyzing the various elements of the work, the reader should be able to arrive at an indirectly stated theme.

(Average) (Skill 8.2)
41. In the following quotation, addressing the dead body of Caesar as though he were still a living being is to employ an:

    O, pardon me, though
    Bleeding piece of earth
    That I am meek and gentle with
    These butchers.
    —Marc Antony, from *Julius Caesar*

    A. Apostrophe
    B. Allusion
    C. Antithesis
    D. Anachronism

(Rigorous) (Skill 8.2)
42. In the sentence, "The Cabinet conferred with the president," "Cabinet" is an example of a/an:

    A. Metonym
    B. Synecdoche
    C. Metaphor
    D. Allusion

(Easy) (Skill 8.6)

43. Which is the best definition of diction?

   A. The specific word choices of an author to create a particular mood or feeling in the reader
   B. Writing that explains something thoroughly
   C. The background, or exposition, for a short story or drama
   D. Word choices that help teach a truth or moral

DIRECTIONS: In sentences 43–46, circle the choice that best corrects the error (underlined) without changing the meaning of the original sentence.

(Average) (Skill 8.6)

44. Wally <u>groaned, "Why do I have to do an oral interpretation of "The Raven."</u>

   A. groaned, "Why… of 'The Raven'?"
   B. groaned, "Why… of "The Raven"?
   C. groaned ", Why… of "The Raven?"
   D. groaned, "Why… of "The Raven."

(Rigorous) (Skill 8.6)

45. Walt Whitman was famous <u>for his composition *Leaves of Grass*, serving as a nurse during the Civil War, and a devoted son.</u>

   A. for his composition *Leaves of Grass*, his service as a nurse during the Civil War, and a devoted son.
   B. for composing *Leaves of Grass*, serving as a nurse during the Civil War, and being a devoted son.
   C. for his composition *Leaves of Grass*, his nursing during the Civil War, and his devotion as a son.
   D. for his composition *Leaves of Grass*, serving as a nurse during the Civil War and a devoted son.
   E. for his composition *Leaves of Grass*, serving as a nurse during the Civil War, and a devoted son.

(Rigorous) (Skill 8.6)

46. There were <u>fewer pieces</u> of evidence presented during the second trial.

   A. fewer peaces
   B. less peaces
   C. less pieces
   D. fewer pieces

(Easy) (Skill 9.1)

47. Mr. Smith <u>respectfully submitted his resignation and had</u> a new job.

   A. respectfully submitted his resignation and has
   B. respectfully submitted his resignation before accepting
   C. respectfully submitted his resignation because of
   D. respectfully submitted his resignation and had

(Average) (Skill 9.1)

48. Charles Dickens, Robert Browning, and Robert Louis Stevenson were:

    A. Victorians
    B. Medievalists
    C. Elizabethans
    D. Absurdists

(Easy) (Skill 9.2)

49. Considered one of the first feminist plays, this Ibsen drama ends with a door slamming, symbolizing the lead character's emancipation from traditional societal norms.

    A. *The Wild Duck*
    B. *Hedda Gabler*
    C. *Ghosts*
    D. *A Doll's House*

(Rigorous) (Skill 9.2)

50. Which of the following is the best definition of existentialism?

    A. The philosophical doctrine that matter is the only reality and that everything in the world, including thought, will, and feeling, can be explained in terms of matter
    B. A philosophy that views things as they should be or as one would wish them to be
    C. A philosophical and literary movement, variously religious and atheistic, stemming from Kierkegaard and represented by Sartre
    D. The belief that all events are determined by fate and are hence inevitable

(Average) (Skill 10.3)

51. American colonial writers were primarily:

    A. Romanticists
    B. Naturalists
    C. Realists
    D. Neoclassicists

Listening and Speaking (Skills 11.1 – 13.4)

(Average) (Skill 11.1)

52. Oral debate is most closely associated with which form of discourse?

    A. Description
    B. Exposition
    C. Narration
    D. Persuasion

(Rigorous) (Skill 11.1)

53. Which of the following types of question will not stimulate higher-level critical thinking?

    A. A hypothetical question
    B. An open-ended question
    C. A close-ended question
    D. A judgment question

(Average) (Skill 11.1)

54. **In preparing a speech for a contest, your student has encountered problems with gender-specific language. Not wishing to offend either women or men, she seeks your guidance. Which of the following is not an effective strategy?**

    A. Use the generic "he" and explain that people will understand and accept the male pronoun as all-inclusive

    B. Switch to plural nouns and use "they" as the gender-neutral pronoun

    C. Use passive voice so that the subject is not required

    D. Use male pronouns for one part of the speech, and then use female pronouns for the other part of the speech

(Average) (Skill 11.2)

55. **Which of the following is NOT an advanced communication skill?**

    A. Clarification

    B. Reflection

    C. Pronunciation

    D. Summarization

(Easy) (Skill 11.2)

56. **What is true of effective communicators?**

    A. They are also good listeners.

    B. They are well-liked by their students.

    C. They speak more than one language.

    D. They have a poor understanding of effective body language.

(Average) (Skill 11.3)

57. **What is NOT a way that speaking and listening can be integrated?**

    A. Storytelling

    B. Role playing

    C. Memorization

    D. Readers' Theatre

(Average) (Skill 12.1)

58. **What is included in the process of preparing to speak on a topic?**

    A. Research, reading, recovery

    B. Discovery, organization, editing

    C. Drafting, revising, editing

    D. Choice, research, time management

(Average) (Skill 12.3)

59. **Which of the following words does NOT indicate a premise for an argument?**

    A. Since

    B. Then

    C. Because

    D. Afterward

(Easy) (Skill 12.3)

60. **Which of the following phrases may be an indication that the conclusion is beginning?**

    A. Implies that

    B. Later

    C. Fortunately

    D. It follows that

(Average) (Skill 12.5)

61. Which nonverbal communication technique suggests that students maintain a straight but not stiff posture, refrain from shifting from hip to hop, point feet directly at the audience, and distribute weight evenly?

   A. Posture
   B. Movement
   C. Gestures
   D. Eye contact

(Rigorous) (Skill 12.5)

62. How can eye contact help someone who is speaking publicly?

   A. It doesn't help the speaker—it helps the audience feel comfortable.
   B. It only helps if someone makes eye contact with the audience for 3 – 5 seconds.
   C. It can help the speaker overcome speech anxiety.
   D. It keeps the speaker still if eye contact is maintained with the audience.

(Easy) (Skill 12.5)

63. How can problems with volume be overcome when making an oral presentation?

   A. Presentations can be taped and the volume can then be controlled easily.
   B. The presenter must simply present two times louder than he or she would normally speak.
   C. The presenter must simply adjust their pitch.
   D. Practice

(Rigorous) (Skill 12.5)

64. What additional benefit do people gain by becoming good oral presenters?

   A. They have a chance at becoming politicians.
   B. They will develop self-confidence for higher levels of communication.
   C. Voice, volume, and pitch errors will be corrected.
   D. They will sound more educated because they have the ability to practice speaking.

(Average) (Skill 12.5)

65. Posture, movement, gestures, and eye contact are all under the umbrella of:

   A. Verbal communication
   B. Effective presentation communications
   C. Nonverbal communication techniques
   D. Speech delivery techniques

Components of Writing (Skills 14.1 – 16.7)

DIRECTIONS: In sentences 66–67, circle the choice that best corrects the error (underlined) without changing the meaning of the original sentence.

(Easy) (Skill 14.3)

66. The Taj Mahal <u>has been designated</u> one of the Seven Wonders of the World, and people <u>know it</u> for its unique architecture.

    A. The Taj Mahal has been designated one of the Seven Wonders of the World, and it is known for its unique architecture.

    B. People know the Taj Mahal for its unique architecture, and it has been designated one of the Seven Wonders of the World.

    C. People have known the Taj Mahal for its unique architecture, and it has been designated of the Seven Wonders of the World.

    D. The Taj Mahal has designated itself one of the Seven Wonders of the World.

(Rigorous) (Skill 14.3)

67. Which sentence below best minimizes the impact of bad news?

    A. We have denied you permission to attend the event.

    B. Although permission to attend the event cannot be given, you are encouraged to buy the video.

    C. Although you cannot attend the event, we encourage you to buy the video.

    D. Although attending the event is not possible, watching the video is an option.

(Average) (Skill 14.5)

68. **DIRECTIONS: In the sample paragraph below, choose the underlined transition that is not used effectively.**

    Autumn is my favorite time of year. <u>First</u>, the crisp, clean air is refreshing after the humid days of summer. <u>In addition</u>, I love the cinnamon smells in the kitchen of apple pies and cider. I <u>also</u> enjoy the beautiful colors of the trees in autumn, too. <u>In contrast</u>, October brings my favorite holiday, Halloween, when everyone dresses up! <u>In sum</u>, the holidays, smells, and sights make autumn the best time of year.

    A. First
    B. In addition
    C. In contrast
    D. In sum

(Average) (Skill 14.5)

69. Transitional words and phrases help to:

    A. Add structure to a text
    B. Signal relationships between ideas in a text
    C. Enhance the flow of writing
    D. All of the above

(Easy) (Skill 15.1)

70. An advertisement seen on television or in as a magazine print ad takes on what form of writing structure?

    A. Narrative
    B. Persuasive
    C. Descriptive
    D. Expository

(Rigorous) (Skill 15.1)

71. The imaginations of children seem to be dwindling before our very eyes. What happened to the good 'ol days when boys would be outside using sticks as make-believe daggers and large cardboard boxes as castles. Girls would stand on their front porches and pretend that they were on stage—performing some sort of skit for the neighborhood parents. Now, electronic games and gizmos are taking over the minds of our young people and robbing them of vital imagination.

    The above piece of writing is most likely the introduction to what type of writing?

    A. A narrative
    B. A descriptive piece
    C. A persuasive piece
    D. An expository piece

(Easy) (Skill 15.1)

72. Which type of writing is meant to tell a story?

    A. Narrative
    B. Descriptive
    C. Persuasive
    D. Expository

(Average) (Skill 15.2)

73. Writing ideas quickly without interruption of the flow of thoughts or attention to conventions is called:

    A. Brainstorming
    B. Mapping
    C. Listing
    D. Free writing

(Rigorous) (Skill 15.2)

74. In preparing a report about William Shakespeare, students are asked to develop a set of interpretive questions to guide their research. Which of the following would not be classified as an interpretive question?

    A. What would be different today if Shakespeare had not written his plays?
    B. How will the plays of Shakespeare affect future generations?
    C. How does Shakespeare view nature in *A Midsummer's Night Dream* and *Much Ado About Nothing*?
    D. During the Elizabethan age, what roles did young boys take in dramatizing Shakespeare's plays?

(Rigorous) (Skill 15.3)

75. In this paragraph from a student essay, identify the sentence that provides a detail.

    (1) The poem concerns two different personality types and the human relation between them. (2) Their approach to life is totally different. (3) The neighbor is a very conservative person who follows routines. (4) He follows the traditional wisdom of his father and his father's father. (5) The purpose in fixing the wall and keeping their relationship separate is only because it is all he knows.

    A. Sentence 1
    B. Sentence 3
    C. Sentence 4
    D. Sentence 5

(Easy) (Skill 15.3)

76. Which of the following should not be included in the opening paragraph of an informative essay?

    A. Thesis sentence

    B. Details and examples supporting the main idea

    C. Broad, general introduction to the topic

    D. A style and tone that grabs the reader's attention

(Average) (Skill 15.3)

77. Middle and high school students are more receptive to studying grammar and syntax:

    A. Through worksheets and end-of-lesson practices in textbooks

    B. Through independent homework assignments

    C. Through analytical examination of the writings of famous authors

    D. Through application to their own writing

DIRECTIONS: In sentences 78–79, choose the most effective word within the context of the sentence.

(Average) (Skill 15.4)

78. When a student is expelled from school, the parents are usually _____ in advance.

    A. rewarded

    B. congratulated

    C. notified

(Average) (Skill 15.4)

79. Before appearing in court, the witness was _____ the papers requiring her to show up.

    A. condemned

    B. served

    C. criticized

(Rigorous) (Skill 16.7)

80. Which of the following situations is not an ethical violation of intellectual property?

    A. A student visits ten different Web sites and writes a report to compare the costs of downloading music. He uses the names of the Web sites without their permission.

    B. A student copies and pastes a chart verbatim from the Internet but does not document it because it is available on a public site.

    C. From an online article found in a subscription database, a student paraphrases a section on the problems of music piracy. She includes the source in her Works Cited but does not provide an in-text citation.

    D. A student uses a comment from M. Night Shyamalan without attribution, claiming the information is common knowledge.

Modes of Writing
(Skills 17.1 – 20.5)

(Average) (Skill 17.4)
81. Which of the following is most true of expository writing?

   A. It is mutually exclusive of other forms of discourse

   B. It can incorporate other forms of discourse in the process of providing supporting details

   C. It should never employ informal expression

   D. It should only be scored with a summative evaluation

(Average) (Skill 17.4)
82. Explanatory or informative discourse is:

   A. Exposition

   B. Narration

   C. Persuasion

   D. Description

(Rigorous) (Skill 17.4)
83. Which of the following is an example of the *post hoc* fallacy?

   A. When the new principal was hired, student reading scores improved; therefore, the principal caused the increase in scores.

   B. Why are we spending money on the space program when our students don't have current textbooks?

   C. You can't give your class a 10-minute break. Once you do that, we'll all have to give our students a 10-minute break.

   D. You can never believe anything he says because he's not from the same country as we are.

(Rigorous) (Skill 17.5)
84. What syntactic device is most evident from Abraham Lincoln's "Gettysburg Address"?

   It is rather for us to be here dedicated to the great task remaining before us—that from these honored dead we take increased devotion to that cause for which they gave the last full measure of devotion—that we here highly resolve that these dead shall not have died in vain—that this nation, under God, shall have a new birth of freedom—and that government of the people, by the people, for the people, shall not perish from the earth.

   A. Affective connotation

   B. Informative denotations

   C. Allusion

   D. Parallelism

(Easy) (Skill 17.6)
85. In the paragraph below, which sentence does not contribute to the overall task of supporting the main idea?

   (1) The Springfield City Council met Friday to discuss new zoning restrictions for the land to be developed south of the city. (2) Residents who opposed the new restrictions were granted 15 minutes to present their case. (3) Their argument focused on the dangers that increased traffic would bring to the area. (4) It seemed to me that the Mayor Simpson listened intently. (5) The council agreed to table the new zoning until studies would be performed.

   A. Sentence 2

   B. Sentence 3

   C. Sentence 4

   D. Sentence 5

QUESTIONS

(Rigorous) (Skill 18.3)

86. For their research paper on the use of technology in the classroom, students have gathered data that shows a sharp increase in the number of online summer classes over the past five years. What would be the best way for them to depict this information visually?

   A. A line chart
   B. A table
   C. A pie chart
   D. A flow chart

(Rigorous) (Skill 18.4)

87. Identify the type of appeal used by Molly Ivins in this excerpt from her essay "Get a Knife, Get a Dog, But Get Rid of Guns."

   As a civil libertarian, I, of course, support the Second Amendment. And I believe it means exactly what it says: A well-regulated militia being necessary to the security of a free state, the right of the people to keep and bear arms shall not be infringed.

   A. Ethical
   B. Emotional
   C. Rational
   D. Literary

(Rigorous) (Skill 18.5)

88. What type of reasoning does Henry David Thoreau use in the following excerpt from "Civil Disobedience"?

   Unjust laws exist; shall we be content to obey them, or shall we endeavor to amend them, and obey them until we have succeeded, or shall we transgress them at once? Men generally, under such a government as this, think that they ought to wait until they have persuaded the majority to alter them. They think that, if they should resist, the remedy would be worse than the evil. But it is the fault of the government itself that the remedy is worse than the evil … Why does it always crucify Christ, excommunicate Copernicus and Luther, and pronounce Washington and Franklin rebels?

   A. Ethical reasoning
   B. Inductive reasoning
   C. Deductive reasoning
   D. Intellectual reasoning

(Average) (Skill 19.1)

89. Modeling is a practice that requires students to:

   A. Create a style unique to their own language capabilities
   B. Emulate the writing of professionals
   C. Paraphrase passages from good literature
   D. Peer evaluate the writings of other students

(Average) (Skill 19.2)

90. The English department is developing strategies to encourage all students to become a community of readers. From the list of suggestions below, which would be the least effective way for teachers to foster independent reading?

    A. Each teacher sets aside a weekly, 30-minute, in-class reading session during which the teacher and students read a magazine or book for enjoyment.

    B. The teacher and the students develop a list of favorite books to share with each other.

    C. The teacher assigns at least one book report each grading period to ensure that students are reading from the established class list.

    D. The students gather books for a classroom library so that books can be shared with each other.

(Average) (Skill 19.3)

91. The new teaching intern is developing a unit on creative writing and is trying to encourage her freshman high school students to write poetry. Which of the following would not be an effective technique?

    A. In groups, students draw pictures to illustrate "The Love Song of J. Alfred Prufrock" by T.S. Eliot

    B. Either individually or in groups, students compose a song, writing lyrics that try to use poetic devices

    C. Students bring to class the lyrics of a popular song and discuss the imagery and figurative language

    D. Students read aloud their favorite poems and share their opinions of and responses to the poems

(Rigorous) (Skill 19.5)

92. In order to make the plot of a story interesting and balanced, the author must include:

    A. Characters

    B. Descriptive words

    C. Strong nouns, verbs, and adjectives

    D. Character's thoughts, feelings, and actions

(Easy) (Skill 19.5)

93. The following passage is written from which point of view?

    As she mused, the pitiful vision of her mother's life laid its spell on the very quick of her being—that life of commonplace sacrifices closing in final craziness. She trembled as she heard again her mother's voice saying constantly with foolish insistence: Dearevaun Seraun! Dearevaun Seraun!*

    * "The end of pleasure is pain!" (Gaelic)

    A. First-person narrator

    B. Second-person direct address

    C. Third-person omniscient

    D. First-person omniscient

(Rigorous) (Skill 19.6)

94. **For students to prepare for a their roles in a dramatic performance:**

    A. They should analyze their characters to develop a deeper understanding of the character's attitudes and motivations.

    B. They should attend local plays to study settings and stage design.

    C. They should read articles and books on acting methodology.

    D. They should practice the way other actors have performed in these roles.

(Average) (Skill 20.4)

95. **If a student uses slang and expletives, what is the best course of action to take to improve the student's formal communication skills?**

    A. Ask the student to paraphrase his writing—that is, to translate it into language appropriate for the school principal to read.

    B. Refuse to read the student's papers until he conforms to a more literate style.

    C. Ask the student to read his work aloud to the class for peer evaluation.

    D. Rewrite the flagrant passages to show the student the right form of expression.

(Easy) (Skill 20.4)

96. **In "inverted triangle" introductory paragraphs, the thesis sentence occurs:**

    A. At the beginning of the paragraph

    B. In the middle of the paragraph

    C. At the end of the paragraph

    D. In the second paragraph

(Average) (Skill 20.4)

97. **Students need to be aware that an email message:**

    A. Should be written according to formal business letter guidelines

    B. May eventually reach a wider audience than intended

    C. Should be written using all capital letters

    D. Should not be used to send large documents or multimedia files

(Rigorous) (Skill 20.5)

98. **Which might be true if a story has an unreliable narrator?**

    A. A character will be revealed subtly through dialogue, interior monologue, description, and behavior

    B. A character will be revealed through dialogue only

    C. The writer will tell the reader directly what a character is like

    D. There will be discrepancies between what the narrator tells the reader and what is revealed through the character's actions

(Average) (Skill 20.5)

99. **Which of the following is NOT an example of fiction?**

    A. Biography

    B. Mythology

    C. Poetry

    D. Science fiction

(Rigorous) (Skill 20.5)

100. An idealized model of a person, object, or concept from which similar instances are derived is called:

    A. A theme

    B. An archetype

    C. A protagonist

    D. An antagonist

Answer Key

ANSWER KEY						
1. D	16. C	31. C	46. D	61. A	76. B	91. A
2. C	17. A	32. D	47. C	62. C	77. D	92. D
3. B	18. D	33. C	48. A	63. D	78. C	93. C
4. A	19. D	34. A	49. D	64. B	79. B	94. A
5. C	20. B	35. D	50. C	65. C	80. A	95. A
6. B	21. D	36. A	51. D	66. A	81. B	96. C
7. B	22. B	37. C	52. D	67. B	82. A	97. B
8. C	23. A	38. C	53. C	68. C	83. A	98. D
9. A	24. A	39. A	54. A	69. D	84. D	99. A
10. C	25. A	40. A	55. C	70. B	85. C	100. B
11. A	26. B	41. A	56. A	71. D	86. A	
12. C	27. A	42. B	57. C	72. A	87. A	
13. D	28. A	43. A	58. B	73. D	88. C	
14. C	29. A	44. A	59. A	74. D	89. B	
15. B	30. B	45. B	60. D	75. C	90. C	

Rigor Table

Rigor level	Questions
Easy 20%	1, 4, 19, 25, 26, 27, 37, 43, 47, 49, 56, 60, 63, 66, 70, 72, 76, 85, 93, 96
Average 40%	3, 6, 9, 11, 15, 16, 17, 18, 20, 28, 30, 31, 33, 38, 40, 41, 44, 48, 51, 52, 54, 55, 57, 58, 59, 61, 63, 65, 68, 69, 73, 77, 78, 79, 81, 82, 89, 90, 91, 95, 97, 99
Rigorous 40%	2, 5, 7, 8, 10, 12, 13, 14, 21, 22, 23, 24, 29, 32, 34, 35, 36, 39, 42, 45, 46, 50, 53, 62, 64, 67, 71, 74, 75, 80, 83, 84, 86, 87, 88, 92, 94, 98, 100

Sample Test with Rationales

Media Literacy (Skills 1.1 – 2.5)

(Easy) (Skill 1.1)

1. What is not a characteristic of an effective editorial cartoon?

    A. It presents a message or point of view concerning people, events, or situations using caricature and symbolism to convey the cartoonist's ideas

    B. It has wit and humor, which is usually obtained by exaggeration that is slick and not used merely for comic effect

    C. It has a foundation in truth; that is, the characters must be recognizable to the viewer, and the point of the drawing must have some basis in fact even if it has a philosophical bias

    D. It seeks to reflect the editorial opinion of the newspaper that carries it

    Answer: D. It seeks to reflect the editorial opinion of the newspaper that carries it

    An editorial cartoon does not necessarily reflect the opinion of the newspaper that publishes it.

(Rigorous) (Skill 1.1)

2. What is the common advertising technique used by these advertising slogans?

    "It's everywhere you want to be."
    —Visa

    "Have it your way."
    —Burger King

    "When you care enough to send the very best."
    —Hallmark

    "Be all you can be."
    —U.S. Army

    A. Peer approval

    B. Rebelion

    C. Individuality

    D. Escape

    Answer: C. Individuality

    All of these ads associate products with people who can think and act for themselves. Products are linked to individual decision making. With peer approval, the ads would associate their products with friends and acceptance. For rebellion, the ads would associate products with behaviors or lifestyles that oppose society's norms. Escape would suggest the appeal of getting away from it all.

(Average) (Skill 1.1)

3. **Why are posters no longer as effective as they used to be?**

   A. No one takes the time to look at them like they used to because people are too busy.

   B. Video and multimedia have taken over as a more popular method of persuading people.

   C. The cost of paper has become more than many politicians and companies can afford now that video and multimedia are more affordable.

   D. People no longer have the manpower to hang them in high-traffic locations.

Answer: B. Video and multimedia have taken over as a more popular method of persuading people.

The barrage of electronic campaigning, reporting, and persuading has taken over as a way to campaign and draw attention.

(Easy) (Skill 1.2)

4. **What is a positive aspect about print messages?**

   A. They have longevity and are easily portable.

   B. They are understood by everyone.

   C. Print messages must be actively read.

   D. They appeal to a wider range of people.

Answer: A. They have longevity and are easily portable.

A print message has unique features. Some seem to be positive. For instance, print messages have longevity; they are also easily portable. Print messages appeal almost exclusively to the mind and allow students to recursively read sections that warrant more thought.

(Rigorous) (Skill 1.2)

5. **Compared with print, what is better about a graphic message?**

   A. It is easier to create a graphic message.

   B. It takes less time to create a graphic message.

   C. Graphic messages convey a shorter range of information

Answer: C. Graphic messages convey a shorter range of information

Compared to print, graphic messages convey a much shorter range of information. If a particular graphic is inspiring, the inspirations conveyed are subject to the descriptions of the various readers who view it. With print, the inspired scripts are already there for the reader, provided the reader is applying active reading skills.

(Average) (Skill 1.3)

6. **How does the media influence consumers and their behavior?**

   A. Through news and documentary programming

   B. Primarily through advertising

   C. Shows and other sitcoms

   D. By influencing body image

Answer: B. Primarily through advertising

One of the main venues in which the media exert a profound influence on personal and societal values, opinions, and behaviors is through advertizing.

(Rigorous) (Skill 1.4)

7. The literary device of personification is used in which example below?

    A. "Beg me no beggary by soul or parents, whining dog!"

    B. "Happiness sped through the halls, cajoling as it went."

    C. "O wind thy horn, thou proud fellow."

    D. "And that one talent which is death to hide."

Answer: B. "Happiness sped through the halls, cajoling as it went."

"Happiness," an abstract concept, is described as if it were a person.

(Rigorous) (Skill 2.1)

8. In presenting a report to peers about the effects of Hurricane Katrina on New Orleans, the students wanted to use various media in their argument to persuade their peers that more needed to be done. Which of these would be the most effective?

    A. A PowerPoint presentation showing the blueprints of the levees before the flood and redesigned now for current construction

    B. A collection of music clips made by the street performers in the French Quarter before and after the flood

    C. A recent video showing the areas devastated by the floods and the current state of rebuilding

    D. A collection of recordings of interviews made by the various government officials and local citizens affected by the flooding

Answer: C. A recent video showing the areas devastated by the floods and the current state of rebuilding

For maximum impact, a video would offer dramatic scenes of the devastated areas. A video by its very nature is more dynamic than a static PowerPoint presentation. Furthermore, the condition of the levees would not provide as much impetus for change as seeing the devastated areas. Oral messages, such as music clips and interviews, provide another way of supplementing the message; but again, they are not as dynamic as video.

SAMPLE TEST

(Average) (Skill 2.1)

9. What is NOT included in still visual media?

   A. Speeches
   B. Pictures
   C. Drawings
   D. Charts and tables

Answer: A. Speeches

Still visual media include pictures, drawings, photographs, tables, charts, maps, and diagrams.

(Rigorous) (Skill 2.3)

10. What is necessary in the development of moving visual media presentations?

    A. A storyboard must be utilized before the presentation can be developed.
    B. Capable designers must be employed at a fair rate of pay.
    C. A storyline or presentation rationale must be decided upon.
    D. An appropriate volume, pitch, voice, and rhythm must be utilized to increase the effectiveness of the presentation.

Answer: C. A storyline or presentation rationale must be decided upon.

A moving presentation needs to have an understandable beginning, development, and conclusion. Obviously, choosing effective transitions between scenes and installing a reasonable pace of image movement figure importantly in visual media.

(Average) (Skill 2.4)

11. When making or preparing a presentation, what are some key aspects to keep in mind?

    A. Aesthetics, principals of communication, effective use of technology
    B. Font size, vocabulary used, and a receptive audience
    C. Whether films or filmstrips will be used
    D. The amount of audience engagement desired

Answer: A. Aesthetics, principals of communication, effective use of technology

Effective graphics should be pleasing to the eye. This is especially true if the graphic is some type of picture. Oral communication as it applies in the classroom includes formal and informal speaking and listening. Principles of oral communication include attention to such issues as vocabulary levels, appropriate volume, repetition of key points, and active listening. Speaking clearly is, of course, critical to any communication effort. Technologies that incorporate interactive dimensions of audiovisual material are especially effective in communicating information and ensuring adequate audience focus.

Reading (Skills 3.1 – 6.4)

(Rigorous) (Skill 3.2)

12. Mr. Martin has a bag of letter tiles for every student in his class. He tells the students to make the word "cat" with their letter tiles. Next, Mr. Martin tells the students to change the word "cat" to "sat." Mr. Martin continues changing the first letter of the words to create rhyming words. This is an activity in:

    A. Phonics
    B. Fluency
    C. Phonemic awareness
    D. Comprehension

    Answer: C. Phonemic awareness

    Phonemic awareness requires students to hear phonemes. In our example, "at" must be heard and students must realize that is needs to remain the same and only the first letter needs to be adjusted in order to change the word.

(Rigorous) (Skill 3.2)

13. A first grade student is reading a level D guided reading book aloud and his teacher is listening. The student gets stuck on one of the words and looks to the teacher for help. The teacher says, "What is the first sound?" Then she says, "Sound out the rest of the letters as you blend the sounds together." The teacher is teaching the student:

    A. Phonemic awareness
    B. Fluency
    C. Comprehension
    D. Phonics

    Answer: D. Phonics

    Phonics is a student's connection between the sounds and letters on a page. Students learning phonics might see the word "bad" and sound each letter out slowly until they recognize that they just said the word.

(Rigorous) (Skill 3.2)

14. Mr. Miller is having his students participate in a reader's theater activity. Mr. Miller first read the short play aloud to the students in class. For the remainder of the week students read the play to themselves, with a partner, and at home for homework. The teacher is helping to develop:

    A. Phonemic awareness
    B. Phonics
    C. Fluency
    D. Comprehension

    Answer: C. Fluency

    Fluency is a student's ability to read connected pieces of text and comprehend what is read. If a student is not fluent in reading, he would sound each letter or word out slowly and pay more attention to the phonics of each word.

(Average) (Skill 3.6)

15. Written on the sixth-grade reading level, most of S. E. Hinton's novels (for instance, *The Outsiders*) have the greatest reader appeal with:

    A. Sixth graders
    B. Ninth graders
    C. Twelfth graders
    D. Adults

Answer: B. Ninth graders

Adolescents are concerned with their changing bodies, their relationships with each other and adults, and their place in society. Reading *The Outsiders* makes them confront different problems that they are only now beginning to experience as teenagers, such as gangs and social identity. The book is universal in its appeal to adolescents.

(Average) (Skill 3.6)

16. Which teaching method would best engage underachievers in the required senior English class?

    A. Assign use of glossary work and extensively footnoted excerpts of great works

    B. Have students take turns reading aloud the anthology selection

    C. Let students choose which readings they'll study and write about

    D. Use a chronologically arranged, traditional text, but also assign group work, panel presentations, and portfolio management

Answer: C. Let students choose which readings they'll study and write about

Allowing students to choose the readings they'll study encourages them to react honestly to literature. Students should take notes on what they're reading so they will be able to discuss the material. They should not only react to literature, but also experience it. Small-group work is a good way to encourage them. The other answers are not fit for junior high or high school students. They should be encouraged, however, to read critics of works in order to understand critical work.

DIRECTIONS for Questions 17 and 18: Read the following sentences and attempt to determine the meanings of the underlined words.

(Average) (Skill 4.1)

17. Farmer John got a two-horse plow and went to work. Straight furrows stretched out behind him.

    The word <u>furrows</u> means:

    A. Long cuts made by plow

    B. Vast, open fields

    C. Rows of corn

    D. Pairs of hitched horses

Answer: A. Long cuts made by plow

"Long cuts made by plow" is the correct answer. The words "straight" and the expression "stretched out behind him" are your clues.

(Average) (Skill 4.1)

18. The survivors struggled ahead, shambling through the terrible cold, doing their best not to fall.

    The word <u>shambling</u> means:

    A. Frozen in place

    B. Running

    C. Shivering uncontrollably

    D. Walking awkwardly

Answer: D. Walking awkwardly

"Walking awkwardly" is the correct answer. The words "ahead" and "through" are your clues.

The context for a word is the written passage that surrounds it. Sometimes the writer offers synonyms—words that have nearly the same meaning. Context clues also can appear within the sentence itself, within the preceding and/or following sentence(s), or in the passage as a whole.

(Easy) (Skill 4.2)

19. **To understand the origins of a word, one must study its:**

    A. Synonyms

    B. Inflections

    C. Phonetics

    D. Etymology

Answer: D. Etymology

Etymology is the study of word origins. A synonym is an equivalent of another word and can substitute for it in certain contexts. Inflection is a modification of words according to their grammatical functions, usually by employing variant word endings to indicate such qualities as tense, gender, case, and number. Phonetics is the science devoted to the physical analysis of the sounds of human speech, including their production, transmission, and perception.

(Average) (Skill 4.2)

20. **The synonyms "gyro," "hero," and "submarine" reflect which influence on language usage?**

    A. Social

    B. Geographical

    C. Historical

    D. Personal

Answer: B. Geographical

These words are interchangeable, but their use depends on the region of the United States, not on the social class of the speaker. Nor is there any historical context around any of them. The usage can be personal, but it will most often vary with the region.

(Rigorous) (Skill 4.2)

21. **Which word in the following sentence is a bound morpheme: "The quick brown fox jumped over the lazy dog"?**

    A. The

    B. Fox

    C. Lazy

    D. Jumped

Answer: D. Jumped

The suffix "–ed" is an affix that cannot stand alone as a unit of meaning. Thus it is bound to the free morpheme "jump." "The" is always an unbound morpheme since no suffix or prefix can alter its meaning. As written, "fox" and "lazy" are unbound, but their meaning is changed with affixes, such as "foxes" or "laziness."

(Rigorous) (Skill 4.8)

22. In order for someone to make an inference they must rely on:

   A. Literal comprehension
   B. Background knowledge
   C. Context clues
   D. Conclusions

Answer: B. Background knowledge

In order for someone to comprehend, whether the information is presented verbally or the information is read, listeners must rely on their background knowledge, or what they already know, in order to infer meaning.

(Rigorous) (Skill 5.1)

23. Factors that have caused the decline of newspaper readership include which of the following?

   A. People are now relying on the Internet for their news, causing a decline in newspaper advertising
   B. Because of environmental concerns and the high cost of paper, people are turning to the radio and television to keep current with the news
   C. Many people think newspapers are too biased in their coverage and seek their information from more credible sources
   D. Newspaper unions have negotiated tough contracts for their workers, and the profits are being negated by high salaries

Answer: A. People are now relying on the Internet for their news, causing a decline in newspaper advertising

Although the death knell for newspapers has sounded before with the advent of radio and television, more analysts are skeptical about the newspaper industry's ability to compete with the Internet. Certainly, the paper supply has an impact on the environment, but this has not caused the decline in newspaper readership. Reading an unbiased newspaper is next to impossible, but responsible readers are critical readers who learn to identify fact from opinion and rely on a variety of sources for their information. Although high wages may affect a newspaper's profit, they do not affect the number of readers.

(Rigorous) (Skill 5.2)

24. Which aspect of language is innate?

   A. Biological capability to articulate sounds understood by other humans
   B. Cognitive ability to create syntactical structures
   C. Capacity for using semantics to convey meaning in a social environment
   D. Ability to vary inflections and accents

Answer: A. Biological capability to articulate sounds understood by other humans

Language ability is innate, and the biological capability to produce sounds lets children learn semantics and syntactical structures through trial and error. Linguists agree that language is first a vocal system of word symbols that enable a human to communicate his or her feelings, thoughts, and desires to other human beings.

(Easy) (Skill 5.4)
25. The Inca were a group of Indians who ruled an empire in South America.
    A. Fact
    B. Opinion

Answer: A. Fact

Research can prove this statement true.

(Easy) (Skill 5.4)
26. The Inca were clever.
    A. Fact
    B. Opinion

Answer: B. Opinion

It is doubtful that all people who have studied the Inca agree with this statement. Therefore, no proof is available.

(Easy) (Skill 5.4)
27. The Inca built very complex systems of bridges.
    A. Fact
    B. Opinion

Answer: A. Fact

As with question number one, research can prove this statement true.

(Average) (Skill 5.5)
28. What is one way to make an irrelevant sentence relevant?
    A. Add an example.
    B. Add a connotation.
    C. Make the sentence ambiguous.
    D. Take out transitions.

Answer: A. Add an example.

Examples can support the main idea and give the document overall credibility. This is especially important in passages in which information is being argued, compared, or contrasted.

(Rigorous) (Skill 5.6)
29. Which of the following is not a fallacy in logic?
    A. All students in Ms. Suarez's fourth period class are bilingual.
       Beth is in Ms. Suarez's fourth period.
       Beth is bilingual.
    B. All bilingual students are in Ms. Suarez's class.
       Beth is in Ms. Suarez's fourth period.
       Beth is bilingual.
    C. Beth is bilingual.
       Beth is in Ms. Suarez's fourth period.
       All students in Ms. Suarez's fourth period are bilingual.
    D. If Beth is bilingual, then she speaks Spanish.
       Beth speaks French.
       Beth is not bilingual.

Answer: A. All students in Ms. Suarez's fourth period class are bilingual. Beth is in Ms. Suarez's fourth period. Beth is bilingual.

The second statement, or premise, is tested against the first premise. Both premises are valid and the conclusion is logical. In Answer B, the conclusion is invalid because the first premise does not exclude other students. In Answer C, the conclusion cannot be logically drawn from the preceding premises—that is, you cannot conclude that all students are bilingual based on one example. In Answer D, the conclusion is invalid because the first premise is faulty.

(Average) (Skill 5.7)
30. Which of the following responses to literature typically gives middle school students the most problems?

   A. Interpretive
   B. Evaluative
   C. Critical
   D. Emotional

Answer: B. Evaluative

Middle school readers will exhibit both emotional and interpretive responses. In middle/junior high school, organized study models enable students to identify main ideas and supporting details, to recognize sequential order, to distinguish fact from opinion, and to determine cause/effect relationships. Also, a child's ability to say why a particular book was boring or why a particular poem made him/her sad evidences critical reactions on a fundamental level. It is a bit early for evaluative responses, however. These depend on the reader's consideration of how the piece represents its genre, how well it reflects the social/ethical mores of a given society, and how well the author has approached the subject for freshness and slant. Evaluative responses are made only by a few advanced high school students.

(Average) (Skill 5.7)
31. Which of the following is not one of the four forms of discourse?

   A. Exposition
   B. Description
   C. Rhetoric
   D. Persuasion

Answer: C. Rhetoric

Rhetoric is an umbrella term for techniques of expressive and effective speech. Rhetorical figures are ornaments of speech such as anaphora, antithesis, metaphor, and so on. The other three choices are specific forms of discourse.

(Rigorous) (Skill 5.7)
32. The arrangement and relationship of words in sentences or sentence structures best describes:

   A. Style
   B. Discourse
   C. Thesis
   D. Syntax

Answer: D. Syntax

Syntax is the grammatical structure of sentences. Style refers to the way something is written. Discourse, broadly, means communication. A thesis is the main idea that holds an essay together.

Literature (Skills 7.1 – 10.4)

(Average) (Skill 7.1)

33. Which is the best definition of free verse, or *vers libre*?

   A. Poetry that consists of an unaccented syllable followed by an unaccented sound
   B. Short, lyrical poetry written to entertain but with an instructive purpose
   C. Poetry that does not have a uniform pattern of rhythm
   D. Poetry that tells the story and has a plot

Answer: C. Poetry that does not have a uniform pattern of rhythm

Free verse has lines of irregular length (but it does not run on like prose).

(Rigorous) (Skill 7.1)

34. Which sonnet form describes the following?

   My galley charg'd
      with forgetfulness,
   Through sharp seas, in
      winter night doth pass
   'Tween rock and rock; and
      eke mine enemy, alas,
   That is my lord steereth with
      cruelness.
   And every oar a thought with
      readiness,
   As though that death were
      light in such a case.
   An endless wind doth tear
      the sail apace
   Or forc'ed sighs and trusty
      fearfulness.
   A rain of tears, a cloud of dark
      disdain,
   Hath done the wearied
      cords great hinderance,
   Wreathed with error and eke
      with ignorance.
   The stars be hid that led me
      to this pain
   Drowned is reason that
      should me consort,
   And I remain despairing
      of the poet

   A. Petrarchan or Italian sonnet
   B. Shakespearian or Elizabethan sonnet
   C. Romantic sonnet
   D. Spenserian sonnet

Answer: A. Petrarchan or Italian sonnet

The Petrarchan sonnet, also known as the Italian sonnet, is named after the Italian poet Petrarch (1304–1374). It is divided into an octave rhyming abbaabba and a sestet normally rhyming cdecde.

(Rigorous) (Skill 7.1)

35. Which term best describes the form of the following poetic excerpt?

> And more to lulle him in his slumber soft,
> A trickling streake from high rock tumbling downe,
> And ever-drizzling raine upon the loft.
> Mixt with a murmuring winde, much like a swowne
> No other noyse, nor peoples troubles cryes.
> As still we wont t'annoy the walle'd towne,
> Might there be heard: but careless Quiet lyes,
> Wrapt in eternall silence farre from enemyes.

A. Ballad

B. Elegy

C. Spenserian stanza

D. Ottava rima

Answer: D. Ottava rima

The ottava rima is a specific eight-line stanza, the rhyme scheme of which is *abababcc*.

(Rigorous) (Skill 7.1)

36. Which poem is typified as a villanelle?

A. "Do not go gentle into that good night"

B. "Dover Beach"

C. *Sir Gawain and the Green Knight*

D. *The Pilgrim's Progress*

Answer: A. "Do not go gentle into that good night"

This poem by Dylan Thomas typifies the villanelle because it was written as such. A villanelle is a form that was invented in France in the sixteenth century and was used mostly for pastoral songs. It has an uneven number (usually five) of tercets rhyming aba, with a final quatrain rhyming abaa. This poem is the most famous villanelle written in English. "Dover Beach," by Matthew Arnold, is not a villanelle, while *Sir Gawain and the Green Knight* was written in alliterative verse by an unknown author usually referred to as The Pearl Poet around 1370. *The Pilgrim's Progress* is a prose allegory by John Bunyan.

(Easy) (Skill 7.2)

37. The substitution of "went to his rest" for "died" is an example of a:

A. Bowdlerism

B. Jargon

C. Euphemism

D. Malapropism

Answer: C. Euphemism

A euphemism replaces an unpleasant or offensive word or expression with a more agreeable one. It also alludes to distasteful things in a pleasant manner, and it can even paraphrase offensive texts.

(Average) (Skill 7.2)

38. In literature, evoking feelings of pity or compassion is to create:

    A. Colloquy

    B. Irony

    C. Pathos

    D. Paradox

    Answer: C. Pathos

    A very well known example of pathos is Desdemona's death in *Othello*, but there are many other examples of pathos. In *King Lear*, Cordelia accepts defeat with this line: "We are not the first / Who with best meaning have incurred the worst."

(Rigorous) (Skill 8.2)

39. Which of the following is a characteristic of blank verse?

    A. Meter in iambic pentameter

    B. Clearly specified rhyme scheme

    C. Lack of figurative language

    D. Unspecified rhythm

    Answer: A. Meter in iambic pentameter

    An iamb is a metrical unit of verse having one unstressed syllable followed by one stressed syllable. This is the most commonly used metrical verse in English and American poetry. An iambic pentameter is a ten-syllable verse made of five of these metrical units, either rhymed as in sonnets or unrhymed as in free or blank verse.

(Average) (Skill 8.2)

40. Which is an untrue statement about a theme in literature?

    A. The theme is always stated directly somewhere in the text.

    B. The theme is the central idea in a literary work.

    C. All parts of the work (plot, setting, mood) should contribute to the theme in some way.

    D. By analyzing the various elements of the work, the reader should be able to arrive at an indirectly stated theme.

    Answer: A. The theme is always stated directly somewhere in the text.

    The theme may be stated directly, but it can also be implicit in various aspects of the work, such as the interaction between characters, symbolism, or description.

(Average) (Skill 8.2)

41. In the following quotation, addressing the dead body of Caesar as though he were still a living being is to employ an:

    O, pardon me, though
    Bleeding piece of earth
    That I am meek and gentle with
    These butchers.
    　　—Marc Antony, from *Julius Caesar*

    A. Apostrophe

    B. Allusion

    C. Antithesis

    D. Anachronism

Answer: A. Apostrophe

This rhetorical figure addresses personified things, absent people, or gods. An allusion, on the other hand, is a quick reference to a character or event known to the public. An antithesis is a contrast between two opposing viewpoints, ideas, or presentations of characters. An anachronism is the placing of an object or person out of its time with the time of the text. The best-known example is the clock in Shakespeare's *Julius Caesar*.

(Rigorous) (Skill 8.2)

42. In the sentence, "The Cabinet conferred with the president," "Cabinet" is an example of a/an:

    A. Metonym
    B. Synecdoche
    C. Metaphor
    D. Allusion

Answer: B. Synecdoche

In a synecdoche, a whole is referred to by naming a part of it. Also, a synecdoche can stand for a whole of which it is a part, as in this example.

(Easy) (Skill 8.6)

43. Which is the best definition of diction?

    A. The specific word choices of an author to create a particular mood or feeling in the reader
    B. Writing that explains something thoroughly
    C. The background, or exposition, for a short story or drama
    D. Word choices that help teach a truth or moral

Answer: A. The specific word choices of an author to create a particular mood or feeling in the reader

Diction refers to an author's choice of words, expressions, and style to convey his or her meaning.

DIRECTIONS: In sentences 43–46, circle the choice that best corrects the error (underlined) without changing the meaning of the original sentence.

(Average) (Skill 8.6)

44. Wally <u>groaned, "Why do I have to do an oral interpretation of "The Raven."</u>

    A. groaned, "Why… of 'The Raven'?"
    B. groaned, "Why… of "The Raven"?
    C. groaned ", Why… of "The Raven?"
    D. groaned, "Why… of "The Raven."

Answer: A. groaned, "Why… of 'The Raven'?"

The question mark in a quotation that is an interrogation should be within the quotation marks. Also, when quoting a work of literature within another quotation, one should use single quotation marks ('…') for the title of this work, and they should close before the final quotation mark.

(Rigorous) (Skill 8.6)

45. Walt Whitman was famous <u>for his composition *Leaves of Grass*, serving as a nurse during the Civil War, and a devoted son.</u>

    A. for his composition *Leaves of Grass*, his service as a nurse during the Civil War, and a devoted son.

    B. for composing *Leaves of Grass*, serving as a nurse during the Civil War, and being a devoted son.

    C. for his composition *Leaves of Grass*, his nursing during the Civil War, and his devotion as a son.

    D. for his composition *Leaves of Grass,* serving as a nurse during the Civil War and a devoted son.

    E. for his composition *Leaves of Grass*, serving as a nurse during the Civil War, and a devoted son.

    Answer: B. for composing *Leaves of Grass*, serving as a nurse during the Civil War, and being a devoted son.

    In order to be parallel, the sentence needs three gerunds. The other sentences use both gerunds and nouns, which demonstrates a lack of parallelism.

(Rigorous) (Skill 8.6)

46. There were <u>fewer pieces</u> of evidence presented during the second trial.

    A. fewer peaces
    B. less peaces
    C. less pieces
    D. fewer pieces

Answer: D. fewer pieces

Use "fewer" for countable items; use "less" for amounts and quantities, such as in "fewer minutes but less time." "Peace" is the opposite of war, not a "piece" of evidence.

(Easy) (Skill 9.1)

47. Mr. Smith <u>respectfully submitted his resignation and had</u> a new job.

    A. respectfully submitted his resignation and has
    B. respectfully submitted his resignation before accepting
    C. respectfully submitted his resignation because of
    D. respectfully submitted his resignation and had

Answer: C. respectfully submitted his resignation because of

Answer A eliminates any relationship of causality between submitting the resignation and having the new job. Answer B just changes the sentence and, by omission, does not indicate the fact that Mr. Smith had a new job before submitting his resignation. Answer D means that Mr. Smith first submitted his resignation, and then got a new job.

(Average) (Skill 9.1)

48. Charles Dickens, Robert Browning, and Robert Louis Stevenson were:

    A. Victorians
    B. Medievalists
    C. Elizabethans
    D. Absurdists

Answer: A. Victorians

The Victorian period is remarkable for the diversity and quality of its literature. Robert Browning wrote chilling monologues such as "My Last Duchess" and long poetic narratives such as *The Pied Piper of Hamlin*. Robert Louis Stevenson wrote his works partly for young adults, whose imaginations were quite taken by his *Treasure Island* and *The Case of Dr. Jekyll and Mr. Hyde*. Charles Dickens tells of the misery of the time and the complexities of Victorian society in novels such as *Oliver Twist* and *Great Expectations*.

(Easy) (Skill 9.2)

49. Considered one of the first feminist plays, this Ibsen drama ends with a door slamming, symbolizing the lead character's emancipation from traditional societal norms.

    A. *The Wild Duck*
    B. *Hedda Gabler*
    C. *Ghosts*
    D. *A Doll's House*

Answer: D. *A Doll's House*

Nora in *A Doll's House* leaves her husband and her children when she realizes her husband is not the man she thought he was. Hedda Gabler, another feminist icon, shoots herself. *The Wild Duck* deals with the conflict between idealism and family secrets. *Ghosts*, considered one of Ibsen's most controversial plays, deals with many social ills, some of which include alcoholism, incest, and religious hypocrisy.

(Rigorous) (Skill 9.2)

50. Which of the following is the best definition of existentialism?

    A. The philosophical doctrine that matter is the only reality and that everything in the world, including thought, will, and feeling, can be explained in terms of matter
    B. A philosophy that views things as they should be or as one would wish them to be
    C. A philosophical and literary movement, variously religious and atheistic, stemming from Kierkegaard and represented by Sartre
    D. The belief that all events are determined by fate and are hence inevitable

Answer: C. A philosophical and literary movement, variously religious and atheistic, stemming from Kierkegaard and represented by Sartre

Even though there are other very important thinkers in the movement known as Existentialism, such as Camus and Merleau-Ponty, Sartre remains the main figure in this movement.

(Average) (Skill 10.3)

51. American colonial writers were primarily:

    A. Romanticists
    B. Naturalists
    C. Realists
    D. Neoclassicists

Answer: D. Neoclassicists

The early colonists had been schooled in England, and even though their writing became quite American in content, their emphasis on clarity and balance in their language remained British. This literature reflects the lives of the early colonists, such as William Bradford's excerpts from "The Mayflower Compact," Anne Bradstreet's poetry, and William Byrd's journal *A History of the Dividing Line*.

Listening and Speaking (Skills 11.1 – 13.4)

(Average) (Skill 11.1)

52. **Oral debate is most closely associated with which form of discourse?**

    A. Description
    B. Exposition
    C. Narration
    D. Persuasion

Answer: D. Persuasion

It is extremely important to be convincing while having an oral debate. This is why persuasion is so important—because this is the way that you can influence your audience.

(Rigorous) (Skill 11.1)

53. **Which of the following types of question will not stimulate higher-level critical thinking?**

    A. A hypothetical question
    B. An open-ended question
    C. A close-ended question
    D. A judgment question

Answer: C. A close-ended question

A close-ended question requires a simple answer, like "yes" or "no." An open-ended question can generate an extended response that would require critical thinking. Both a hypothetical question and a judgment question require deeper thinking skills.

(Average) (Skill 11.1)

54. **In preparing a speech for a contest, your student has encountered problems with gender-specific language. Not wishing to offend either women or men, she seeks your guidance. Which of the following is not an effective strategy?**

    A. Use the generic "he" and explain that people will understand and accept the male pronoun as all-inclusive
    B. Switch to plural nouns and use "they" as the gender-neutral pronoun
    C. Use passive voice so that the subject is not required
    D. Use male pronouns for one part of the speech, and then use female pronouns for the other part of the speech

Answer: A. Use the generic "he" and explain that people will understand and accept the male pronoun as all-inclusive

No longer is the male pronoun considered the universal pronoun. Speakers and writers should choose gender-neutral words and avoid nouns and pronouns that inaccurately exclude one gender or the other.

(Average) (Skill 11.2)

55. Which of the following is NOT an advanced communication skill?

   A. Clarification
   B. Reflection
   C. Pronunciation
   D. Summarization

Answer: C. Pronunciation

Pronunciation is how clearly one speaks and pronounces words. It is not considered an *advanced* communication skill.

(Easy) (Skill 11.2)

56. What is true of effective communicators?

   A. They are also good listeners.
   B. They are well-liked by their students.
   C. They speak more than one language.
   D. They have a poor understanding of effective body language.

Answer: A. They are also good listeners.

Effective communicators are also good listeners. Teachers who exhibit such behaviors as eye contact, focusing on student body language, clarifying students' statements, and using "I" messages are effective listeners.

(Average) (Skill 11.3)

57. What is NOT a way that speaking and listening can be integrated?

   A. Storytelling
   B. Role playing
   C. Memorization
   D. Readers' Theatre

Answer: C. Memorization

Memorization is not a way to blend speaking and listening. All memorization requires is repetition or drill and practice.

(Average) (Skill 12.1)

58. What is included in the process of preparing to speak on a topic?

   A. Research, reading, recovery
   B. Discovery, organization, editing
   C. Drafting, revising, editing
   D. Choice, research, time management

Answer: B. Discovery, organization, editing

Discovery means to settle on a topic or subject. While organizing, one needs to think of the purpose of the speech. Then a thesis must be developed. The introductions and conclusions must be written. Then the speech must be edited or looked at with, or by, a fresh pair of eyes.

(Average) (Skill 12.3)

59. Which of the following words does NOT indicate a premise for an argument?

   A. Since
   B. Then
   C. Because
   D. Afterward

   Answer: A. Afterward

   Premises (or assertions) are often indicated by phrases such as "because," "since," and "obviously."

(Easy) (Skill 12.3)

60. Which of the following phrases may be an indication that the conclusion is beginning?

   A. Implies that
   B. Later
   C. Fortunately
   D. It follows that

   Answer: D. It follows that

   Conclusions are often indicated by phrases such as "therefore," "it follows that," "we conclude," and so on. The conclusion is often stated as the final stage of inference.

(Average) (Skill 12.5)

61. Which nonverbal communication technique suggests that students maintain a straight but not stiff posture, refrain from shifting from hip to hop, point feet directly at the audience, and distribute weight evenly?

   A. Posture
   B. Movement
   C. Gestures
   D. Eye contact

   Answer: A. Posture

   Posture is the way that we hold our bodies. It is part of nonverbal communication and it can affect the way a presentation is understood.

(Rigorous) (Skill 12.5)

62. How can eye contact help someone who is speaking publicly?

   A. It doesn't help the speaker—it helps the audience feel comfortable.
   B. It only helps if someone makes eye contact with the audience for 3 – 5 seconds.
   C. It can help the speaker overcome speech anxiety.
   D. It keeps the speaker still if eye contact is maintained with the audience.

   Answer: C. It can help the speaker overcome speech anxiety.

   Interestingly, eye contact usually helps the speaker overcome speech anxiety by connecting with the attentive audience and easing feelings of isolation.

(Easy) (Skill 12.5)

63. How can problems with volume be overcome when making an oral presentation?

    A. Presentations can be taped and the volume can then be controlled easily.

    B. The presenter must simply present two times louder than he or she would normally speak.

    C. The presenter must simply adjust their pitch.

    D. Practice

Answer: D. Practice

Problems with volume can be overcome with practice. Those who speak softly can have someone stand in the back of the room and signal when the volume is strong enough. Conversely, if someone speaks too loudly, they can have a person in the front of the room signal when their voice is soft enough.

(Rigorous) (Skill 12.5)

64. What additional benefit do people gain by becoming good oral presenters?

    A. They have a chance at becoming politicians.

    B. They will develop self-confidence for higher levels of communication.

    C. Voice, volume, and pitch errors will be corrected.

    D. They will sound more educated because they have the ability to practice speaking.

Answer: B. They will develop self-confidence for higher levels of communication.

By speaking in front of people and making oral presentations, speakers develop self-confidence and a higher level of communication.

(Average) (Skill 12.5)

65. Posture, movement, gestures, and eye contact are all under the umbrella of:

    A. Verbal communication

    B. Effective presentation communications

    C. Nonverbal communication techniques

    D. Speech delivery techniques

Answer: C. Nonverbal communication techniques

None of these communication techniques require speaking. Therefore, they are all nonverbal communication techniques. Nonverbal communication can affect the way a presentation is understood.

Components of Writing (Skills 14.1 – 16.7)

DIRECTIONS: In sentences 66–67, circle the choice that best corrects the error (underlined) without changing the meaning of the original sentence.

(Easy) (Skill 14.3)

66. The Taj Mahal <u>has been designated</u> one of the Seven Wonders of the World, and people <u>know it</u> for its unique architecture.

   A. The Taj Mahal has been designated one of the Seven Wonders of the World, and it is known for its unique architecture.

   B. People know the Taj Mahal for its unique architecture, and it has been designated one of the Seven Wonders of the World.

   C. People have known the Taj Mahal for its unique architecture, and it has been designated of the Seven Wonders of the World.

   D. The Taj Mahal has designated itself one of the Seven Wonders of the World.

   Answer: A. The Taj Mahal has been designated one of the Seven Wonders of the World, and it is known for its unique architecture.

   In the original sentence, the first clause is passive voice and the second clause is active voice, causing a voice shift. Answer B merely switches the clauses but does not correct the voice shift. In Answer C, only the verb tense in the first clause has been changed but is still active voice. Sentence D changes the meaning. In Answer A, both clauses are passive voice.

(Rigorous) (Skill 14.3)

67. Which sentence below best minimizes the impact of bad news?

   A. We have denied you permission to attend the event.

   B. Although permission to attend the event cannot be given, you are encouraged to buy the video.

   C. Although you cannot attend the event, we encourage you to buy the video.

   D. Although attending the event is not possible, watching the video is an option.

   Answer: B. Although permission to attend the event cannot be given, you are encouraged to buy the video.

   Subordinating the bad news and using passive voice minimizes the impact of the bad news. In Answer A, the sentence is in active voice and thus too direct. The word "denied" sets a negative tone. In Answer C, the bad news is subordinated, but it is still in active voice with negative wording. In Answer D, the sentence is too unclear.

(Average) (Skill 14.5)

68. **DIRECTIONS: In the sample paragraph below, choose the underlined transition that is not used effectively.**

    Autumn is my favorite time of year. <u>First</u>, the crisp, clean air is refreshing after the humid days of summer. <u>In addition</u>, I love the cinnamon smells in the kitchen of apple pies and cider. I <u>also</u> enjoy the beautiful colors of the trees in autumn, too. <u>In contrast</u>, October brings my favorite holiday, Halloween, when everyone dresses up! <u>In sum</u>, the holidays, smells, and sights make autumn the best time of year.

    A. First
    B. In addition
    C. In contrast
    D. In sum

Answer: C. In contrast

In this paragraph, the transition *in contrast* is not used properly, because the statement that follows does not contrast with the other supporting sentences. Instead, a transition such as *finally* would have been more suitable.

(Average) (Skill 14.5)

69. **Transitional words and phrases help to:**

    A. Add structure to a text
    B. Signal relationships between ideas in a text
    C. Enhance the flow of writing
    D. All of the above

Answer: D. All of the above

Transitions are words or phrases that signal relationships between ideas in a text. Proper use of transitional words and phrases add flow, fluency, and structure to a text.

(Easy) (Skill 15.1)

70. **An advertisement seen on television or in as a magazine print ad takes on what form of writing structure?**

    A. Narrative
    B. Persuasive
    C. Descriptive
    D. Expository

Answer: B. Persuasive

Advertisements are normally trying to persuade the reader to take a certain course of action or to purchase something.

(Rigorous) (Skill 15.1)

71. *The imaginations of children seem to be dwindling before our very eyes. What happened to the good 'ol days when boys would be outside using sticks as make-believe daggers and large cardboard boxes as castles. Girls would stand on their front porches and pretend that they were on stage—performing some sort of skit for the neighborhood parents. Now, electronic games and gizmos are taking over the minds of our young people and robbing them of vital imagination.*

    The above piece of writing is most likely the introduction to what type of writing?

    A. A narrative

    B. A descriptive piece

    C. A persuasive piece

    D. An expository piece

    Answer: D. An expository piece

    An expository piece contains a thesis statement that alerts the readers to what they will read in the rest of the piece. This is most likely the introduction to an expository piece on video games and how they are doing a disservice to the children of today.

(Easy) (Skill 15.1)

72. Which type of writing is meant to tell a story?

    A. Narrative

    B. Descriptive

    C. Persuasive

    D. Expository

    Answer: A. Narrative

    Although all forms of writing may tell some sort of story, narratives are usually meant to tell a story by stringing together a series of events in sequential order.

(Average) (Skill 15.2)

73. Writing ideas quickly without interruption of the flow of thoughts or attention to conventions is called:

    A. Brainstorming

    B. Mapping

    C. Listing

    D. Free writing

    Answer: D. Free writing

    Free writing for ten or fifteen minutes allows students to write out their thoughts about a subject. This technique allows students to develop ideas that they are conscious of, but it also helps them develop ideas that are lurking in the subconscious. It is important to let the flow of ideas run through the hand. If students get stuck, they can write the last sentence over again until inspiration returns.

(Rigorous) (Skill 15.2)

74. In preparing a report about William Shakespeare, students are asked to develop a set of interpretive questions to guide their research. Which of the following would not be classified as an interpretive question?

    A. What would be different today if Shakespeare had not written his plays?

    B. How will the plays of Shakespeare affect future generations?

    C. How does Shakespeare view nature in *A Midsummer's Night Dream* and *Much Ado About Nothing*?

    D. During the Elizabethan age, what roles did young boys take in dramatizing Shakespeare's plays?

Answer: D. During the Elizabethan age, what roles did young boys take in dramatizing Shakespeare's plays?

This question requires research into the historical facts; the movie *Shakespeare in Love* notwithstanding, women did not act in Shakespeare's plays, and their parts were taken by young boys. Answers A and B are hypothetical questions requiring students to provide original thinking and interpretation. Answer C requires comparison and contrast, which are interpretive skills.

(Rigorous) (Skill 15.3)

75. In this paragraph from a student essay, identify the sentence that provides a detail.

    (1) The poem concerns two different personality types and the human relation between them. (2) Their approach to life is totally different. (3) The neighbor is a very conservative person who follows routines. (4) He follows the traditional wisdom of his father and his father's father. (5) The purpose in fixing the wall and keeping their relationship separate is only because it is all he knows.

    A. Sentence 1

    B. Sentence 3

    C. Sentence 4

    D. Sentence 5

Answer: C. Sentence 4

Sentence 4 provides a detail to sentence 3 by explaining how the neighbor follows routine. Sentence 1 is the thesis sentence, which is the main idea of the paragraph. Sentence 3 provides an example to develop that thesis. Sentence 5 is a reason that explains why.

(Easy) (Skill 15.3)

76. Which of the following should not be included in the opening paragraph of an informative essay?

    A. Thesis sentence

    B. Details and examples supporting the main idea

    C. Broad, general introduction to the topic

    D. A style and tone that grabs the reader's attention

Answer: B. Details and examples supporting the main idea

The introductory paragraph should introduce the topic, capture the reader's interest, state the thesis, and prepare the reader for the main points in the essay. Details and examples, however, should be given in the second part of the essay, so as to help develop the thesis presented at the end of the introductory paragraph, following the inverted triangle method consisting of a broad general statement followed by some information, and then the thesis at the end of the paragraph.

(Average) (Skill 15.3)

77. Middle and high school students are more receptive to studying grammar and syntax:

    A. Through worksheets and end-of-lesson practices in textbooks
    B. Through independent homework assignments
    C. Through analytical examination of the writings of famous authors
    D. Through application to their own writing

Answer: D. Through application to their own writing

At this age, students learn grammatical concepts best through practical application in their own writing.

DIRECTIONS: In sentences 78–79, choose the most effective word within the context of the sentence.

(Average) (Skill 15.4)

78. When a student is expelled from school, the parents are usually _____ in advance.

    A. rewarded
    B. congratulated
    C. notified

Answer: C. notified

Notified means informed or told, which fits into the logic of the sentence. The words *rewarded* and *congratulated* are positive actions, which do not make sense regarding someone being expelled from school.

(Average) (Skill 15.4)

79. Before appearing in court, the witness was _____ the papers requiring her to show up.

    A. condemned
    B. served
    C. criticized

Answer: B. served

Served means given, which makes sense in the context of the sentence. *Condemned* and *criticized* do not make sense within the context of the sentence.

(Rigorous) (Skill 16.7)

80. Which of the following situations is not an ethical violation of intellectual property?

   A. A student visits ten different Web sites and writes a report to compare the costs of downloading music. He uses the names of the Web sites without their permission.

   B. A student copies and pastes a chart verbatim from the Internet but does not document it because it is available on a public site.

   C. From an online article found in a subscription database, a student paraphrases a section on the problems of music piracy. She includes the source in her Works Cited but does not provide an in-text citation.

   D. A student uses a comment from M. Night Shyamalan without attribution, claiming the information is common knowledge.

Answer: A. A student visits ten different Web sites and writes a report to compare the costs of downloading music. He uses the names of the Web sites without their permission.

In this scenario, the student is conducting primary research by gathering the data and using it for his own purposes. He or she is not violating any principle by using the names of the Web sites. In Answer B, students who copy and paste from the Internet without documenting the sources of their information are committing plagiarism, a serious violation of intellectual property. Even when a student puts information in his or her own words by paraphrasing or summarizing, as in Answer C, the information is still secondary and must be documented. Although dedicated movie buffs might consider anything that M. Night Shyamalan says to be common knowledge in Situation D, his comments are not necessarily known in numerous places or known by many people.

Modes of Writing (Skills 17.1 – 20.5)

(Average) (Skill 17.4)

81. Which of the following is most true of expository writing?

   A. It is mutually exclusive of other forms of discourse

   B. It can incorporate other forms of discourse in the process of providing supporting details

   C. It should never employ informal expression

   D. It should only be scored with a summative evaluation

Answer: B. It can incorporate other forms of discourse in the process of providing supporting details

Expository writing sets forth an explanation or an argument about any subject.

(Average) (Skill 17.4)

82. Explanatory or informative discourse is:

   A. Exposition

   B. Narration

   C. Persuasion

   D. Description

Answer: A. Exposition

Exposition sets forth a systematic explanation of any subject. It can also introduce the characters of a literary work and their situations in the story.

(Rigorous) (Skill 17.4)

83. Which of the following is an example of the *post hoc* fallacy?

    A. When the new principal was hired, student reading scores improved; therefore, the principal caused the increase in scores.

    B. Why are we spending money on the space program when our students don't have current textbooks?

    C. You can't give your class a 10-minute break. Once you do that, we'll all have to give our students a 10-minute break.

    D. You can never believe anything he says because he's not from the same country as we are.

Answer: A. When the new principal was hired, student reading scores improved; therefore, the principal caused the increase in scores.

A *post hoc* fallacy assumes that because one event preceded another, the first event caused the second event. In this case, student scores could have increased for other reasons. Answer B is a red herring fallacy, in which one raises an irrelevant topic to side track from the first topic. In this case, the space budget and the textbook budget have little effect on each other. Answer C is an example of a slippery slope, in which one event is followed precipitously by another event. Answer D is an ad hominem ("to the man") fallacy, in which a person is attacked rather than the concept or interpretation he or she puts forth.

(Rigorous) (Skill 17.5)

84. What syntactic device is most evident from Abraham Lincoln's "Gettysburg Address"?

    It is rather for us to be here dedicated to the great task remaining before us—that from these honored dead we take increased devotion to that cause for which they gave the last full measure of devotion—that we here highly resolve that these dead shall not have died in vain—that this nation, under God, shall have a new birth of freedom—and that government of the people, by the people, for the people, shall not perish from the earth.

    A. Affective connotation

    B. Informative denotations

    C. Allusion

    D. Parallelism

Answer: D. Parallelism

Parallelism is the repetition of grammatical structure. In speeches such as this and the speeches of Martin Luther King, Jr., parallel structure creates a rhythm and balance of related ideas. Lincoln's repetition of clauses beginning with "that" ties four examples back to "the great task." Connotation is the emotional attachment of words; denotation is the literal meaning of words. Allusion is a reference to a historic event, person, or place.

(Easy) (Skill 17.6)

85. In the paragraph below, which sentence does not contribute to the overall task of supporting the main idea?

    (1) The Springfield City Council met Friday to discuss new zoning restrictions for the land to be developed south of the city. (2) Residents who opposed the new restrictions were granted 15 minutes to present their case. (3) Their argument focused on the dangers that increased traffic would bring to the area. (4) It seemed to me that the Mayor Simpson listened intently. (5) The council agreed to table the new zoning until studies would be performed.

    A. Sentence 2
    B. Sentence 3
    C. Sentence 4
    D. Sentence 5

Answer: C. Sentence 4

The other sentences provide detail to the main idea of the new zoning restrictions. Because sentence 4 provides no example or relevant detail, it should be omitted.

(Rigorous) (Skill 18.3)

86. For their research paper on the use of technology in the classroom, students have gathered data that shows a sharp increase in the number of online summer classes over the past five years. What would be the best way for them to depict this information visually?

    A. A line chart
    B. A table
    C. A pie chart
    D. A flow chart

Answer: A. A line chart

A line chart is used to show trends over time and would emphasize the sharp increase. A table is appropriate to show the exact numbers, but it does not have the same impact as a line chart. Not appropriate is a pie chart, which shows the parts of a whole, or a flow chart, which details processes or procedures.

(Rigorous) (Skill 18.4)

87. Identify the type of appeal used by Molly Ivins in this excerpt from her essay "Get a Knife, Get a Dog, But Get Rid of Guns."

    As a civil libertarian, I, of course, support the Second Amendment. And I believe it means exactly what it says: A well-regulated militia being necessary to the security of a free state, the right of the people to keep and bear arms shall not be infringed.

    A. Ethical
    B. Emotional
    C. Rational
    D. Literary

Answer: A. Ethical

An ethical appeal is using the credentials of a reliable and trustworthy authority. In this case, Ivins cites the Constitution.

(Rigorous) (Skill 18.5)

88. What type of reasoning does Henry David Thoreau use in the following excerpt from "Civil Disobedience"?

    Unjust laws exist; shall we be content to obey them, or shall we endeavor to amend them, and obey them until we have succeeded, or shall we transgress them at once? Men generally, under such a government as this, think that they ought to wait until they have persuaded the majority to alter them. They think that, if they should resist, the remedy would be worse than the evil. But it is the fault of the government itself that the remedy is worse than the evil … Why does it always crucify Christ, excommunicate Copernicus and Luther, and pronounce Washington and Franklin rebels?

    A. Ethical reasoning
    B. Inductive reasoning
    C. Deductive reasoning
    D. Intellectual reasoning

Answer: C. Deductive reasoning

Deductive reasoning begins with a general statement that leads to the particulars. In this essay, Thoreau begins with the general question about what should be done about unjust laws. His argument leads to the government's role in suppressing dissent.

(Average) (Skill 19.1)

89. Modeling is a practice that requires students to:

    A. Create a style unique to their own language capabilities
    B. Emulate the writing of professionals
    C. Paraphrase passages from good literature
    D. Peer evaluate the writings of other students

Answer: B. Emulate the writing of professionals

Modeling has students analyze the writing of a professional writer and try to reach the same level of syntactical, grammatical, and stylistic mastery as the author whom they are studying.

(Average) (Skill 19.2)

90. The English department is developing strategies to encourage all students to become a community of readers. From the list of suggestions below, which would be the least effective way for teachers to foster independent reading?

    A. Each teacher sets aside a weekly, 30-minute, in-class reading session during which the teacher and students read a magazine or book for enjoyment.
    B. The teacher and the students develop a list of favorite books to share with each other.
    C. The teacher assigns at least one book report each grading period to ensure that students are reading from the established class list.
    D. The students gather books for a classroom library so that books can be shared with each other.

Answer: C. The teacher assigns at least one book report each grading period to ensure that students are reading from the established class list.

Teacher-directed assignments such as book reports appear routine and unexciting. Students will be more excited about reading when they can actively participate. In Answer A, the teacher is modeling reading behavior and providing students with a dedicated time during which time they can read independently and still be surrounded by a community of readers. In Answers B and D, students share and make available their reading choices.

(Average) (Skill 19.3)
91. The new teaching intern is developing a unit on creative writing and is trying to encourage her freshman high school students to write poetry. Which of the following would not be an effective technique?

    A. In groups, students draw pictures to illustrate "The Love Song of J. Alfred Prufrock" by T.S. Eliot
    B. Either individually or in groups, students compose a song, writing lyrics that try to use poetic devices
    C. Students bring to class the lyrics of a popular song and discuss the imagery and figurative language
    D. Students read aloud their favorite poems and share their opinions of and responses to the poems

Answer: A. In groups, students draw pictures to illustrate "The Love Song of J. Alfred Prufrock" by T.S. Eliot

Although drawing is creative, it will not accomplish as much as the other activities to encourage students to write their own poetry. Furthermore, "The Love Song of J. Alfred Prufrock" is not a freshman-level poem. The other activities involve students in music and their own favorites, which will be more appealing.

(Rigorous) (Skill 19.5)
92. In order to make the plot of a story interesting and balanced, the author must include:

    A. Characters
    B. Descriptive words
    C. Strong nouns, verbs, and adjectives
    D. Character's thoughts, feelings, and actions

Answer: D. Character's thoughts, feelings, and actions

The best plots are driven by the characters. To develop an effective plot, the writer must incorporate, and balance, meaningful dialogue, interior thoughts of the characters, and character's actions and reactions.

(Easy) (Skill 19.5)

93. The following passage is written from which point of view?

    As she mused, the pitiful vision of her mother's life laid its spell on the very quick of her being—that life of commonplace sacrifices closing in final craziness. She trembled as she heard again her mother's voice saying constantly with foolish insistence: Dearevaun Seraun! Dearevaun Seraun!*

    * "The end of pleasure is pain!" (Gaelic)

    A. First-person narrator
    B. Second-person direct address
    C. Third-person omniscient
    D. First-person omniscient

    Answer: C. Third-person omniscient

    The passage is clearly in the third person (the subject is "she"), and it is omniscient since it gives the characters' inner thoughts.

(Rigorous) (Skill 19.6)

94. For students to prepare for a their roles in a dramatic performance:

    A. They should analyze their characters to develop a deeper understanding of the character's attitudes and motivations.
    B. They should attend local plays to study settings and stage design.
    C. They should read articles and books on acting methodology.
    D. They should practice the way other actors have performed in these roles.

Answer: A. They should analyze their characters to develop a deeper understanding of the character's attitudes and motivations.

By examining how their characters feel and think, students will understand the characters' attitudes and motivation.

(Average) (Skill 20.4)

95. If a student uses slang and expletives, what is the best course of action to take to improve the student's formal communication skills?

    A. Ask the student to paraphrase his writing—that is, to translate it into language appropriate for the school principal to read.
    B. Refuse to read the student's papers until he conforms to a more literate style.
    C. Ask the student to read his work aloud to the class for peer evaluation.
    D. Rewrite the flagrant passages to show the student the right form of expression.

Answer: A. Ask the student to paraphrase his writing—that is, to translate it into language appropriate for the school principal to read.

Asking the student to write for a specific audience will help him become more involved in his writing. If he continues writing to the same audience—the teacher—he will continue seeing writing as just another assignment and will not apply grammar, vocabulary, and syntax the way they should be. By rephrasing his own writing, the student will learn to write for a different public.

(Easy) (Skill 20.4)

96. In "inverted triangle" introductory paragraphs, the thesis sentence occurs:

    A. At the beginning of the paragraph
    B. In the middle of the paragraph
    C. At the end of the paragraph
    D. In the second paragraph

Answer: C. At the end of the paragraph

The introduction to an essay should begin with a broad general statement, followed by one or more sentences adding interest and information to the topic. The thesis should be written at the end of the introduction.

(Average) (Skill 20.4)

97. Students need to be aware that an email message:

    A. Should be written according to formal business letter guidelines
    B. May eventually reach a wider audience than intended
    C. Should be written using all capital letters
    D. Should not be used to send large documents or multimedia files

Answer: B. May eventually reach a wider audience than intended

E-mail messages, even if intended for just one reader, may eventually reach a much wider audience. In recent years, a number of e-mail writers have found themselves in embarrassing situations or legal troubles because of the circulation of their personal e-mail messages on the Internet.

(Rigorous) (Skill 20.5)

98. Which might be true if a story has an unreliable narrator?

    A. A character will be revealed subtly through dialogue, interior monologue, description, and behavior
    B. A character will be revealed through dialogue only
    C. The writer will tell the reader directly what a character is like
    D. There will be discrepancies between what the narrator tells the reader and what is revealed through the character's actions

Answer: D. There will be discrepancies between what the narrator tells the reader and what is revealed through the character's actions

Sometimes there will be discrepancies between what the narrator tells the reader about a character and what is revealed through the character's actions. In this case, the narrator is unreliable, and that unreliability becomes an important and significant device for understanding the story.

(Average) (Skill 20.5)

99. Which of the following is NOT an example of fiction?

    A. Biography
    B. Mythology
    C. Poetry
    D. Science fiction

Answer: A. Biography

The term fiction is generally synonymous with literature. Fiction refers only to novels, short stories, and other writing that is not based on fact. A biography is factual, so it is not a form of fiction.

(Rigorous) (Skill 20.5)

100. **An idealized model of a person, object, or concept from which similar instances are derived is called:**

    A. A theme

    B. An archetype

    C. A protagonist

    D. An antagonist

Answer: B. An archetype

An archetype is an idealized model of a person, object, or concept from which similar instances are derived, copied, patterned, or emulated. An image, character, or pattern of circumstances that recurs frequently in literature can be considered an archetype.

SAMPLE TEST

www.ingramcontent.com/pod-product-compliance
Lightning Source LLC
Chambersburg PA
CBHW080535300426
44111CB00017B/2740